The Psychology of Mature Spiritu

At the threshold of the twenty-first century many people are encountering a spiritual dilemma. Enlightened secularism and humanism no longer seem adequate for living an ethical life, but religious practices and spiritual paths still seem at odds with intelligence and rationality.

The Psychology of Mature Spirituality addresses this dilemma. Its three sections—integrity, wisdom, and transcendence—describe and analyze a mature form of spirituality that will be a hallmark of future years. Distinguished contributors develop these three themes, showing the reader how human development over the lifespan can lead to a belief system that places neither god(s) nor humankind at the metaphorical centre of the universe. What they describe is a new 'skeptical spirituality'.

Combining developmental psychology, depth psychology, and religious studies, *The Psychology of Mature Spirituality* is a timely and accessible volume which will appeal not only to those involved in psychology, psychoanalysis, and religious studies, but also to the interested general reader.

Polly Young-Eisendrath is Clinical Associate Professor of Psychiatry at University of Vermont College of Medicine, Burlington. **Melvin E. Miller** is Professor of Psychology at Norwich University, Northfield, VT.

The Psychology of Mature Spirituality

Integrity, wisdom, transcendence

Edited by Polly Young-Eisendrath and
Melvin E. Miller

London and Philadelphia

First published 2000 by Routledge
11 New Fetter Lane, London EC4P 4EE

Simultaneously published in the USA and Canada
by Taylor & Francis Inc.,
325 Chestnut Street, Philadelphia, PA 19106

Routledge is an imprint of the Taylor & Francis Group

Typeset in Times by Mayhew Typesetting, Rhayader, Powys
Printed and bound in Great Britain by Biddles Ltd, www.biddles.co.uk

British Library Cataloguing in Publication Data
A catalogue record for this book is available from the British Library

Library of Congress Cataloging in Publication Data

The psychology of mature spirituality : integrity, wisdom, transcendence / edited by
Polly Young-Eisendrath and Melvin E. Miller.
     p. cm.
   Includes bibliographical references and index.
   ISBN 0–415–17959–9—ISBN 0–415–17960–2 (pbk.)
   1. Spirituality—Psychology.   2. Psychology, Religious.   I. Young-Eisendrath, Polly,
1947– II. Miller, Melvin E.
   BL624.P79 2000
   291.4—dc21   00-025538

ISBN 0–415–17959–9 (hbk)
ISBN 0–415–17960–2 (pbk)

Lovingly dedicated to my teacher,
Roshi Philip Kapleau—P.Y.-E.

To my wife, Loren, companion
and friend—M.E.M.

Contents

Figures and tables

FIGURES

TABLES

The contributors

John Beebe, MD, a Clinical Assistant Professor in Psychiatry at the University of California, San Francisco, is a Jungian analyst and international lecturer in analytical psychology. Founding Editor of *The San Francisco Jung Institute Library Journal* and the first United States co-editor of *The Journal of Analytical Psychology*, Dr Beebe has frequently published on personal character and its imagery, including the book *Integrity in Depth* (1992). He is past chairperson of the Ethics and Certifying Committees of the C. G. Jung Institute of San Francisco; as President-elect of his Institute, he currently chairs its Training Coordinating Committee.

Roger Brooke, Ph.D., is a Professor of Psychology and Director of Training in Clinical Psychology at Duquesne University, Pittsburgh. He is in private practice as a psychotherapist, but in recent years he has also been working in clinical neuropsychology and gerontology. He is adjunct faculty of the C. G. Jung Institute Analyst Training Program of Pittsburgh. Until 1994, Dr Brooke was at Rhodes University, South Africa, where he spent his formative years. He was deeply influenced there by the Jungian analysts Renos Papadopoulos and the late Vera Buhrmann, but his training in psychoanalytically oriented psychotherapy was at the University of the Witwatersrand. Brooke is the author of the internationally acclaimed *Jung and Phenomenology* (Routledge, 1991), and of numerous papers in analytical psychology, phenomenology, and psychotherapy. He has a passion for long-distance running and the wilderness, and is married with three youngsters.

Ellen M. Crouse, BA, is a Registered Nurse who recently earned her undergraduate degree in psychology at Texas A&M University. Currently, she is a graduate student in clinical psychology at the University of Montana at Missoula. Her research interests include analytical psychology, history of psychology, and how resilience develops within or acts as a mediator for survivors of trauma or abuse.

Terrill L. Gibson, Ph.D., is a pastoral psychotherapist and Jungian analyst who practices individual and family therapy in Tacoma, Washington. He lectures widely on the integration of psychotherapy and spirituality, especially from a Christian perspective. His articles have appeared in *The Journal of Religion and Health*, *Pastoral Psychology*, and *The Journal of Pastoral Care*. He is a frequent consultant, faculty member, and clinical supervisor and facilitator at a variety of Pacific Northwest universities, social services, corporations, and religious congregations. His book, co-edited with Laura Dodson, *Psyche and Family*, will be published soon.

Charles Guignon, Ph.D., received both his BA and Ph.D. degrees in philosophy at the University of California, Berkeley. His writings include *Heidegger and the Problems of Knowledge*, *The Cambridge Companion to Heidegger*, *Re-envisioning Psychology*, readers on existentialism, Dostoyevsky, and 'the good life,' and papers on hermeneutics, narrative explanation, Heidegger, Wittgenstein, and Rorty. He has taught at Princeton University, the University of Texas at Austin, and Berkeley, and is currently professor of philosophy at the University of Vermont.

Richard P. Hayes, Ph.D., is an associate professor of Buddhism at McGill University, where he also serves as Buddhist chaplain. He completed his Ph.D. in Sanskrit and Indian Studies in 1982 at the University of Toronto, specializing in Indian philosophy. He has published a book and several articles on Indian Buddhist philosophy and was subject editor of Indian and Tibetan philosophy for the *Routledge Encyclopedia of Philosophy*. He is currently a co-editor of the Indian philosophy section of the *Stanford Encyclopedia of Philosophy*. His *Land of No Buddha* (Windhorse, 1998) is a collection of popular essays on Buddhism in the West.

Ruthellen Josselson, Ph.D., is a Professor of Psychology at Fielding Institute and Forchheimer Professor of Psychology at Hebrew University in Jerusalem. Recipient of the APA Henry Murray Award and a Fullbright Research Fellowship, she has also been Visiting Professor at the Harvard Graduate School of Education. She is author of *Revising Herself: The Story of Women's Identity from College to Midlife* and *The Space Between Us: Exploring the Dimensions of Human Relationships*. She is also co-editor of the annual *The Narrative Study of Lives*.

Michael C. Kalton, Ph.D., is currently Professor and Director of the Liberal Studies program at the University of Washington, Tacoma. He holds a Ph.D. from Harvard University (1977) in the joint fields of Comparative Religion and East Asian Languages and Civilization. His research specialization has been the Korean Neo-Confucian tradition, about which he has published two books and numerous articles and book chapters. His book on Korea's leading Neo-Confucian thinker, *To*

Become a Sage, won the international T'oegye Study Society prize in 1998.

Gisela Labouvie-Vief, Ph.D., was born in Germany and received her graduate training at West Virginia University. A graduate of one of the first and most vigorous lifespan developmental programs, she began to work on theory and research on development across adulthood. In particular, she proposed that in middle to late adulthood, individuals integrate cognition and emotion to form a unique form of thinking that transcends the opposites of reason and emotion to form thinking that is capable of embodied abstraction. In her research, she has tracked this form of thinking and is researching how its development is supported or delayed by certain experiences. Her pioneering work has been supported by continuous funds through the National Institute on Aging and it is recognized internationally.

Melvin E. Miller, Ph.D., has been interested in philosophy, narrative, and world religions throughout his adult life. His longitudinal research on the development of worldviews and religious perspectives naturally evolved from such concerns. In addition to postdoctoral psychotherapy and psychoanalytic studies at the Boston Institute for Psychotherapy and the National Training Program in Contemporary Psychoanalysis, he has twice been a Visiting Scholar at Harvard Divinity School. He is presently Professor of Psychology, Director of Psychological Services, and Director of Doctoral Training at Norwich University. Among his publications is a book co-edited with Susanne Cook-Greuter entitled *Transcendence and Mature Thought in Adulthood: The Further Reaches of Adult Development*, and a recently co-edited book with Alan N. West entitled *Spirituality, Ethics, and Relationship in Adulthood: Clinical and Theoretical Explorations*. He is on the Editorial Board of the *Bulletin of the Boston Institute for Psychotherapy*. Dr Miller has a part-time clinical practice in Montpelier, Vermont.

David H. Rosen, MD, is the McMillan Professor of Analytical Psychology, Professor of Psychiatry and Behavioral Science, and Professor of Humanities in Medicine at Texas A&M University. He has a BA degree from the University of California (Berkeley) in Psychological-Biological Sciences, and a MD from the University of Missouri (Columbia). Dr Rosen's psychiatric training was at the Langley Porter Institute, University of California Medical Center (San Francisco), where he remained on the faculty until 1982. From 1982 until 1986, when he went to Texas A&M University, he was Associate Professor of Psychiatry and Medicine at the University of Rochester Medical Center in New York. Dr Rosen's research interests include analytical psychology, psychology of religion, evolutionary psychology, depression, suicidology, healing, and the psychosocial, psychiatric, and human aspects of medicine. His seventy publications include six books, the most recent of which are *Evolution of the Psyche* (co-edited with Michael Luebbert) (1999), *The Tao of Jung: The Way of Integrity* (1997), and *Transforming Depression: Healing the Soul through Creativity* (1996).

Sherry Salman, Ph.D., is a Jungian psychoanalyst and psychologist in Rhinebeck, NY, and New York City, who is a faculty member and supervising analyst at the C. G. Jung Training Institute in New York. Her recent publications include 'The creative psyche: Jung's major contributions' (1997), in *The Cambridge Companion to Jung*, and 'Dissociation and the Self in the magical pre-Oedipal field' (1999), in *The Journal of Analytical Psychology*.

Judith Stevens-Long, Ph.D., is a member of the faculty at the Fielding Institute in Santa Barbara, where she also directs the Master's program in Organizational Design and Effectiveness (MODE). The MODE is designed to deliver on-line education to working professionals all over the globe. Students, as well as faculty, have been recruited in Europe, Asia, and Australia, and recruitment efforts are currently under way in South America. Judith received her Ph.D. from the University of California at Los Angeles in 1971 and began her teaching career at California State University, Los Angeles. She was asked to join the founding faculty at the University of Washington, Tacoma, where she helped develop curriculum and teaching methods in Human and Organizational Development. She left UWT to take an administrative post at Fielding, where she had consulted to the Ph.D. program since 1984. Dr Stevens-Long has written a best-selling textbook called *Adult Life* (now in its 4th edition), has published numerous articles on human development and group process, and has written a new book on communication in the workplace.

Demaris S. Wehr, Ph.D., has a doctorate in Religion and Psychology. She currently teaches courses in Spirituality and Psychology, Women's Studies, and Jungian Psychology at Andover Newton Theological School and Lesley College. She is also a psychotherapist in private practice, and is the author of *Jung and Feminism: Liberating Archetypes* (Boston: Beacon, 1987). She is currently working on a book about healing from spiritual abuse.

Polly Young-Eisendrath, Ph.D., is a psychologist and Jungian psychoanalyst practicing in Burlington, Vermont. Clinical Associate Professor of Psychiatry at the University of Vermont, she has published ten books, and many chapters and articles, and lectures widely on topics of resilience, women's development, couple relationship, and the interface of contemporary psychoanalysis and spirituality. Her most recent books are *The Cambridge Companion to Jung* and *The Resilient Spirit: Transforming Suffering into Insight and Renewal*. She has just completed *Women and Desire: Beyond Wanting to Be Wanted*. In 1971, she became a student of Roshi Philip Kapleau.

Beyond enlightened self-interest

The psychology of mature spirituality in the twenty-first century

Polly Young-Eisendrath and Melvin E. Miller

The opening of the twenty-first century is marked by a peculiar situation in regard to religion and spirituality. On one hand, most people are weary and even demoralized by our constant focus on 'enlightened self-interest.' To paraphrase biblical scholar Miles (Revel and Ricard 1999: x), we are becoming bored and more than a little frightened by the widely held belief in the moral code that the world is real and the world's goods are really worth acquiring. Intense enthusiasm for everything from a credit card to a new baby, a foreign vacation to a museum membership has replaced what, in another period of time, might have been a curiosity or even a sense of awe about existence itself and our purpose within it.

On the other hand, people of the twenty-first century are wary of religious dogma and oppressive creeds and politics that too often require adults to behave intellectually and emotionally as though they were children. Most institutionalized religions have demanded that we fill certain roles that reward us—if they do at all—only with social experiences of community and family traditions, not with spiritual meaning. Many Americans and Europeans no longer engage in formal religious practices within the confines of traditional Western religious institutions—with the exception of some forms of fundamentalism, especially Christian fundamentalism. Most educated people are loath to define themselves by religious dogma that does not reflect their authentic experience of life.

And yet what of this 'authentic experience' of life? Often it is overloaded with self-interest and anxiety, especially if one is living in an industrialized society and enjoying the wealth and security of a life free from hunger and physical threat. People living under stressful conditions of poverty, terror, or major health threats do not have the freedom to think about their lifestyle. They may find that more traditional religious practices are helpful because these tend to reduce fear. On the other hand, they may find that traditional practices do not help, but rather abandon them to fear, resentment, and despair. Some people living under the most stressful conditions—for example, the Mother Teresas—become resilient in the process of transforming their suffering into a sense of purpose and meaning through traditional or non-traditional spiritual and religious means. They are the exceptions.

The typical educated individual at the beginning of the twenty-first century is likely to feel demoralized about the chances of finding any larger purpose or meaning in human life. Those of us who are trying to live in tune with the rational empiricism and scientific achievements of our era face a double bind in regard to our spirituality. If we pursue the old paths of institutionalized religion, we often end up pretending to be convinced of something that seems inherently illogical and unpersuasive: religious dogma. Or, if we pursue the path of enlightened scientific reasoning, we end up in despair and apathy about humanity and its inhumanity. So we attempt to soothe our despair and anxiety through acquiring material things, trying Prozac or its cousins, taking exotic vacations, believing in our own or our children's achievements, and the like. These latter are the cultural imperatives of the educated individual at the beginning of the twenty-first century.

In the midst of such a double bind, many tend to cling to superstitions and unscientific spiritual practices such as astrology and oracular psychic methods. These and other New Age activities can be added to bolster one's self-interest, without disrupting the material longings and acquisitiveness of a poor soul in distress. Beliefs in paranormal phenomena of all sorts (for instance, alien abductions at this Millennium) have always characterized the *fin de siècle* consciousness of the masses. But this current cultural moment has its peculiar brand of spiritualism interspersed with self-interest. This mix expresses the dilemma of a new millennium in which many imagine that the greatest spiritual adventures are taking place in the natural sciences (e.g. chaos theory, quantum mechanics, systems theory, etc.), but cannot be understood by those who are not scientists, and so exclude the ordinary individual who no longer believes in the powers of theism, but has nothing to replace them.

This volume of essays was designed to address this dilemma. Is it possible to embrace spiritual meaning and not become either childish or irrational, while increasing one's genuine awe, inspiration, gratitude, *and* intellectual appreciation of living now in this period of scientific skepticism?

The idea of 'spirituality' is somewhat contemporary itself. Even a few decades ago, an interest in the sacred would typically not be separated from being religious. For example, in 1938 in his Terry Lectures at Princeton University on the topic of 'Psychology and Religion,' Jung strove to give a broad and inclusive definition of 'religion.' He said,

> Religion appears to me to be a peculiar attitude of the human mind . . . a careful consideration and observation of certain dynamic factors, understood to be 'powers,' spirits, demons, gods, laws, ideas, ideals or

whatever name man has given to such factors as he has found in his world powerful, dangerous, or helpful enough to be taken into careful consideration, or grand, beautiful and meaningful enough to be devoutly adored and loved.

(1938/1958: 8)

Jung was alert to include any cause to which a person might be 'religiously devoted' in his definition of a religious attitude. At the turn of the new century, many of us have stopped referring to religion, but simply talk about spiritual experiences outside of any religious context. We (the editors) were hopeful to formalize such individual enagement with spiritual life by asking psychologists, psychiatrists, religious educators, and philosophers to write about the sacred from the perspective of what genuinely challenged them in their personal and professional lives.

For the purposes of this volume, we asked our contributors to address 'spirituality' in the broadest way possible—in terms of anything that seemed to enhance the sense of the sacred in human life. We also asked them to speak especially to the complexity, nuance, and integrity of what would seem to them a 'mature' spirituality. We were interested in assisting psychotherapists, like ourselves, and others who teach or help people to encounter essential existential questions that demand a spiritual answer: Who are we as humans? What is our purpose here? What is the meaning of death in our lives? and Can we develop an enduring sense of meaning? These are the life questions that emerge in effective long term psychotherapy; they are the existential issues of adulthood in general.

MATURE SPIRITUALITY

We decided to organize these essays into three groupings that reflect, in our view, the components of mature spirituality. The three section titles are Integrity, Wisdom, and Transcendence. We ask how each of these relate to maturity in spiritual development. *Integrity*—referring as it does to both an ethical commitment and an integration of diverse states—was the easiest and the first quality that came to mind as 'mature spirituality.' We assumed that the person who had reached a complex, multifaceted perspective on life and humanity would have encountered the question of how to bring together all sides of her or his feelings and points of view. We also took a cue from Loevinger's (1976) 'stages of ego development' in which the highest stage is called 'integrated' and refers to the capacity to pull together multiple meanings with a tolerance for ambiguity and paradox.

The chapters in the next section were grouped around the concept of *Wisdom*. This is a quality that has traditionally been associated with spiritual elders, and thus it was a more difficult one to define and include in a book on contemporary spiritual development. How does wisdom fit with the dilemma of enlightened self-interest and spiritual longing in the context of skeptical or cynical secularism? Does wisdom have to be mired-down in New Age formulas or antiquated mysticism? Can it be freed from our prejudices about how it 'should' look and take on an appearance that fits with our experience of contemporary people? Ancient Western philosophical teachings (ending perhaps with Spinoza) and Eastern philosophies of Buddhism include 'wisdom practice' that could help individuals increase their capacity for sustained and sustaining insight. Is there something today that does the same or a similar thing? Or must we return to ancient teachings in order to develop wisdom? Most of the contributors to this project seem to believe that wisdom can be achieved by contemporary means; some have developed persuasive arguments to this end.

And finally, we felt that we needed to address this quality called *Transcendence*—especially since it is sought willy-nilly by many people in contemporary mind-expanding practices. By this term, we mean extending or expanding the limits of our ordinary consciousness or experience in ways that connect us with a symbolic or phenomenal reality beyond the ordinary. Transcendence may mean extending our ordinary sense of ourselves as autonomous individuals. It may even mean transcending our usual confines of space–time–causality, or transcending our usual habits of fear and self-protectiveness.

In Christian theology, especially, transcendence is often contrasted with immanence. In terms of such theology, transcendence goes beyond our common world of reality, while immanence remains within it. In our contemporary understanding of transcendence, as these essays attest, there is no dualism of the two qualities; they merge in our experience of the present moment. And so the issues that are included under the topic of transcendence encompass questions about how and why we should want to expand our ordinary reality in order to glimpse into something else—and about how that something else must contribute to the here-and-now dilemmas of truth and compassion for ourselves, for others, and for the world/environment in which we live.

When we collected these essays we did not imagine that there would be an underlying theme that developed throughout. We were astonished to find one clearly traced as the early drafts arrived and we first read them through. The central theme that emerged was one that expressed the outline of mature spirituality in our time: acceptance of one's limitations, groundedness in the ordinary, and willingness to be surprised. We might call this a 'skeptical spirituality' that places neither god(s) nor humankind at the metaphorical center of the universe. These essays seem to imply that neither divinity nor humanity can save us from ourselves. And so we must get used to working with ourselves as we are—with blindspots and imperfections—so that we can become more truthful and compassionate in our development.

In reading this volume, there are two suggested approaches. First, it might be read from beginning to end. In doing so, the reader will find some chapters overlap and contradict each other. In such a reading, it would be useful to find the underlying argument in each chapter and see how it is expanded or dismissed in another. On the other hand, one might choose to read the first couple of chapters in each section and then read randomly—according to your interests. The chapters have been arranged so that the first of each section serves as an introduction to the section theme. The second in each section was chosen to counter and/or expand upon the first. The chapters that follow take up specific concerns and issues that emerge in the development of mature spirituality in regard to the topic of the section and a particular activity or domain.

Like the other contributors to this volume, we regard spiritual development to be a necessary component of a healthy, effective life as a human being. By spiritual development, we mean a lifetime of engagement with a transcendent source that is intimate and Other. This development begins in childhood, out of our dependence on others. In our early years we are awed by our parents and elders, whose power seems supreme: Who are They? They are our earliest encounter with an Otherness that sustains and protects us. The images and meanings that we accrue in those early contacts with Otherness introduce us to, or block us from, a later respect for and interest in a spiritual life (cf. McDargh [1983]; Rizzutto [1974, 1976]).

If we mature psychologically as we grow older, we come to see that we are responsible for sustaining and protecting ourselves. This is a fearful prospect. Some adults never wholly assume this responsibility but continue to hope for protection and favors from a powerful Otherness (God, Goddess, divinities). Their spiritual development remains in a childish form.

Assuming responsibility for our own (and eventually others') lives is a transformation that should lead to the next phase of spiritual development as we begin to address, in a more focused manner, questions such as: What is my purpose here? How do I fit into the intimate Otherness of family, society, the world? If we discover satisfactory answers to these questions—and some may not, the search may be lifelong—then we naturally turn our attention to the last great inquiry: Who are we? What does it mean to be human? Mature spirituality is the honing of integrity, wisdom, and transcendence in the service of the question of what it means to be human in the Otherness of our universe.

As noted earlier, religions have traditionally guided spiritual development; symbolic connections were regulated by images and processes that were automatically made available to the developing child as well as the mature adult. But in our era, spiritual development proceeds more randomly and can be more easily derailed as families and individuals operate in their own idiosyncratic ways. Widespread symbolic connections come more from TV and movies than from religious practices.

Many question whether any kind of religious practices are needed in today's world. After all, we say, religions have clearly oppressed (and still oppress) many people. So if religions have been harmful, and if narrowly conceived religious dogmas can impede—even damage—psychological development, why is spirituality important at all in this period?

These essays offer an affirmative, albeit complex, response to such queries. Most contributors agree, in general, that a mature spirituality is important for good psychological health. Spiritual engagement with a larger meaning is an essential dimension of being fully alive and fully human. By the time we reach adulthood—and certainly by midlife—we have all encountered some pain and adversity that has prompted anguish and suffering at a personal level. If we haven't been confronted with serious illness, loss, or accident, we have at least had to contend with the hassles and imperfections of everyday life. The confrontation with aging also brings painful awareness of time's passage and the decline of physical health. Without some practice or meaning that transcends our own self-interest, no matter how enlightened it is, we face our future with despair, inner emptiness, or constant restlessness. The experience that 'I'm useful here and I have a larger purpose than promoting my own identity' is radically important to self-esteem and self-determination over the adult years.

Mature spirituality in no way attempts to erase the difficulties of suffering or adversity. In fact, it embraces them as part of human life. And it gives us a new perspective that helps to make them bearable and even interesting. They become part of the fate that we embrace because we are engaged in an adventure—a mystery—of understanding an Otherness that can never be wholly grasped, but must be acknowledged if we are to thrive. Ultimately we learn that our pain, suffering, blindspots, and other difficulties can become the royal road to transcending our self-interest, in the process of witnessing the interdependence and wonder that are the core of our existence. These essays show us how the domain and process of mature spirituality can be described, fostered, and taught in ways that help us come to terms with the spiritual issues facing humankind as we stand on the threshold of a new century. Moreover, they show us how to celebrate spirituality in its many forms; they help us exalt the spiritual side of self-exploration, relationship, and engagement with the Other. Ideally, these essays will contribute to our collective integrity and wisdom.

REFERENCES

Jung, C. G. (1938/1958) *The Collected Works of C. G. Jung*, vol. 11: *Psychology and religion*, trans. R. F. C. Hull, Princeton, NJ: Princeton University Press.

Loevinger, J. (1976) *Ego Development: Conceptions and Theories*, San Francisco: Jossey Bass.

McDargh, J. (1983) *Psychoanalytic Object Relations Theory and the Study of Religion: On Faith and the Imaging of God*, Lanham, MD: University Press of America.

Revel, J.-F. and Ricard, M. (1999) *The Monk and the Philosopher: A Father and Son Discuss the Meaning of Life*, New York: Schocken Books.

Rizzuto, A.-M. (1974) 'Object relations and the formation of the image of God,' *British Journal of Medical Psychology*, 47: 83–9.

Rizzuto, A.-M. (1976) 'Freud, God, the devil and the theory of object representation,' *International Journal of Psycho-analysis*, 57/3: 165–80.

PART I

Integrity

Chapter 1

The place of integrity in spirituality

John Beebe

If integrity could be reduced to purity, then its relation to spirituality would be obvious. Purity of heart, as Kierkegaard famously told us, is to will one thing, and the pure heart that wills only the relation to God is by definition securely on the spiritual path. However, 'integrity is a complex notion' (Kekes, 1989: 219, 222–30). After Freud and Jung it must include an orientation toward responsible integration of unacceptable desires—Jung's *shadow* and Freud's *id*.

As a Jungian analyst, I am concerned to bring all of the parts of the person into view, not just the strivings towards being a better individual. Yet I do not consider the practice of depth psychotherapy simply an X-ray or MRI of the stationary soul in which the only attitude that matters is to see it all as clearly and with as much texture as possible. I am ever trying to foster an attitude in my patient and myself that seeks to find the right relation to each new and sometimes disturbing revelation of the self. I have learned that on my part neither a strongly moralistic conscious stance nor the neutral, non-judgmental posture of the traditional, analytically oriented psychotherapist brings forth the attitude from the unconscious that I am seeking.

What works, I have discovered, is a nearly continuous monitoring of the psyche for its ethical intentions. That is, it is necessary in the midst of listening to any feeling or account of behavior to consider the impact of that feeling or behavior on some object, for the psyche is nothing if not a subjectivity that intends to do something with and to its objects. Different psychological theories, using different languages, seem to be converging in agreement that all psychic life implies a dialectic between *self* and *other*. It is no longer possible to imagine an effective therapy of this dialectic that would consider only one of these at the expense of the other pole. Yet depth psychology has tended to describe the discovery of self in therapy in a moral vacuum, assuming that those who learn to be true to themselves will automatically avoid dealing falsely with others.

My own work has been an effort to consider the impact on the implied other of the various states of self that Jung describes as archetypal. It has led me finally to consider the nature of what I have called moral process, meaning particularly the way in which the responsibility to other is imagined and lived by the self. In my book *Integrity in Depth* (1992), I refer to certain philosophers who have been motivated to push philosophy past its usual concerns with ontology (the nature of being) and epistemology (the way we know things) into a more practical focus on the impact of persons as moral agents. The new moral psychology has much in common with contemporary interactional depth psychology, and I believe the common ground lies in the concern for the self's accountability. That accountability is described by names like *sincerity*, *responsibility*, *morality*, and *ethics*, but I have found the best word to be *integrity*.

As the moral philosopher Calhoun has noted, integrity means 'standing for something' beyond 'the integration of "parts" of oneself into a whole,' 'fidelity to those projects and principles which are constitutive of one's core identity,' and 'maintaining the purity of one's own agency, especially in dirty-hands situations.' Integrity is a 'social virtue' (Calhoun 1995: 235, 258). This view goes back in the West at least as far as Hegel, who understood integrity as an aspect of good citizenship (Crittenden 1992: 254), but in the East we can find it in the *Analects* of Confucius.

What has given new impetus to the social dimension of integrity in the West is the crisis of recognition that human beings carry the power to destroy the planet on which they live. Integrity involves a willing sensitivity to the needs of the whole, an ethic that combines caring for others in the world with a sense of justice in insisting that others treat us and we treat them as we would all like to be treated. The psychological question is how such sensitivity may be nurtured.

Psychotherapy has much experience to share if it can recognize that it is a practice that promotes integrity. The simple act of trying to put feelings into words is itself an act of integrity. We should note that with the verbalization of affect two very different things are brought into relationship. One is a psychological function which directly experiences and gives value to affect or emotion without the intercession of words, exactly as one registers the impact of music. Jung, following a long tradition that he also clarifies, calls this the *feeling* function of human consciousness. The act of naming, on the other hand, which he calls *thinking*, is a cognitive procedure that invokes the discriminated use of language to give a defined meaning to the emotion. According to Jung's landmark book, *Psychological Types* (1971), thinking and feeling are opposites on a rational axis that permits the discrimination of givens in experience. When the two poles of this axis are brought together, as in that moment when an upsetting feeling is appropriately named, a small miracle occurs: a union of opposites in which a whole is sensed. Psychotherapists call this *insight* and, tracking such moments of heightened consciousness over the course of an analytic hour, take the pulse of individuation.

The Jungian ideal of individuation is that the consciousness of the person will become psychologically undivided, with no part of the self so split off in the unconscious that it is inaccessible to dialogue with the ego. In analysis, the analyst is looking for a self-coherent narrative in the patient undergoing treatment. Unfortunately, this not unreasonable expectation can be confused with the utopian ideal of personality as a continuous state of consciousness in which no characterologic defenses are evident. This goal is surely impossible, because, as depth psychology has shown, it is the continuing fate of any human being to experience at least some psycho-pathology (Hillman 1975: 55) in which split-off complexes set up 'a shadow government of the ego' (Jung 1966a: 87) or what Jungians often call a state of 'possession by complexes' (Sandner and Beebe 1995: 317).

INTEGRITY AS THE HOLDING ENVIRONMENT

What actually individuates is not the total personality, with its inevitable blind spots, but the willingness of the person being analyzed to face them. In a previous essay, I have written:

> Character as a whole does not individuate, although we may make great progress in overcoming our susceptibility to possession by par-ticular complexes and thus [become] more aware of our character. Character belongs to our embodied nature, and has a structure which allows for permanent strengths and permanent shadow attributes. Parts of our character may develop, but its basic nature is present in us very early . . . What *can* individuate out of a person's character is integrity, that accountability which makes the work on the rest of character—recognizing it, allowing for it, compensating it, training it—possible.
>
> (Beebe 1998: 60)

Another way to say this is that integrity 'holds character.'[1]

Within psychoanalysis, Winnicott was the first to conceptualize psycho-therapy as a holding environment. His use of the word *holding* was an analogy to child-rearing, which as a pediatrician he had had long occasion to observe. '"It took a long time," he wrote, "for the analytic world . . . to look, for example, at the importance of the way a baby is held and yet when you come to think of it, this is of primary significance. The question of holding and handling brings up the whole issue of human reliability"' (Winnicott quoted in Phillips 1988: 30).

The image of holding can also apply to the need to carry an awareness of one's moral responsibility to others, as in the healthy development of a sense of shame. The ancient Chinese classic, the *I Ching*, which is essentially a manual of how to think about integrity across a range of human situations, speaks in a recent translation of 'embracing the shameful' (Wu 1998: 97). The more familiar translation of this line is 'They bear shame' (Wilhelm and Baynes 1967: 54). The actual pictographs in the Chinese text are *bao*, which 'shows a fetus in the womb, a symbol for holding and caring for what is within,' and *xiu*, which 'shows an offering of a sacrificial sheep' (Wu 1991: 86). Bringing this image into Western idiom, I tend to think of it as holding sheepishness close to oneself, as when one allows oneself to feel ashamed or guilty when one has mishandled another. The line is tradi-tionally interpreted as a sign of a turn for the better, since it suggests that people who have been using their power illegitimately are beginning to feel that expiation is called for.

Recently, the integrity of the United States has been challenged to come to terms with an admitted character defect in its President. From the beginning of President Clinton's emergence on the national scene, the word 'character' has been invoked by his opponents to convey anxiety about his fitness for office. When finally the President admitted not only to an extra-marital affair, but to lying about it to his wife and members of the Cabinet even after it had become exposed, many felt that the 'smoking gun' had surfaced which would surely doom his popular reputation. Strangely, the President's approval ratings did not drop. Instead, the major leader of the opposing party, who had campaigned on a platform of moral indignation, was forced to resign after the midterm Congressional elections failed to produce a mandate for his party. Many people were perplexed by this outcome—as they were later when the Republican leadership failed in its effort to have the President removed from office—and wondered if it represented a moral indifference on the part of the populace.

I think it did not. America remains the most church-going nation in the world, and a country in which extra-marital affairs are still widely dis-approved of. Rather the way in which the country held the President's shadow seems to me to illustrate a psychological process in which the people, without denying the character problem of the President, elected silently to carry it in consciousness without being drawn into the kind of punitive reaction which makes the sinner both a scapegoat and a martyr. The people seemed to be reacting with great discrimination at a feeling level, approaching the commonly stated ideal of hating the sin and loving the sinner. A leading novelist even suggested that Clinton's own 'tolerance for ambiguity within the self' made Clinton a more 'rounded' character in the moral imagination than his prosecutor, the 'flat' Ken Starr, with his 'zealous and chillingly unambiguous morality' (Canin 1998: 39).

This is obviously a more complex stance than the superego attitude that Bennett recommended in *The Death of Outrage*, his angry response to what he viewed as a failure of American morality (Bennett 1998). Interestingly, President Clinton began to speak of his need to work on his character through spiritual ministry and to atone for the damage he caused to his family and to the public trust. Never previously had this President admitted a defect in himself that needed work, and in some ways this was a first for the Presidency itself.

THE IMPORTANCE OF SHADOW IN SPIRITUAL MATURITY

It is impossible to know very much about what actually happens in the lives of public figures, but such collective dramas have always been the stuff of our culture's fantasies about the nature of human transformation. The lesson of our literary tradition seems to be that it is not the particular character flaw that a hero may possess, but rather the attitude toward it that matters. There seems to be something especially attractive, spiritually speaking, about owning of the parts of oneself that do not fit into the usual gestalt of one's moral identity.

Jung taught that the god of Western Europe is Respectability (Jung 1989: 68) and that respectability's archetype is *persona*, that mask with which we so frequently confuse ourselves. Under the spell of the persona, the shadow is truly other to the ego. When the shadow is held in consciousness, an opportunity for spiritual development presents itself. Jung says as much in his essay, 'The Philosophical Tree,' when he writes, 'Filling the conscious mind with ideal conceptions is a characteristic feature of Western theosophy, but not the confrontation with the shadow and the world of darkness. One does not become enlightened by imagining figures of light, but by making the darkness conscious' (Jung 1967: 265, para. 335).

This is not naively to equate shadow with spirit or the unconscious with God, although Jung teaches that spirit enters the psyche through the shadow. This is one way to understand Jung's enormous difference from Freud, which Jung unsparingly articulated on the occasion of Freud's death amidst otherwise quite appreciative reflections on his former teacher's contributions to the Western understanding of psyche:

> Ludwig Klages' saying that 'the spirit is the adversary of the soul' might serve as a . . . motto for the way Freud approached the possessed psyche. Whenever he could, he dethroned the 'spirit' as the possessing and repressing agent by reducing it to a 'psychological formula.' . . . In a crucial talk with him I once tried to get him to understand the admonition: 'Try the spirits whether they are of God' (1 John 4:1). In vain . . .
>
> Freud's 'psychological formula' is only an apparent substitute for the daemonically vital thing that causes a neurosis. In reality, only the spirit can cast out the 'spirits'—not the intellect, which is at best a mere assistant . . . and scarcely fitted to play the role of an exorcist.
>
> (Jung 1966b: 48–9)

Jung implies here that Freud fell victim in some way to the shadow that
Freud was the first to investigate, because he could not discover his own
purpose in investigating it. We know from many biographers that the key
motivation Freud himself offered was 'ambition' (Gay 1988: 442), the
ambition of a discoverer and liberator, which was linked in his imagination
to the heroic figure of Oedipus saving Thebes by answering the Sphinx's
riddle. Hillman has pointed out that Freud's very methods were Oedipal:
'inquiry as interrogation, consciousness as seeing, dialogue to find out, self-
discovery by recall of early life, oracular reading of dreams' (Hillman 1991:
130–1). But Jung was wary of Freud's assumption that the unconscious was
simply a Sphinx's riddle to be deciphered and mastered by a heroic ego.
Jung felt that an effective solution to the problem of the unconscious
required an active willingness to consider the possibility that what comes
from the unconscious to interfere with our conscious functioning may have
a positive, transformative purpose. Thus, his insistence on the psychological
value of the religious idea that we must inquire of a possessing spirit (what
Jung would have called a *complex*) whether it be 'of God.'

To get to the point that one can inquire of the spirits what source they
spring from and what they intend is a major purpose of the spiritual
exercises of St Ignatius of Loyola, which Jung was lecturing on at the time
he composed his memorial to Sigmund Freud. The exercises are actually a
form of psychotherapy often conducted by trained spiritual directors within
the Jesuit order of the Catholic Church, even today. They seek to cultivate
a vigilant receptivity to images in dreams and fantasy that may guide an
individual at a time of crisis.

To Jung, these exercises seemed to represent a forerunner of his own
technique of active imagination in which particular troublesome states of
mind are asked to personify themselves so that the individual can enter into
an active dialogue with them. What is interesting about both the exercises
and Jung's technique is the insistence by both upon the ethical attitude of
the ego. It is the spiritual director's duty in conducting the exercises to
assure that the particular fantasy image is of God and not of the Devil. It is
the ego's duty in Jung's technique to take an appropriate attitude toward
the possessing complex. Here we can see the role of integrity in discrimi-
nating spiritual experience. Spirit emerges out of the shadowy background
of consciousness, but it is the integrity of consciousness that assures our
ability to see if the spirit is capable of moving us in the direction of greater
awareness or condemning us to repetitive impulse.

THE STRANGER AND OUR INTEGRITY

A practical illustration of the process has been offered by Marcus in her
classic paper, 'The Stranger in Women's Dreams' (1956), in which the

common theme of the 'intruding stranger' is amplified. The stranger, usually male and often of another race and class than the dreamer, somehow forces his way into the dreamer's personal space. Not surprisingly, he is initially perceived as quite dangerous, although his actual behavior, aside from intruding, often turns out not to be destructive. Marcus's interpretation is that this figure represents a spiritual opportunity to the woman who is capable of accepting his entrance on her psychological scene. It obviously takes a psychological leap of faith for the woman to imagine the appearance of an image who may well signal the robber, rapist, or murderer within as an opportunity for development. Yet this is what Marcus suggests in her discussion of the dream figure as an indicator of the *animus*, the female archetype of spirit, pressing for integration into the dreamer's conscious life. Although linked to Jung's classical notion of the *anima* as a soul figure mediating the contents of the unconscious to a man in a tutelary fashion, the woman's animus had traditionally conjured up the image of a hostile, irritated, obsessive state of mind, as in its *Oxford English Dictionary* meaning. Yet Jungians have made clear that the animus is often an unrecognized aspect of a woman's strength (Young-Eisendrath and Wiedemann 1987), and her bridge to the wider self (Ulanov 1992: 25). First encounters with images of this psychological function may be frightening, dark, and overwhelming to the ego.

Contemporary readers may gain insight into this paradox at the heart of the Jungian notion of individuation by studying John Guare's drama, *Six Degrees of Separation*, about the spiritual effect of an intruding stranger. The play, which has been made into a movie, shows the development of integrity in a middle-aged, upper-class woman whose attitude toward life is changed after a homeless young black man talks his way into her Manhattan apartment on the pretext that he is the son of Sidney Poitier and the friend of her children at Harvard. In fact, he has gleaned all of his information about her family from a former classmate of her children who had picked him up in a gay encounter in a Boston alley. The protagonist Ouisa Kittredge is, at the beginning of the play, totally identified with the ego ambitions of her art dealer husband, Flanders. The appearance of the young man in their apartment is fortuitous because they are entertaining a South African financier who has a strong anti-apartheid ethos: the young man's presence makes him willing to trust the Kittredges with 2 million dollars toward the purchase of a Cézanne which they will be able to sell at a great profit. But when the young imposter, Paul, proceeds to pick up a hustler and bring him back to the Kittredge's apartment after they have gone to sleep, the Kittredges are horrified and kick both Paul and the hustler out.

What makes the story interesting is that Ouisa does not give up wondering about the meaning of Paul's appearance in her life. As the play progresses, she takes the lead in teasing out how Paul managed to create a relation to her family, and in the play's most philosophic scene muses:

I read somewhere that everybody on this planet is separated by only six other people. Six degrees of separation. Between us and everybody else on this planet. The President of the United States. A gondolier in Venice. Fill in the names. I find that a) tremendously comforting that we're so close and b) like Chinese water torture that we're so close. Because you have to find the right six people to make the connection. It's not just big names. It's *anyone*. A native in a rain forest. A Tierra del Fuegan. An Eskimo. I am bound to everyone on this planet by a trail of six people. It's a profound thought. How Paul found us. How to find the man whose son he pretends to be. Or perhaps *is* his son, although I doubt it. How every person is a new door, opening up into other worlds. Six degrees of separation between me and everyone else on this planet. But to find the right six people.

(Guare 1994: 81)

This is a realization of what Jung describes in the language of the alchemist Dorn as the 'union of the whole man with the *unus mundus*,' the underlying unity of the world (Jung 1963: 534, 538).

In alchemy, which was a spiritual discipline in the midst of proto-chemical practice, the realization of the *unus mundus* was conceived as the highest possible state of conjunction, the ultimate goal of the alchemical work, given in the image of the 'philosophers' stone.' Although today we tend to see alchemy as the forerunner of physical chemistry and its *mysterium tremendum* as the nature of chemical combination which gives material substances their integrity, Jung taught us to recognize the stone as an image of the integrity of the psychologically unified self. It is precisely at that self's stage of highest integrity that it realizes its connection to all other selves on the planet.

Nowhere does this come home to developed individuals more than in their relationship to the chance happenings of their lives. It is the individual's integrity that enables such chance happenings to have the force of truly meaningful coincidences. Indeed there is a Chinese tradition that genuine synchronicities, such as the meaningful answers one gets in casting the *I Ching*, only occur for people who are already possessed of the highest integrity (Wilhelm 1977: 13).

But as Guare's character Ouisa so effectively personifies, the requisite attitude is not one of austere stand-offish moral purity, but rather a vigorous feeling of potential connection between the human and the divine which is offered to us by the intrusion of uncanny coincidence. In the film version of *Six Degrees of Separation* this is beautifully illustrated when Ouisa, with her husband, Flan, is allowed to ride a lift to the top of the Sistine Chapel, where workmen are still cleaning Michelangelo's master-piece. The matchless image on the ceiling of the chapel shows God's finger on the point of touching man's. Ouisa is invited by one of the workmen to slap the hand of God, in effect to complete its contact with that of Adam. This represents the moment in the film when Ouisa advances from the passive stance of a witty, intuitive woman, musing on life, to a moral agent capable of direct participation in it. Psychologically her integrity is signalled by a union of opposites of archetypal image-sense and spontaneous action—a linking within the awakened soul of what Jung called the intuitive and sensation functions. She touches the meaning of God's having beckoned to her sleeping spirit through the intrusion of the young stranger, Paul. Ouisa's slap of God's hand is like a black hero's 'high five' and suggests her own personal integration of the irreverent African trans-gressivity of the trickster Paul: it is the signal of a mature integrity. Such an integrity, as Chinese philosophy has always seemed to know, and as the Western mind is just beginning to discover, has the capacity to recognize the spirit of God in experience that is unexpectedly meaningful and to celebrate that spirit by uniting the world.

NOTE

1. The relationship between character and integrity in the development of spirituality has been developed by Tarrant (1998: 171–204).

REFERENCES

Beebe, J. (1992) *Integrity in Depth*, College Station, TX: Texas A & M Press.
Beebe, J. (1997) 'Attitudes toward the unconscious,' *Journal of Analytical Psychology* 42/1: 3–20.
Beebe, J. (1998) 'Toward a Jungian analysis of character', in A. Casement (ed.), *Post-Jungians Today*, London and New York: Routledge.
Bennett, W. (1998) *The Death of Outrage*, New York: The Free Press.
Calhoun, C. (1995) 'Standing for something', *Journal of Philosophy*, 92/5: 235–60.
Canin, E. (1998) in 'The talk of the town,' *The New Yorker* (5 October 1998) 74/30: 39.
Crittenden, P. (1992) *Learning to Be Moral*, Atlantic Highlands, NJ, and London: Humanities Press International.
Gay, P. (1988) *Freud: A Life for Our Time*, New York and London: W. W. Norton.
Guare, J. (1994) *Six Degrees of Separation*, New York: Vintage Books.
Hillman, J. (1975) *Revisioning Psychology*, New York: Harper & Row.
Hillman, J. (1991) 'Oedipus revisited' in K. Kerenyi and J. Hillman, *Oedipus Variations*, Woodstock, CT: Spring Publications.
Jung, C. G. (1963) *Mysterium Coniunctionis*, New York: Bollingen Foundation.
Jung, C. G. (1966a) *The Practice of Psychotherapy*, 2nd edn, rev., Princeton, NJ: Princeton University Press.
Jung, C. G. (1966b) *The Spirit in Man, Art, and Literature*, Princeton, NJ: Princeton University Press.

Jung, C. G. (1967) *Alchemical Studies*, Princeton, NJ: Princeton University Press.

Jung, C. G. (1971) *Psychological Types*, Princeton, NJ: Princeton University Press.

Jung, C. G. (1989) *Analytical Psychology: Notes of the Seminar Given in 1925*, ed. W. McGuire, Princeton, NJ: Princeton University Press.

Kekes, J. (1989) *Moral Tradition and Individuality*, Princeton, NJ: Princeton University Press.

Marcus, K. (1956) 'The stranger in women's dreams,' Paper 7, Los Angeles: Analytical Psychology Club of Los Angeles.

Phillips, A. (1988) *Winnicott*, Cambridge, MA: Harvard University Press.

Sandner, D. and Beebe, J. (1995) 'Psychopathology and analysis', in M. Stein (ed.), *Jungian Analysis*, Chicago: Open Court.

Tarrant, J. (1998) *The Light Inside the Dark*, New York: HarperCollins.

Ulanov, A. (1992) 'Disguises of the anima', in N. Schwartz-Salant and M. Stein (eds), *Gender and Soul in Psychotherapy*, Wilmette, IL: Chiron Publications.

Wilhelm, H. (1977) *Heaven, Earth and Man in the Book of Changes*, Seattle: University of Washington Press.

Wilhelm, R., and Baynes, C. (trans.) (1967) *The I Ching*, 3rd edn, Princeton, NJ: Princeton University Press.

Wu, J. (1991) *Yi Jing*, Washington: The Taoist Center.

Wu, Y. (1998) *I Ching: The Book of Changes and Virtues*, San Bruno, CA: Great Learning Publishing Co.

Young-Eisendrath, P., and Wiedemann, F. (1987) *Female Authority: Empowering Women Through Psychotherapy*, New York: Guilford Press.

Chapter 2

A Buddha and his cousin

Richard P. Hayes

Like most religions, the Buddhist tradition is rich in stories that are designed to illustrate key principles and values. Stories of the Buddha himself offer a verbal portrait of an ideal human being that followers of the tradition can aspire to emulate; his story offers a picture of a person with a perfectly healthy mind. Stories of other people (and of gods, ghosts and ghouls) portray a wide range of beings from the nearly perfect to the dreadfully imperfect, all presented as models of what one could eventually become oneself through gradual transformations from one's present mentality. In what follows, I shall first tell a brief story about myself and will then recount the stories of two men who were cousins with similar but importantly different mentalities. And I shall conclude with a few observations about what I see as the significance of the difference between these two cousins.

First, a word about the storyteller. Several decades ago, my life was dominated by my need to make a decision about whether I would do the military service that I had been told my entire life was a duty and a privilege. While in the midst of making that decision, I happened to read Plato's account of the trial and death of Socrates. During that same month, I happened to attend a series of talks on Buddhism, all given by Asian Buddhists who also happened to be scientists working in the United States. Both Socrates and the Buddha had the same advice: find out who you really are, and then have the moral courage to be yourself.

After giving the matter more thought than I have ever given to anything since, I impulsively decided not to do military service and not to stay in the country that required it of me. Ever since that time, I have kept near me a worn copy of Plato's account of the death of Socrates and a shelf full of Buddhist texts.

Curiosity about the Buddhist texts led to my going back to university to take up the study of Sanskrit, Pali, and Tibetan. It also led me into a variety of Buddhist temples and centers to train in various kinds of Buddhist meditation. I now teach Buddhist studies at McGill University, and my wife and I guide people, mostly young adults, in Buddhist meditation at our home.

Also woven into the Socratic Buddhist tapestry has been a thread of intermittent interest in psychology. During recent years, circumstances have permitted the fulfillment of a lifelong dream of working with an analyst. (The dream was for a Freudian, but it came true with a Jungian, which is close enough for dreams.) Socrates, the Buddha, and Jung now seem to me like a tripod on which my mind is, for the time being, delicately balanced. A great deal of what this mind does is to think about the tripod on which it is balanced. What follows is some of that thinking.

WHAT THE BUDDHA ATTAINED

My current affiliation with a Buddhist group is with the Friends of the Western Buddhist Order (FWBO), an order founded in the late 1960s by Sangharakshita, a British man who had been a Buddhist monk for almost two decades. In the book of chants and recitations used by the FWBO, there is a verse that reads:

> We reverence the Buddha, and aspire to follow him.
> The Buddha was born as we are born.
> What the Buddha overcame, we too can overcome.
> What the Buddha attained, we too can attain.

Aspiring to follow the Buddha, of course, requires having some understanding of what he overcame and what he attained. Such understanding is imparted in a number of ways, one of the most common being to tell the story of his life and to reflect on the events that served as major turning-points. It is not my aim to retell that whole story here but rather to touch on a few episodes within it that have a particular relevance to myself and, I think, to many people living now in Western culture. By looking at these episodes I hope at least to give some idea of what one aspires to overcome and to attain through Buddhist practice.

A TALE OF TWO COUSINS

Cousin Gotama

Perhaps the best-known feature of the traditional account of the life of the Buddha is that he was born into luxury and privilege. According to ancient canonical sources, the young man called Gotama had three palaces and a beautiful wife and a large retinue of servants and attendants. Despite all this affluence, he was uneasy and restless. A poignant story is told of how, as a boy, Gotama saw his father and a team of farmers plowing the earth. On seeing how hard the oxen struggled under the drag of the plows, and how difficult it was for the men to guide the beasts, and especially on seeing all the insects and grubs and eggs that had been disturbed by the plows, the boy was filled with a profound sadness. Realizing that it is impossible to maintain life without disturbing the lives of others, sometimes even depriving others of their lives, the boy was overcome with grief of the type that Jungian analyst James Hollis calls existential guilt, which arises when 'we understand that the principle that underlies life is death' (Hollis 1996: 30).

Part of what it means to say that the Buddha was born as we were born is that he, like many of us, was disturbed by the recognition that his life entailed the destruction of others, and that this is so no matter what one chooses to eat. Some degree of pain and suffering, in other words, is unavoidable so long as one is alive. It is impossible to achieve a painless trajectory through life. At best, one can aspire to achieve a path through life that reduces the amount of unnecessary suffering that one's existence inflicts on others.

It could be said that the principal task of a Buddhist is to figure out somehow which kinds of pain are avoidable and which are inevitable and to learn how to avoid as much as possible inflicting and being afflicted by those that can be avoided. Inflicting no pain at all on others can result only in making one's own life impossible; inflicting too much makes the burden of guilt unbearable. Thinking that one must do what is impossible, namely, to avoid all pain, only increases one's own pain. Above all else, what one must do is to be realistic in one's aspirations.

The point that pain is unavoidable in any worthwhile enterprise in life is illustrated in traditional accounts of Gotama's decision to leave home. When Gotama reached the age of twenty-nine, say the texts, his first and only son was born. In celebration of the event, a large party was arranged at which all the best food and drink was served. Entertainment for the evening was provided by the most accomplished singers and dancers, most of them women, who stayed until very late in the evening. The festivities went on for so many hours that most of the guests fell asleep, as did the entertainers. On seeing all these women lying around in various states of disarray, some of them drooling and others snoring and yet others sleeping with their eyes wide open so that they appeared like dead fish, the new father was horrified by their appearance. All these women, who had been so alluring only a few hours earlier, were now arranged in such repelling postures with their once-attractive cosmetics now smeared unappealingly over their faces and clothing, the young man realized that beauty is not absolute but depends entirely on circumstances and perceptions.

On coming to this sad recognition, Gotama lost all interest in the pleasures and opulence of the only kind of life he had known, for this life no longer brought him satisfaction. And so, not knowing what he might find as an alternative, he left. His leave-taking proved to be a source of grief to his father and to his wife and to all those who loved him. Fully acknowledging the pain caused by his decision, Buddhists traditionally say that so long as people have emotional dependencies on others, they are bound to suffer. It is only by breaking free of those dependencies that one can become liberated from suffering, and yet the very act of breaking free causes pain of its own. Among the many unrealistic expectations that can cause unnecessary pain is that of expecting freedom from hardship without undergoing some more hardship.

The point that a realistic balance must be found is further emphasized in another episode in the traditional story of Gotama's life. According to this story, he tried to win freedom from his distress by avoiding destroying anything at all. So as to harm nothing, he avoided all but the smallest amounts of food. He ate so little that he became too weak to think clearly or do anything but sit still. It was only when Gotama, then aged thirty-five, abandoned the extreme self-denial of a rigorously ascetic life that he finally became a Buddha, that is, someone who had awakened to the true nature of things and adjusted his expectations accordingly.

Cousin Devadatta

Shortly after this awakening, the Buddha returned to his home town and visited his family for the first time since he had fled home at the age of twenty-nine. It was during this visit that he became reacquainted with his cousin, Devadatta, who was convinced of the soundness of what the Buddha was teaching and made the decision to become a monk in the newly founded Buddhist order. For nearly forty-five years the Buddha and his cousin Devadatta lived the life of wandering mendicants, within a community that preached to people wherever they went and that inspired others by exemplifying the joy that comes of material simplicity, integrity, and virtue.

According to all accounts, Devadatta was popular and effective as a teacher. He was, in nearly all respects, a model monk. And yet, towards the end of his life, things went dramatically wrong between him and the Buddha, and their falling out had repercussions for nearly everyone in the Buddhist community. The rest of this story will be devoted to reflecting on how this falling out occurred, and what it means for anyone who takes up serious contemplative practice.

From the very beginning of his career as a Buddhist monk, Devadatta distinguished himself through his attainment of psychic powers. This accomplishment in itself was not seen by the Buddha as a sign of spiritual attainment, for the Buddha made it clear that a person could attain psychic powers, and the ability to perform miracles, without being virtuous. What should matter to a Buddhist is just the purification of the mind through the elimination of harmful and unrealistic desire and animosity. The ability to read the thoughts of others or perform miraculous physical healing is something that one can acquire without becoming free of desire and anger. And freedom from desire and anger is something that one can attain without developing psychic powers. Therefore, said the Buddha in such canonical texts as the Kevaddha Sutta (part of the Pali canon, which is the scripture of the Theravada school of Buddhism), such powers are irrelevant to the real goal of Buddhist practice; since, however, such powers have the capacity to confuse people, the Buddha says that he despises them (Walshe 1987: 176).

Later scholastics, such as the fifth-century Theravadin commentator Buddhaghosa, list psychic powers as one of the principal obstacles to insight. 'Like a child lying on its back and like tender corn it is difficult to manage. It is broken by the slightest thing. . . . Therefore, one who desires insight should cut off the impediment of psychic powers' (Buddhaghosa 1975: 113). It is possible that this wariness of psychic powers stems from the fact that Devadatta was well known for having them, but even better known for not having the attainments that are the real goal of Buddhist meditative practice. It is worth noting that the wariness of achievements like those of Devadatta extends well beyond psychic powers and covers a wide range of attractive qualities that are popularly known as charisma. In most Buddhist traditions, personal charisma, whether it is one's own or someone else's, is something to beware. The ways in which Devadatta displayed his charisma, along with his lack of good character, makes up one of the best-known cautionary tales in Buddhist lore.

Eight years before the Buddha died at the age of eighty, Devadatta's lack of good character began to manifest itself in ways that could no longer be ignored. According to the canonical sources, the Buddha had become a well-known teacher by this time. During the thirty-seven years that had elapsed since he began his teaching career, the Buddha had attracted a number of prominent monks as well as wealthy and famous patrons. As his fame increased, so did the material quality of the gifts that were given to the Buddhist community. Monks who had once dressed in robes made of discarded rags were now being given robes made of new cloth. Monks who had once begged their meals by going from house to house were being invited to dine with kings and merchants. Monks who had once lived outdoors in makeshift huts were now living in monastic compounds in permanent buildings. The Buddha, who had been called the great ascetic, was no longer living a life of obvious asceticism. It was this shift in lifestyle that became the explicit substance of Devadatta's grievance against the Buddha, although the texts hint that the explicit issue was masking a more personal agenda. About this more will be said later.

An ambitious son

One of the Buddha's most powerful patrons was King Bimbisara, who had been on the throne for fifty-two years and had known Gotama well before the latter came to be known as the Buddha. Bimbisara had a son named Ajatasattu. Devadatta reportedly talked Ajatasattu into seizing power from his father. The prince would seize control of the state at the same time that Devadatta seized control of the monastic order, and the new king would become the patron of the new spiritual leader. The stories of the two rebellions are told with obvious parallelism. In each case, the person to be deposed learned of the plot to overthrow him and refused to take measures against the conspirators who were planning the coup.

The outcomes of the two conspiracies, however, were different. The *coup d'état* succeeded. Bimbisara was imprisoned, and his son took power. Because he understood the Buddha's teachings about impermanence, however, Bimbisara was not alarmed at being thrown in prison. He even thrived there. He took his confinement as an opportunity to meditate and live a life of simplicity, and every day he grew more contented with his new life. Finally Ajatasattu gave orders to torture Bimbisara, with the result that Bimbisara died, and the usurping son was left with the dread stain of parricide on his hands.

To make matters worse, Ajatasattu found out only after his father had died that his mother had planned to have an abortion while pregnant with Ajatasattu, and Bimbisara had prevented the abortion and then shown the greatest of love for the baby prince, once saving the child from infant death by taking heroic measures. And so the usurper had not only killed his father but had taken the life of the man who had more than once saved his life. As if this were not enough of a burden of guilt, Ajatasattu also learned that his father, even in dying, had forgiven his son.

An ambitious cousin

Devadatta's attempt to take leadership of the Buddhist community was less successful. He tried three times to murder the Buddha, but each time the plot failed, although on one occasion the Buddha was seriously injured. Even after Devadatta had tried to kill the Buddha, the Buddha forgave him. And then Devadatta went to the Buddha and made five requests, all having to do with the way that Buddhist monks should live. The five requests were that all monks should be required (1) to live in the forest rather than in cities, (2) to eat only begged alms rather than food provided at feasts to which monks were invited guests, (3) to wear only sewn rags rather than robes made of new cloth donated by the laity, (4) to sleep only under trees rather than in buildings with a roof, and (5) to follow a strict vegetarian diet, avoiding all flesh and fish, even when this was given to a monk on his begging rounds. The Buddha responded to these requests for stricter discipline by saying that any monk who wished to follow those austerities was welcome to do so, but adhering to such a life was to be purely voluntary for Buddhist monks and nuns.

When the Buddha refused to make Devadatta's proposed rules for more stringent asceticism mandatory, Devadatta mounted a campaign throughout the Buddhist community. Proclaiming that the Buddha had grown soft and was no longer interested in renouncing the luxuries of a settled life, Devadatta managed to win five hundred monks and nuns over to his side, all of them dedicated to the ideal of living a truly homeless life free of any of the domestic comforts. The defections, however, proved to be short-lived.

Before long all the monks and nuns returned to the Buddha. Upon realizing that his attempts to seize power had utterly failed, Devadatta fell ill to a disease that so weakened him that he could no longer walk. His condition deteriorated steadily for several months.

Finally, when he realized that he was about to die, he sent word to the Buddha with a request that he be allowed to see him one last time. The Buddha responded by saying that the two men had no further need to see each other in this life. Devadatta, thinking that the Buddha would surely see him, arranged to have some men carry him on a stretcher to where the Buddha was then staying. On the way to see the Buddha one last time, Devadatta became thirsty and asked the stretcher-bearers to set him down near a stream so that he could bathe and have a drink. When he stepped off his portable bed onto the earth, the earth opened up and swallowed him.

TRADITIONAL COMMENTS ON DEVADATTA'S STORY

In discussing the story of Devadatta and the Buddha, there are several points to which the Buddhist tradition has added comments. Let me discuss these briefly before explaining what they mean to me personally. One point that traditional commentators have made is that even when one becomes liberated from the root causes of suffering, suffering does not stop. What is said to stop at the moment of liberation, which Buddhists call Nirvana, is the formation of new karma. Karma, according to Buddhist scholasticism, is any action that is performed with the intention of some kind of personal gain. An act of kindness, for example, that is done with the hopes of gaining some benefit as a reward for the kindness done, is a karma. In this case, it is a good karma, one that will ripen into happiness for the person who does it. Even as a good karma, however, it is a karma, and one of the features of a karma is that one has expectations. Whenever there are expectations, there is the risk of disappointment, and disappointment is a kind of pain. The only way to be liberated from this kind of pain is to have no further expectations. Even when this kind of liberation from expectations has been achieved, however, the effects of all the karma that one had accumulated before being liberated must still be experienced. If one had malevolent thoughts in the past, then the negativity of those malicious motivations must be experienced in the form of some kind of pain. And so the commentators tell us that the Buddha's difficulties with Devadatta, and the injuries he received at Devadatta's instigation, were the final results of maliciousness and anger that Gotama had felt before becoming a Buddha.

A second point, which I alluded to above, was that Devadatta's ostensible reasons for wishing to take control of the Buddhist monastic community were a result of his failure to have control over his own mind. One who fails to control his own mind compensates for this lack of control by trying to seize control of external factors.

One canonical text called the Devadatta Sutta, found in the fourth volume of *The Book of Gradual Sayings*, specifies all the ways in which Devadatta had failed to gain control over his own mind. This text reports that shortly after Devadatta had left the Buddhist community, the Buddha said of his cousin that he was overcome by desires for material gain, by a dread of material loss, by a desire for fame, by a fear of obscurity, by a desire for honor, and by a fear of blame. He was overcome, says this text, by evil intentions from within and corrupted by bad companionship from without (Hare 1935: 109). He and Ajatasattu, both overwhelmed by their own lust for power, naturally fell into league with one another, each reinforcing the other's ill-conceived desires. One's mentality influences one's taste in friends, and the company one keeps affects one's mentality.

A third point that the tradition makes is that Ajatasattu, because of the gravity of his crime against his father, was never able to benefit from the Buddha's teachings. Even when he later became a patron of the Buddha and was given inspirational discourses by the Buddha, the king's mind was so vitiated by the heavy burden of parricide that he was still confused, even when he heard the most lucid teacher in the land. In other words, the traditional Buddhist moral of the story is that a mentality can become so diseased and corrupted that even the greatest healer of the human psyche cannot make it healthy and whole again.

BRINGING THE TRADITION DOWN TO MY LEVEL

Let me now try to explain what the story of the Buddha and Devadatta has meant in my own practice of Buddhism. As I said above, my interest in Buddhism began when I was a 21-year-old man trying to make a decision about whether to answer my country's call to military service, and while thinking about that issue, I happened to read Plato's account of the trial of Socrates. What I recall most vividly was that when Socrates was found guilty of corrupting the youth of Athens and was sentenced to death by hemlock, his friends tried to talk him into fleeing to another country. Socrates refused. My interpretation of his refusal to flee was that he felt that he had benefited by the laws of his country his entire life and could not disregard those same laws when they worked to his personal inconvenience. (He also said that for a philosopher, death is no inconvenience, but in my youth I tended not to trust people who say such things while still alive.)

Applying Socrates's line of reasoning to my own situation, I decided that I had no choice; the only honorable thing for me to do was to stay in the country and obey its laws, or face the prescribed penalty for breaking the law. This conclusion seemed inescapable to me, and my newfound love of Socrates made me feel determined either to do my military service or to refuse to do my duty and go to prison as a criminal. Having made this very firm decision, I then surprised myself by making a sudden and spontaneous decision to take the next bus across the border into a country I knew next to nothing about. There is more than one way to escape a conclusion.

Every escape has a price. The price I paid for escaping the wisdom of Socrates was a heavy burden of feeling that I had failed to be honorable. I had cheated my country. I had taken everything of benefit that my society could offer me and absconded with it to a place where I was a foreigner. I could not honestly claim to have deep convictions, though I tried very hard to cultivate them and to portray myself as a pacifist and a conscientious objector. In my newly adopted country, many people received me almost as a kind of hero, a man who had bravely stood up for his convictions. In my heart, however, I knew that I was just a kid who had no ambition to die a seemingly pointless death in some battle in a foreign land. In my own mind, I was a coward.

To make matters worse, an older cousin, whom I had admired and emulated all my life, had done the honorable thing and gone to war, where he was severely wounded. He has spent the rest of his life in a wracked body, subject daily to pain and inconvenience while I have enjoyed almost perfect health. In this situation I could find nothing fair, nothing that sustained my childhood faith that the universe is fundamentally a moral structure in which virtue is somehow rewarded.

The only consolation I had was that I was unable to return to my country, which seemed at least a form of poetic justice. Even that poetic justice was eventually taken away, however, when a federal court judge sent me a letter saying that he had decided that the warrant for my arrest was so old that my case should be dismissed. I was neither found guilty nor exonerated nor granted an amnesty. My case was simply dismissed as a housekeeping measure, an attempt to keep a court docket from being bloated with too many trivial pending cases.

Legally, it was as if nothing had ever happened. Psychologically, it was as if I had been damned to knowing forever that I had gotten away with evading justice. Years later, when I was sitting in an airport and whiling away the time by reading a Buddhist text, I read that among all the Buddhist hells, the most dreadful is the one in which people receive good fortune that they knew in their hearts they did not deserve. Right away, I recognized that I had been living in that hell for most of my adult life. (Since then, I have moved out of that particular hell, but I still retain visiting rights. My current hell is the lesser one of remembering things I have read but forgetting where I read them.)

DEVADATTA WITHIN

Several of the many Buddhist traditions are based on the doctrine that everyone has a Buddha within, and this inner Buddha is one's true nature. Although for many years I practiced a form of Buddhism built on that very doctrine, I never believed it. I still do not. What I find much easier to believe is that everyone has a Devadatta within—a Devadatta who is lying in wait ready to ambush and destroy the Buddha if he should ever happen along the road. The Devadatta of Buddhist legend was, or claimed to be, a moral perfectionist. He was someone who could not tolerate anything that might be construed as laxity or as a lack of the most rigorous forms of self-discipline. As we saw earlier, the Buddhist tradition has long recognized that this sort of perfectionism in the matter of external form is in fact a mask for a fundamental lack of control.

In the language of modern psychotherapy, the need for stringent rules that everyone must be made to follow is an instance of projection. It is projecting one's own actual but disowned sense of weakness and moral failure onto others. This leads to the conviction that everyone needs a dose of iron discipline, imposed if necessary by a benevolent dictator. In my own case, this projection led me in my younger years to be a stern father, an uncompromising husband, and an overly demanding pedagogue.

It also led me to practice the most severe forms of Buddhism, such as Zen. For many years, the only practice that I recognized as authentic Buddhism was sitting motionless until the pain made tears come to my eyes and then signaling to the monitor to come beat me on the back with a stick the size of a cricket bat. When I now look back on that kind of practice, I am inclined to think that I am not the only Buddhist whose inner Devadatta has gained the upper hand over his inner Buddha.

PERFECTIONISM

The story of Devadatta shows that perfectionism is the enemy of perfection. But when one is caught up in the snares of perfectionism, it is very difficult to appreciate that this is the moral of the story of Devadatta. Failing to grasp the nature of Devadatta's failings, one is inclined to take up a spiritual practice that measures insight and wisdom by one's ability to follow strict forms of externally imposed, and arbitrary, discipline without flinching or complaining.

It is one thing to know that moral perfectionism retards (or even destroys) rather than promotes spiritual growth and maturity; it is another thing to find one's way out of Devadatta's community and back into the Buddha's. As with everything that is truly worth doing, there is no set prescription for how to do it.

That notwithstanding, there are, I think, some important clues in the traditional Buddhist analysis of Devadatta's character. He was, says that analysis, overwhelmed with worldly ambitions. He was conquered by his own desire for recognition, approval, material gain, and comfort. He was afraid of anonymity, disapproval, material loss, and pain. So far, this is a very stock and formulaic list of the foibles of any worldly person. Hundreds of Buddhist texts speak of the ill that comes of these four desires and the corresponding four fears, which collectively are called the eight worldly traits. What is interesting about Devadatta's case, however, is that he seems not to have recognized his own worldly nature. He denied it. He projected it onto others. He insisted that everyone live by the strict discipline that he needed. This is perhaps one of the most common (and most tragic) themes in the entire history of human religions.

What I personally find fascinating about Devadatta's blindness to his own worldliness is that the traditional Buddhist cure for his brand of perfectionism is itself a kind of perfectionism. The preferred alternative in Buddhist tradition to being a Devadatta is to become a Buddha. But how is a Buddha described? A Buddha is described as a person who has gotten entirely beyond the reach of the root causes of avoidable unhappiness; he is someone who has completely exterminated his desires and aversions that are rooted in a failure to see and accept things as they really are. This is the perfection that Devadatta's perfectionism tries to kill.

INTEGRITY

Let us go back and consider once again two lines from the liturgy of a Buddhist order:

What the Buddha overcame, we too can overcome.
What the Buddha attained, we too can attain.

A question that no one with the intellectual integrity of a Socrates or a Buddha would allow us to evade is this: Is it realistic to expect to get entirely beyond the reach of such fundamental drives as the desire for the pleasant and the fear of the unpleasant? I can hear Devadatta prompting us to answer Yes! But is that answer fully in keeping with our own experiences of what it is like to be the owner and operator of a human body run by a human mind?

Unfortunately, I think the majority of Buddhists have listened to Devadatta on this one. Most Buddhists, it seems to me, insist that the Buddha was completely liberated, without even a trace of worldly desire or fear of pain. But the Buddha himself said to listen to oneself, to study one's own reality with an uncompromising determination to discover what one's constitution really is. It is only when one has truly studied oneself and sees what is there, rather than what a spiritual guide or some other authority says ought to be there, that one has taken the Buddha seriously.

My own experience, and my familiarity with the reported experiences of others, has told me again and again that it is unwise to listen to Devadatta on this question of the feasibility of perfect liberation. It is here, I think, that modern depth psychology can come to the rescue of such contemplative traditions as Buddhism that are prone to being undermined by an unhealthily enthusiastic drive for goals that are best seen as unattainable.

It has become my preference to see the goals of Buddhism not as actual possibilities but as similar to mathematical asymptotes, theoretical limits that can be approached but can never be attained. My inclination is now to view Buddhist concepts such as nirvana or enlightenment as navigational stars by which one gets one's bearing and sails in approximately the right direction. Just as no wise sailor ever hopes to reach the stars by which he navigates the world, I would suggest that the wise Buddhist is the one who navigates life by the ideal of liberation without succumbing to the hope of actually reaching that ideal. Ideals have the potential to be liberative. When they are taken too literally, however, there is a real danger of becoming further ensnared in delusion rather than liberated from it.

POSTSCRIPT

Stories have endings. We know how the stories of Socrates, Devadatta, and the Buddha ended. What is not yet known is how the teller of this particular tale will end up, except dead. The current prognosis for the years that remain before that inevitable ending seems to be positive. For the time being, my inner Devadatta seems to have been swallowed up by the earth.

Or has he? There is always the very real possibility that he was not swallowed at all but rather was launched into orbit, where he lives constantly in the earth's penumbra, coming out now and then to offer an overly harsh mythological retelling of his own history. The inner Buddha has become an asymptote, to be approached but never reached. This means

Devadatta cannot lay his hands on him. That leaves only my inner Socrates to account for. He seems to be waiting patiently to be accused of corrupting the youth by calling into question the literal reality of the Buddhas.

REFERENCES

Buddhaghosa (1975) *The Path of Purity*, a translation of the *Visuddhimagga* by Pe Maung Tin, London: Pali Text Society.

Hare, E. M. (1935) *The Book of the Gradual Sayings*, vol. 4, Pali Text Society Translation Series 26, Oxford: Pali Text Society, 1995 (reprint of 1st edn).

Hollis, J. (1996) *Swamplands of the Soul: New Life in Dismal Places*, Toronto: Inner City Books.

Walshe, M. (1987) *Thus Have I Heard: The Long Discourses of the Buddha*, London: Wisdom Publications.

Chapter 3

The mutual influence and involvement of therapist and patient: co-contributors to maturation and integrity

Melvin E. Miller

What is the therapist's role in fostering the maturity and integrity of the patient? How involved should a therapist become, and to what end? We must assume that some level of influence is inevitable, but we must also ask *how much* and *what kind* of influence? One of the principal objectives of any effective psychotherapy, in my view, is to influence and promote the integrity of the patient. To begin with, then, it is essential that we arrive at an acceptable definition of *integrity*.

INTEGRITY DEFINED

The dictionary defines integrity as 'wholeness, entireness, completeness, . . . the condition of having no part or element taken away or wanting' (*Oxford English Dictionary* [*OED*]: 1455). Rike (1999) explains the etymology of the term:

> The word 'integrity' comes from the Latin *integritas*, meaning wholeness, soundness, which (like integral and integrative) come from *integer*, untouched, whole, entire. To have integrity is to possess the mode of unity or wholeness proper to one's nature.
>
> (p. 151)

I believe that human beings should enjoy not only physical integrity, but also psychological and emotional completeness. Yet integrity, in any of its manifestations, may at times be threatened. Integrity may at best be transient. We run head-first into critical ontological issues when we speak of emotional integrity as meaning to 'possess the mode of unity or wholeness proper to one's nature.' To many, such language immediately suggests some essentialist or Platonic sense of human nature. But how can we ever know what is 'proper to one's nature'? Are there universal attributes which characterize our individual and collective humanity?

Certain ways of expressing integrity are most consistent with being fully human. Rike (1999: 151) considers acting with integrity as behaving 'in accordance with certain moral rules or principles or . . . in ways which promote certain values and goals.' This is integrity in the sense of authenticity, honesty—having one's behavior 'at one' with one's beliefs. But integrity means more than this. It is an awareness of harmony and wholeness—and a striving for a differentiated wholeness with meaning and purpose. This 'predisposition to unity' (Young-Eisendrath 1997: 164) unfolds throughout the life experiences of the maturing, individuating self.

Erik Erikson was one of very few psychoanalysts who dared to explore such a philosophically controversial topic (cf. Hoare 1999). Indeed, he argued convincingly for its inclusion in the developmental and psychoanalytic lexicons (cf. Josselson, Chapter 7). He saw the achievement of a sense of integrity as the culmination of a life well-lived, the apex of personal development arrived at through the resolution of the demands of seven preceding stages of growth. He wrote of integrity as a universal potential across humankind, without promoting an essentialist doctrine or dogma. From Erikson:

> [Integrity] . . . is the ego's accrued assurance of its proclivity for order and meaning. It is a post-narcissistic love of the human ego . . . as an experience which conveys some world order and spiritual sense, no matter how dearly paid for. [Integrity] is the acceptance of one's one and only life cycle as something that had to be and that, by necessity, permitted of no substitutions.
>
> (p. 268)

I suggest that we keep such notions of integrity in mind as we ask ourselves: How do we sit with our patients, and what is it that we hope for in the therapy? Admittedly, I attempt to keep some notion of the patient's integrity, wholeness, and potential completeness in mind as I engage the patient during the therapy hour. For example, I usually hold on to the thought that I want to assist patients with becoming more completely themselves—help them experience some kind of differentiated wholeness that has unique meaning for them. All the while, of course, I never presume that I know the exact direction or path they should take, nor the eventual outcome of their therapeutic and growth-oriented strivings. I do this work from a psychoanalytically informed perspective, working primarily with middle-aged adults, seeing them once, twice, or three times per week in a fairly consistent therapeutic frame.

IN SEARCH OF THE OPTIMAL THERAPEUTIC STANCE

Over the years, therapists and analysts have suggested many ways to promote emotional maturity and personal integrity. Few theorists have contended that therapists should be encouraging, directing, or advice-giving (Hoffman 1998), but many held that empathy, warmth, and caring support are primarily requisite (Bacal 1998; Kohut 1977; Wolf 1976). Others argued that a stance approximating 'neutrality' or 'indifference' is essential. Traditional analysts such as Freud argued uncompromisingly that we approach the patient with neutrality and *only neutrality*—that a desire to influence in any way (a desire to be helpful in any way) is off target, and is, in fact, counter-productive, or even destructive to the therapeutic-psychoanalytic enterprise.

Neutrality: history and implications

For the past fifty years or so, a contentious exchange has been brewing around the matter of neutrality. Few authors seem to have adhered pre-cisely to the formulation Freud gave when he introduced the term.[1] There has been considerable discussion as to what the term actually means, and perhaps even more dispute over how to practice it. The controversy has been heated (Alonso 1996; Bacal 1998; Hoffer 1985; Hoffman 1998; Mitchell 1997), taking many forms.

Freud elaborated upon factors he deemed axiomatic: 'I cannot advise my colleagues too urgently to model themselves during psycho-analytic treat-ment on the surgeon, who puts aside all his feelings, even his human sympathy, and concentrates his mental forces on the single aim of perform-ing the operations as skilfully as possible' (1912/1989: 359). The justification for requiring this emotional coldness in the analyst, according to Freud, is that it creates the most advantageous conditions for both parties. Such a stance should enhance the process of free association, permit the full blossoming of the transference, and, at the same time, thwart the develop-ment of an inappropriate countertransference.

One of Freud's clearest formulations of the proper disposition of the analyst appears in his *Recommendations to Physicians Practicing Psycho-Analysis*. Here Freud joined the notion of neutrality with the associated concept, 'evenly-hovering attention.' From Freud: '[Neutrality] consists simply in not directing one's notice to anything in particular and in maintaining the same "evenly-suspended attention" in the face of all that one hears' (1912/1989: 357). Freud continued:

> For as soon as anyone deliberately concentrates his attention to a certain degree, he begins to select from the material before him; . . . and in making this selection he will be following his expectations or inclinations. This, however, is precisely what must not be done. In making the selection, if he follows his expectations he is in danger of never finding anything but what he already knows; and if he follows his inclinations he will certainly falsify what he may perceive.
>
> (1912/1989: 357)

Freud believed that therapists must refrain from contaminating the treat
ment process with their preconceptions and personal issues. Successful
analysis requires the recognition and 'neutralization' of any countertransference, values intrusion, or theoretical objective such as integrity.

Some post-Freudian theorists have remained consistent with Freud's
exacting stance on this issue. Bion may even have taken Freud further in
this direction than Freud ever intended. Bion (1970/1983) is most famous
for his prohibitions against bringing 'memory, desire, and understanding'
into the analytic process. He believed they should be checked at the door of
the consulting room because they interfered so dramatically with the
therapeutic process. Rather, the focus of the analysis should be on the
'present moment' and the 'unknown.' Some have suggested that Bion took
this posture to the extreme (cf. Rubin 1996). From Bion:

> The psychoanalyst should aim at achieving a state of mind so that at
> every session he feels he has not seen the patient before. If he feels he
> has, he is treating the wrong patient.
>
> (1967: 273)

Elsewhere, Bion continued with his emphatic position:

> Now it is clear that if the psycho-analyst has allowed himself the
> unfettered play of memory, desire, and understanding, his preconcep-
> tions will be habitually saturated and his 'habits' will lead him to resort
> to instantaneous and well-practised saturation from 'meaning' rather
> than from O [experience; the thing-in-itself]. . . . If he gives in to this
> tendency he is proceeding in a direction calculated to preclude any
> possibility of union with O.
>
> (1970/1983: 51)

Bion wanted the analyst to connect fully with the patient's experience.
Failure to suspend or bracket memory, desire, and understanding will 'lead
to a steady deterioration in the [analyst's] powers of observation' (p. 51)
and promote an emotional and cognitive disconnect with the patient.
Instead, the immediacy of experience resulting from the suspension of
memory and desire will inform the analyst's interpretations quite
sufficiently:

> His interpretations should gain in force and conviction—both for
> himself and his patient—because they derive from the emotional
> experience with a unique individual and not from generalized theories
> imperfectly 'remembered.'
>
> (Bion 1967: 273)

Harmful influence: neutrality neglected

Freud and Bion together present an enormous challenge to the practicing clinician. Is it ever possible to achieve the kind of neutrality they talk about? The psychotherapy and psychoanalytic literature is replete with examples of patients abused by 'well-meaning' therapists—therapists who have not remained neutral, permitting their memories, desires, understanding (and theories) to interfere with the patient and contaminate the treatment. These abuses can be subtle or quite dramatic.

Kohut (1979) in 'The two analyses of Mr Z' gives examples of common— and not too egregious—limitations to treatment induced by a therapist's too-strict adherence to theoretical principles. In confessing his own limitations in this earlier treatment of Mr Z, Kohut acknowledges: 'All in all, my approach [and perceptions (p. 6)] to Mr. Z's psychopathology . . . can be said to have been fully in tune with the classical theories of psychoanalysis' (p. 7). Kohut believed that his effectiveness in the treatment of Mr Z was limited by his own preoccupation with transference phenomena, and his focus on 'pathogenic conflicts in the area of infantile sexuality and aggression—his Oedipus complex, his castration anxiety, . . . and his preoccupation with the primal scene' (p. 5).

This is an example of somewhat subtle influence by the therapist due to too-strict adherence to the tenets of one's theory. It is as if Kohut acknowledged that he let the 'tail' of his theory 'wag the dog' of mutual discovery and clinical process. The literature is fraught with such examples. We can only wonder about the extent of the harm induced by over-zealous adherence to theory and the ubiquity of this phenomenon.

At the more extreme end of the continuum of untoward influence, we find examples of misuse of the patient by the therapist's moral stance. Rice (1993) relays a story of two therapists who both exercised their personal agendas on the same vulnerable patient. The first therapist had a sexual relationship with the patient, and the second therapist insisted that the patient take legal action against the first. As Rice relays the story, the grieved patient did not want to take legal action against the first therapist because she realized that in some way she desired the affair and invited it. Rice argues that this woman has been abused twice. She suffered at the hands of both therapists; both plied their own agendas and desires. In the case of the first therapist, probably no one would question his inappropriateness. Rice agrees. But then he takes the perhaps controversial position that the second therapist committed a form of moral abuse against the patient as well. The 'acting out of the counter-transference led to technical and ethical errors . . . active in both. Both therapists overlooked the patient's needs and sought to satisfy their own, leading to boundary infringement' (p. 1), and, in turn, impeding the maturational process while contributing to the degradation of the patient's integrity.

Numerous examples of therapists exerting untoward influence—from a clearly non-neutral stance—could be gleaned from both the psychoanalytic archives and the current literature. The damage exacted upon patients by therapists wielding axes of either theoretical or moral influence can be extremely severe. When we take seriously the consequences of these forms of enactments, we might feel that our hands are tied—and, perhaps, that they should be tied. In this context, we likely gain added respect for the more conservative, cautionary perspective upheld by Freud and Bion. Wherein does the solution to this dilemma lie?

Patient responses to a neutral stance

I generally lean toward the more cautious approach voiced by Freud, Bion, and others—those who take the more strict stance around neutrality. I agree that we routinely should not attempt to influence the patient; rather, we should strive to 'sit' in such a way that the patient's issues evolve freely and eventually become resolved in a context and timeframe that is not hurried nor influenced by us.

Sometimes my patients comment on the effect which a relatively neutral stance has on them. Although a few patients have occasionally verbalized their frustrations with my version of neutrality and the concomitant lack of gratification offered, others have reflected upon its salubrious effects—as if the neutrality itself enhanced their sense of well-being, and their integrity. Some patients have reflected upon *both* the frustrations and the beneficial consequences of this somewhat neutral stance. Below is a sampling of patient comments.

Patient 1:   You sit with me with no expectations, no wish for my cure, no wish for change. In some ways, it is hard to bear this. It is difficult, and it is so helpful. You give me space to grow.

Patient 1 (subsequent session):   You let me be in my pain and in my confusion. You let me be wherever I am and that helps so much.

Patient 2:   If I put myself in your shoes, I see that you do not try to exert control over me—over the therapy. And, when I think about it, it seems to me that you have no idea of the outcome, and no control over the outcome either. You try to not exert control over it, nor me. You seem very willing to allow me to wrestle with it all: the pain, the sadness, the confusion. You watch me fall, get up, and fall down again. You don't teach me moves; you let me wrestle with it. You must have faith—faith in me. You must have faith in the process—that I will wrestle with it—that I will work things out.

Patient 3:   You don't encourage, you don't console. That is frustrating, and it's great. You let me struggle with it. Your way lets me keep tiptoeing into this place that I need to go. It makes me work harder; it makes me go deeper.

Patient 4:   I look at you. You don't need me to be cheerful, you don't need me to be a success; you don't need me to be happy nor optimistic. You don't need any of this; you just sit with it. It is so frustrating and so helpful. It forces me to go deeper and deeper into myself—to search for deeper aspects of self.

With responses such as these from patients, one might wonder why I, or any therapist receiving such feedback, would question the usefulness of his or her approach and the efficacy of neutrality. Nonetheless, I submit that there is more going on in these responses than meets the eye. I suggest that neutrality is only part of the picture here. Even in these sessions where I am consciously striving to be neutral, there is considerable mutual interaction and influence taking place.

Ernest Wolf, a contemporary self psychologist, offers some conceptual assistance with these concerns. He makes what I consider to be a useful modification to the Freudian notion of neutrality—a modification that transforms the concept of neutrality into something more lively and inter-active. Wolf (1983) writes about a kind of neutrality that eschews thera-peutic abstinence. He calls it 'ideal neutrality.' To Wolf, ideal neutrality is 'a neutrality of affirmation for the whole person that is experienced sub-jectively as an affirmation of the self' (p. 683). Bacal (1998) in his recent book on *Optimal Responsiveness*, discussed a conversation he had with Wolf, where he suggested that Wolf's definition of (ideal) neutrality con-veys something other than neutrality. Wolf agreed that he was, in essence, 'expressing a view that "being on the patient's side" is the *most* therapeutic stance' (Bacal 1998: 38 [emphasis added]).

Perhaps my 'being on the patient's side' is the felt stance to which my patients were referring. They tacitly implied that I was not really being neutral; they experienced me as being engaged and involved with them, and concerned about their well-being.

THE PARADOX: NEUTRALITY *AND* INFLUENCE

There is a profound and daunting paradox inextricably connected with this entire matter. Neutrality, although often helpful, can never be—and should never be—completely pure nor unalloyed. Neutrality should not be abstin-ence. We cannot be engaged in any interaction with another without exerting some form of influence. In turn, the other will invariably influence us. The inevitability of mutual influence is now recognized in the physical sciences, where we have relativity, quantum theory, and uncertainty theory

(Heisenberg 1958). And in psychoanalytic circles, we have the interrelational and dialectical-constructivist theorists (Hoffman 1998) and the intersubjectivist theorists (Stolorow et al. 1994). In particular, there are the self psychologists (e.g. Kohut, Wolf, Fosshage) who find the roots of their theory in the shift from positivism to a relational, interactive science (Kohut 1977: 31–2). Others describe this movement as the shift from a one-person to a two-person psychology (Mitchell 1997). Members of these contemporary schools of analytic thought accuse Freud, and to some extent Bion, of championing antiquated modes of thinking which promote an outmoded epistemology (cf. Mitchell 1997: 28).

Each camp (i.e. traditional neutrality vs. influence and involvement) grasps only a part of the picture. Each holds important pieces of the puzzle. I believe we must sit with the patient 'neutrally' without attempting to influence. We have to suspend our preconceived notions of what is going on with a patient while placing our 'memory, desire, and understanding' on hold—suspending our theoretical constructs, our morality, and our countertransference, while remaining in a state of not-knowing. But we must also acknowledge our power over the patient and not shy away from the consequences of this inevitable influence. We must acknowledge that we are always 'up to something' as we sit with patients. Why not let it be, in part, about fostering maturity, meaning-making, and integrity? Let us be, in the words of Wolf, 'on the patient's side' as we also strive for something akin to ideal neutrality. We can uphold *both* neutrality and influence as objectives or guides in our sitting with patients. They are not mutually exclusive.

Russell's (1996) thoughts on these matters help ease the transition from Freud's 'evenly hovering attention' and Bion's posture of abstinence to an acceptance of *the fact* of the therapist's *involvement*. Russell insists that 'For therapy to work, the therapist must become involved' (p. 201). Typically, this involvement will be measured, but there are times when patient and therapist together will experience significant crises. Both the relationship and the treatment will undergo crises. Russell goes so far as to say that without crises, there is no therapy; without involvement and influence, there is no therapy.

Russell's perspective is reminiscent of Jung's (1969) writings on countertransference and the *participation mystique*. Jung was one of the first analysts to emphasize the therapist's genuine, emotional involvement in the therapeutic process, and the complex, emotional interrelationship that must develop between analyst and analysand. Jung summed up his position most clearly in his oft-quoted reminder to the clinician: 'You can exert no influence if you are not subject to influence' (1969: 70–2). Searles (1979) took a similar stand with his concept of 'therapeutic symbiosis,' based on his extensive clinical experience with seriously disturbed patients. The 'therapeutic symbiosis' describes the intense, often primitive, emotional interaction and involvement of *both* patient and therapist (conscious-to-conscious and unconscious-to-unconscious).

Recently, a patient described a dream in which she and I were the central figures. The dream was long and involved, and I was an active participant in each scene; there was considerable interaction between us. These interactions took place in my consulting room and in other locations around town. Upon free association to the dream, the patient began to mention how much she felt she was helped by the therapeutic process. She also marveled at the dream's depiction of her helping me—and her changing me. In the dream she described me changing from a cold, withholding person, to someone who was more warm, present, and engaged. She took considerable credit for this shift in me. This dream provided a fortuitous and well-timed opportunity to discuss the mutual interaction of the therapeutic process: patient to therapist and therapist to patient. The patient seemed pleased with her impact upon the therapist—even as she was feeling profoundly changed by the therapist and the therapeutic process. The dream and the attendant associations seem to provide an excellent illustration of the unfolding of the *participation mystique* and the variable, mutual 'interactive influence of two subjectivities' (Fosshage 1994: 273).

There is a delicate balance between neutrality and influence that must be managed here. The position of traditional neutrality offers a degree of safety to therapists, and it prevents novice therapists from making too many egregious mistakes. In addition, it provides safety to the patient. Although becoming more involved in the process may be a necessity, it can be frightening and at times treacherous to both parties. Stark (1996) describes the tightrope walk between involvement and a more neutral kind of abstinence—along with the pitfalls which accompany errors in either direction:

> If therapists never allow themselves to be drawn into participation with patients in their reenactments, then we speak of a failure of empathy. On the other hand, if therapists allow themselves to be drawn into their patient's internal dramas but then get lost in the reenactment, then we speak of a failure of containment.
>
> (p. 243)

How do we do both and stay on course? The challenge of maintaining neutrality while exerting influence is intimidating. Can we have a kind of involvement that is well-tempered and appropriately modulated? Sometimes this involvement will look like 'evenly-hovering attention.' Other times, we will deliberately exert influence — hopefully balanced and guided by a keen sense of what is best for the patient, informed by both empathic attunement and ethical sensibilities, and enhanced by a sense of wisdom and timing achieved through supervision and experience.

RELATIONSHIP, DIALOGUE, AND INFLUENCE

Finally, I shall turn to philosophy and theology to fortify our stance. It is helpful to think of the therapist–patient relationship, not only from the interrelational and intersubjective perspectives, but also from a Buberesque 'I–Thou' position. If we see the patient as a 'Thou,' and as one who is also an 'I,' our obligation to him or her might seem to be clearer. We have a responsibility to be a complete, responsive, caring other for the patient, and to understand that the patient will develop and mature not only from our skill as therapists (informed by and often associated with our neutrality and skilled interventions), but also from our humanity.

The Hebraist and theologian Martin Buber (1970) emphatically stated that a person finds or discovers self in relationship—in dialogue with the other. In fact, Buber proposed that 'relationship' is ontologically prior for human beings; relationship is the medium through which the human being grows, develops, and matures, and it is the vehicle through which the sense of self gradually unfolds:

> In the beginning is the relation—as the category of being, as a readiness, as a form that reaches out to be filled, as a model of the soul: the a priori of relation; the *innate You.* . . . The development of the child's soul is connected indissolubly with his craving for the You. . . . [It develops through] gradually entering into relationships. . . . [The child] becomes an I through a You.
>
> (pp. 78–80)

The contemporary philosopher Charles Taylor agrees with Buber on the pivotal role of relationship, mutual influence, and interactive dialogue in the formation of, and ongoing nourishment of, the human psyche:

> The crucial feature of human life is its fundamentally *dialogical* character. We become full agents, capable of understanding ourselves, and hence of defining our identity through our acquisition of rich human languages of expression. . . . [W]e learn these modes of expression through exchanges with others. People do not acquire the languages needed for self-expression on their own. The genesis of the human mind is in this sense not monological, not something each person accomplishes on his or her own, but dialogical.
>
> (Taylor 1994: 32)

Thus, we find support for the role of mutual influence and involvement from roots that extend beyond the psychoanalytic. Multiple sources provide persuasive evidence not only that interaction and influence from therapist to patient (and from patient to therapist) are unavoidable, but that they are vital to the success of the therapy, and essential to the patient's emerging sense of identity, maturity, and integrity.

Returning to the psychoanalytic perspective one more time, we find that Stephen Mitchell (1997) offers a nutshell encapsulation of our position.

> The most constructive safeguard of the autonomy [maturity and integrity] of the patient is not the denial of the personal impact of the analyst but the acknowledgment, both in our theoretical concepts and in our clinical work, of the interactive nature of the analytic process.
>
> (p. 28)

CONCLUSION

We must be prepared to enter into an engaged dialogue with the patient, though the playing field is not level and the relationship is ritualistically asymmetrical (Hoffman 1998). We must embrace this asymmetry and our inevitable influence upon the patient, and deal with it responsively and responsibly. Moreover, we must respect these inherent relational limitations while still being there, present and involved with the patient in the ways that Russell and others have described it: engaged and immersed in the process. In addition, we must be prepared to disappoint the patient, to weather the intermittent crises that arise in the treatment, and be poised to work through them. We must stand ready to engage the patient with our full humanity while, at the same time, attempting to promote the patient's humanity—even as we augment his or her strivings toward wholeness, maturation, and integrity. In short, we must learn to sit with the patient from a complexly integrated stance that incorporates both neutrality and influence—a stance that both acknowledges and fosters mutual influence. Through this process the patient will change. The therapist must be prepared to change as well. The integrity of both patient and therapist is at stake.

NOTE

1. A dimension of this debate is the accuracy of the term as it is translated from the German. As noted by others, Freud did not use the term 'neutrality' (*Neutralitaet*), but instead used the term *Indifferenz*. It was Strachy who translated it as 'neutrality' (cf. Hoffer 1985).

ACKNOWLEDGMENTS

I would like to thank Susanne Cook-Greuter, John J. McKenna, Loren H. Miller, Alan N. West, and Polly Young-Eisendrath for their helpful comments and suggestions on earlier versions of this chapter.

REFERENCES

Alonso, A. (1996) 'Toward a new understanding of neutrality,' in L. Lifson (ed.), *Understanding Therapeutic Action: Psychodynamic Concepts of Cure*, Hillsdale, NJ: The Analytic Press, 3–19.

Bacal, H. A. (ed.) (1998) *Optimal Responsiveness: How Therapists Heal their Patients*, Northvale, NJ: Jason Aronson.

Bion, W. R. (1967) 'Notes on memory and desire,' *Psychoanalytic Forum* 2: 271–80.

Bion, W. R. (1970/1983) *Attention and Interpretation*, New York: Jason Aronson.

Buber, M. (1970) *I and Thou*, New York: Scribner.

Erikson, E. H. (1950) *Childhood and Society*, New York: Norton.

Fosshage, J. (1994) 'Toward reconceptualizing transference: theoretical and clinical considerations,' *International Journal of Psycho-analysis*, 75/2: 265–80.

Freud, S. (1912/1989) 'Recommendations to physicians practicing psycho-analysis,' in P. Gay (ed.), *The Freud Reader*, New York: Norton, 356–63.

Heisenberg, W. (1958) *Physics and Philosophy: The Revolution in Modern Science*, New York: Harper & Row.

Hoare, C. H. (1999) 'Ethical self; spiritual self: Wisdom and integrity in the writings of Erik H. Erikson,' in M. E. Miller and S. Cook-Greuter (eds), *Creativity, Spirituality, and Transcendence: Paths to Integrity and Wisdom in the Mature Self*, Stamford, CT: Ablex.

Hoffer, A. (1985) 'Toward a redefinition of psychoanalytic neutrality,' *Journal of the American Psychoanalytic Association*, 33: 771–95.

Hoffman, I. Z. (1998) *Ritual and Spontaneity in the Psychoanalytic Process: A Dialectical-Constructivist View*, Hillsdale, NJ: Analytic Press.

Jung, C. G. (1969) 'The practice of psychotherapy,' in H. Mead, M. Fordham, G. Adler, and W. McGuire (eds), and R. F. C. Hull (trans.), *Collected Works*, vol. 16, (Bollingen Series, vol. 20), Princeton, NJ: Princeton University Press.

Kohut, H. (1977) *The Restoration of the Self*, New York: International Universities Press.

Kohut, H. (1979) 'The two analyses of Mr Z,' *International Journal of Psycho-analysis*, 60/3: 4–27.

Mitchell, S. (1997) *Influence and Autonomy in Psychoanalysis*, Hillsdale, NJ: Analytic Press.

Oxford English Dictionary (compact edn) (1971), New York: Oxford University Press.

Rice, C. (1993) 'Prevention of sexual and moral abuse of patients through training,' *BIP BITS: Brief Reports by the Boston Institute for Psychotherapy*, 1/4: 1–3.

Rike, J. L. (1999) 'Loving with integrity: a feminist spirituality of wholeness,' in M. E. Miller and A. N. West (eds), *Spirituality, Ethics, and Relationship in Adulthood: Clinical and Theoretical Explorations*, Madison, CT: Psychosocial Press.

Rubin, J. B. (1996) *Psychotherapy and Buddhism: Toward an Integration*, New York: Plenum Press.

Russell, P. (1996) 'Process with involvement: the interpretation of affect,' in L. Lifson (ed.), *Understanding Therapeutic Action: Psychodynamic Concepts of Cure*, Hillsdale, NJ: Analytic Press, 201–16.

Searles, H. (1979) *Countertransference and Related Subjects: Selected Papers*, New York: International Universities Press.

Stark, M. (1996) 'From structural conflict to relational conflict: a contemporary model of therapeutic action,' in L. Lifson (ed.), *Understanding Therapeutic Action: Psychodynamic Concepts of Cure*, Hillsdale, NJ: Analytic Press, 237–52.

Stolorow, R. D., Atwood, G. E., and Brandchaft, B. (eds), (1994) *The Intersubjective Approach*, Northvale, NJ: Jason Aaronson.

Taylor, C. (1994) *Sources of the Self: The Making of Modern Identity*, Cambridge, MA: Harvard University Press.

Wolf, E. (1976) 'Ambience and abstinence,' *The Annual of Psychoanalysis*, 4: 101–15.

Wolf, E. (1983) 'Aspects of neutrality,' *Psychoanalytic Inquiry*, 3: 675–89.

Young-Eisendrath, P. (1997) 'The self in analysis,' *Journal of Analytical Psychology*, 42: 157–66.

Chapter 4

Spiritual abuse

When good people do bad things

Demaris S. Wehr

This chapter is entitled 'When good people do bad things,' as an obvious play on Rabbi Harold Kushner's book title, *When Bad Things Happen to Good People* (1981). I also intend to make the point that good people endeavoring to do good things for other people sometimes tragically fall into harming the people they would help. Such 'good people' are often found in institutions that do 'good' works. In cases of spiritual abuse, these people undermine the integrity of the ones they would help. By 'integrity,' I mean the ability to act in accordance with one's most deeply held values. In order to act with integrity, one must be acquainted with one's cherished values. Here is where abusive spiritual healers or teachers are particularly undermining. They frequently derail their followers from developmental tasks appropriate to their stage of life. In so doing, they help create a confusion about core issues, such as identity, sense of purpose and direction, and vocational goals. In derailing followers from appropriate developmental tasks, wounding healers divert followers from discovering their own values. Thus, loss of integrity is central in spiritual abuse.

In addition, wounding healers make it nearly impossible for abused followers to trust what sustained them before the abuse. 'Wounding' healers is also a play on words, this time on Henri Nouwen's term 'wounded healer' (Nouwen 1972). Nouwen wished to emphasize that all of us, healers and those seeking healing, are vulnerable and wounded. Often the most effective healers amongst us are those with the greatest awareness of their own woundedness. From this awareness can come a deep compassion for the wounds of others, as well as a skill at addressing them. Wound*ing* healers, by contrast, are not aware of the depth of their own wounds, have not worked on them, and project their issues onto others, sometimes in a most destructive way. Still, this does not make them malicious—a condition which I take to be truly malevolent—on purpose.

The wounding healers you will read about in this chapter were not malicious. They were 'unconscious,' as Jung would say, unaware of their own psychological needs and how these needs could play out in interactions with others. As a result, their own unconscious needs came to dominate the healing work they undertook. This is, in fact, the central identifying characteristic of spiritual abuse: the healer's needs, not those of the one seeking healing, take precedence.

I became interested in the topic of spiritual abuse because of an experience of my own many years ago. Starting in my thirties when I was a single parent and in need of help, I sought consultation with a woman healer and began a relationship that was initially encouraging, uplifting, comforting, joyous, and wonderfully helpful. As time progressed, we became friends. Years after we'd begun, she began having flashbacks of early sexual molestation by her father, which she confided in me. Not yet trained as a therapist, I was flattered to be her confidante. When she entered psychologically turbulent waters, I did my best to listen, freely offering support and counsel. As time went on, she became intermittently enraged at me, while still expressing love. She continued, all the same, in the role of my spiritual advisor. Sensing her fragility, I hesitated to break off the relationship, for fear of hurting or enraging her. The concepts of enmeshment, role reversal, boundary violation, or even the words for them, were not familiar to me at the time. Had they been, they would have helped me identify what was happening. Instead, the relationship became more and more confusing to me and, finally, destructive. I broke it off when I could scarcely recognize myself, having become acutely confused as I began feeling her issues in my own psyche.[1]

It took years to understand what had happened, and to reclaim what I ended up calling my 'self.' I named the lost part my 'self,' because it felt so important, involving my most deeply held values, integrity, and sense of direction and purpose. I had allowed the most personal areas of my life to be taken over by someone else's need. As I progressed in insight and self-awareness, I could see how this role-reversal with my healer, and my acceptance of it, recapitulated my earlier futile, but earnest, attempts to heal my mother of a personality disorder.

Healing from this 'spiritual' relationship involved work with a Jungian psychotherapist, as well as my own advanced study of clinical psychology. Although clinical psychology is itself a discipline with potential for abuse, for me it was liberating. The study of personality disorders gave me a map for understanding bizarre, dominating, confusing, and manipulative behaviors. I learned about 'boundaries,' psychic and physical, and the importance of maintaining appropriate limits. The deficient sense of self with which most middle-class white women in our society grow up became more obvious to me, a deficiency that leaves some women particularly vulnerable to strong direction and potential abuse of that direction from others. I also learned that a deficient sense of self plagues many men as well as women. Eventually it became clear to me that spiritual abuse usually follows on the heels of a psychological 'set-up' from the past, as it had in my own case, although the relationship between the set-up and the abuse may not be easy to see.

Now I am a psychotherapist in private practice with a Jungian and feminist orientation.[2] I am also a professor of psychology and pastoral theology at a theological seminary. In both capacities, people often appear at my door who have been bruised by difficult relationships with healers. I am currently writing a book about healing from spiritual abuse, focusing on dynamics between women seekers and women healers.

SPIRITUAL ABUSE

Spiritual abuse is a misuse of power in a spiritual context. I am using the word 'spiritual' rather than 'religious' because it is broader and more experienced-based. Religion usually refers to institutionalized forms of worship, and spirituality refers to experience of the sacred. In a God-centered environment like a church, spiritual abuse consists of irresponsible behavior such as using the seeker for the healer's own purposes, making unwise pronouncements, abusing the seeker sexually, giving self-serving advice, in the *name of God*. In a non God centered spiritual context, such as Buddhism or psychotherapy, spiritual abuse consists of the same irresponsible uses of power in the name of a sacred practice. Many other examples of unskillful uses of power in spiritual contexts besides these particular ones can be cited. All spiritual abuse brings profound harm where healing and renewal were promised.

Spiritual abuse involves a confusion of kinds of power because it is a use—really a misuse—of *social power* (status automatically conferred by virtue of one's gender, race, or class) and/or *political power* (status and authority because of one's position at the top of a hierarchy) in a *spiritual context*. This social or political power then parades as *spiritual power* and carries spiritual weight and authority.

Most potentially abusive contexts are hierarchical and authoritarian, although of course not all hierarchies, or people in hierarchical positions, are abusive. Hidden hierarchies and hidden authoritarianism also exist. Hidden hierarchies can be even more abusive than overt ones, because they are invisible and denied. Higher-ups in overt or covert hierarchies are endowed with greater spiritual authority than the underlings. Hierarchies thus lend a covert and spiritual legitimacy to abuse if they do not confront abusers in their ranks. The fact that spiritual abuse can be thus 'spiritually' legitimated makes it much harder for a follower to discern when behavior is abusive.

Spiritual abuse plays itself out in many arenas. I include the possibility of some psychotherapists because some of them do 'soul-work' with their clients. Clients entrust therapists with their life stories, their trust, their love, loyalty, and devotion in the effort to find healing. Therapy clients are often seeking meaning and purpose in life. When this level of search shows up in a therapist's office, spiritual work, loosely defined, is going on. Churches, cults, and spiritual communities are also all contexts in which abuse can be played out. Basically, wherever there are spiritual seekers and those designated to help them in their search, the potential for spiritual abuse exists.

Most spiritual paths demand that followers set aside 'self,' by which they mean selfishness, self-centeredness, and the like, and pursue a higher purpose. However, by setting aside self, certain essential attributes may be sacrificed for the greater good. These may include such things as personal goals and desires. There is a very fine line in most spiritual paths, often one that is not sufficiently addressed, between the desirability of being self-abnegating for the greater good and being self-abnegating in a way that sacrifices one's integrity; in other words, that gets one acting in a way that is not in accord with one's deepest, truest values. To be healthy, one's deepest, truest values must include one's own needs.

In spiritual contexts, a seeker is lured in by his or her deepest desires—desires for liberation, healing, self-transcendence, for that which is holy and beyond ordinary sense perception and experience. The environment in which the search takes place is seen as sacred, as is the object of the search. As a result, a seeker tends to be more accepting, more trusting, and less skeptical than he or she might be in a secular setting. The seeker's initial trust is often reinforced by an altered consciousness, by a cleaner, purer sense of self, by renewed energy, by miracles, by healing, by community, and by unusually loving experiences. All these surpass normal, everyday experience and may make everyday experience pale by contrast. When betrayal occurs in such a context, the fall is greater than it would be in more ordinary circumstances.

In this chapter, my focus is on the psychodynamics of spiritual abuse. This topic will be explored via examples from peoples' lives. The examples either are composites or are so well disguised that the actual people involved are unrecognizable. But the stories are real. They illustrate real, and very confusing, dynamics between helpers and seekers in a sacred context.[3]

THE TERRIBLE CHOICE

In all spiritual abuse there comes a time when the follower is faced with a 'terrible choice': a choice between his or her own deepest sense about a situation, intuitions, repressed knowing (which may show up in bodily symptoms), and the abuser's view of the situation. While other elements of spiritual abuse are more specific to particular situations, the terrible choice is generic.

Take for example, 'Loren.' After Loren first talked with me about her experience of spiritual abuse, she had severe shame attacks. The shame was not primarily about what she had allowed to happen to her, but was connected to the taboo against telling other peoples' secrets (her abuser's, in this case). 'Like it's against God,' Loren said. 'I have such a feeling of having transgressed something.'

Loren's feeling of shame already illustrated a terrible choice. It was an example of having internalized her abuser's, and earlier, her mother's, view so thoroughly that their opinions functioned as her own, nearly preventing her from doing what she needed to do—in this case, tell me her story, as she had agreed to do. Although internalization of our parents' views constitutes an important stage in psychological development, there comes a time, usually in one's teens, that one begins to differentiate oneself from one's parents. This may happen in adolescence via rebellion. In Loren's case, such differentiation was arrested for two reasons: one was her religious background that militated against self-expression and rebellion, and the other was the early loss of her parents.

Loren was raised in a fundamentalist Christian family. She lived somewhat 'on the edges' of fundamentalism and of 'right behavior,' having identified with the 'shadow' side of that religion, although she didn't know the term. (The words in quotation marks are Loren's.) Loren first sought therapy from a Jungian-oriented psychotherapist when she was nineteen, attending a church-related college. Consulting a therapist was a dubious affair in the eyes of church authorities, an example of Loren's living on the edge of what was allowed. It is important to know that the therapist had a Jungian bent, because the spiritual aspect of Jungian thought, its orientation toward meaning-making, and especially its affinity for images and metaphors, ended up being very meaningful to Loren.

At the time she sought help from the therapist, her mother and stepfather had recently died in a plane crash, leaving Loren alone with her estranged biological father as her parent. Her world was falling apart. The therapist had a wonderful love of metaphor and poetry, as well as a fluency in Jungian thought. She introduced Loren to a whole new world of poetry and philosophy. Loren loved her therapist. As she put it,

> I had an enormous transference. There was so much energy between us. She was like a muse, she inspired my desire to learn a whole new world. She was a guide, like Persephone, to the underworld. When I'd get afraid because I was exploring the shadow, which was not allowed by my religion, she'd have wonderful images of holding the tension, like in one hand holding a Bible, and in the other, a flashlight. Her presentation was incredibly skilled, strong, solid, articulate, charismatic . . . In some ways she saw me better than anyone had ever seen me. But even in the beginning, there were some ways in which she didn't see me at all. For example, she scoffed at my college major in Religious Education, saying 'that's not you.' That led me to disown that side of myself,

like it was wimpy. I don't think she ever knew how much power she had, so much that I would wipe out a part of me to maintain the alliance. She had no idea. It wasn't that she was all wrong. What she said had some element of truth in it. I was very willing to give up a part of myself for the relationship. It had so much Eros and energy, so no cost was too great.

We can see the conditions for the terrible choice building up, with Loren giving up aspects of herself to maintain the heady, thrilling, erotic alliance with an older woman, a woman old enough to be her mother. It should have been obvious to anyone, let alone a trained therapist, that Loren would be longing for a mother at this important juncture in her life. This woman therapist was becoming her guide to the underworld—a world Loren had not been allowed to explore, and which, to her surprise, she loved. This new mother figure allowed exotic delights which Loren's original mother had not. On one hand, Loren began to thrive in a way she had never dreamed of. On the other hand, she began abandoning part of herself. Self-abandonment in favor of maintaining a relationship was not a new thing for Loren. She realized with hindsight that she had done that all her life in order to maintain a connection with her biological mother. Of course at the time of her therapy, she did not realize any of this consciously. Loren continues:

> In my memory, I'm still grateful for the therapy—not all of it, but for what it summoned in me. At the same time, what my mother couldn't bear in me, the therapist couldn't bear either. For example, my best friend went to this therapist too and I was jealous. I wrote the therapist a letter about this. In the next session, it was clear that there would be no more discussion of this. So I just cringed in shame and thought, 'okay, remember this, jealousy is not acceptable.' This repeated the mother-wound. I became hyper-vigilant, scanning, trying to learn what is acceptable and what is not. I learned my lesson well. It only took one time to be told something. Later this transferred into my becoming the 'perfect friend.' Such forfeiture of self!

A first step toward extricating oneself from a harmful healing relationship is to realize the presence of the terrible choice and to honor one's own perhaps dimly-sensed feeling of violation, validate one's own sense of reality, and claim for oneself the power of definition.

Such choices, in line with what one holds as true and good, have integrity. A good therapist should help, not hinder, with these developmental tasks and should help a person to act with integrity—even to discern what that is. In Loren's case, the realization that she had thoroughly subscribed to another's view, at the expense of her own, would take a long time. That was partly, of course, because her own opinions were still so unformed. Loren was a young person, only nineteen years old when she began therapy.

Later, Loren and her therapist careened from therapy to friendship (with Loren trying to be the therapist's 'perfect friend') to becoming lovers. This was all instigated by the therapist, and never discussed between them. Only after years of mending with the help of another Jungian therapist, this one wise and ethical, holding appropriate boundaries as well as encouraging Loren's appropriate outrage, is Loren managing to reclaim what, in retrospect, she realized she gave away over the years: her growing understanding of who she was as a person, in other words, her sense of self.

PIOUS COERCION

Spiritual abuse can occur when a leader uses his or her spiritual position to control or dominate another person. It often involves overriding the feelings and opinions of another, without regard to what will result in the other person's state of living, emotions or spiritual well-being. In this application, power is used to bolster the position or needs of a leader, over and above one who comes to them in need.

(Johnson and Von Vonderen 1991: 20–1)

It may involve twisting Scripture to get one's own way and to manipulate, or piously coerce, the seeker.

Consider 'Patrick', who was the second of eight children in an Irish Catholic middle-class family. He was seventeen when his mother fell ill with tuberculosis. The illness wrought havoc in the family and ended up in the abandonment of Patrick, his siblings, and their father, when she died two years later. Like many resilient trauma survivors, Patrick carried on, to all outward appearances, successfully. While in college, Patrick began attending Pentecostal healing services. At one particular service, to his amazement, he found himself slain in the Spirit and speaking in tongues. After his next such experience, he was, again to his amazement, healed of a physical disability that had plagued him for the past two years. Intrigued and inspired, Patrick involved himself more and more deeply with this small sect of loving strangers. They seemed to enable him to experience God more deeply than he ever had before. He began speaking in tongues frequently at their evening services. By the time he graduated from college, Patrick was being courted as a potential leader in the Pentecostal movement.

The problem, however, was that although Patrick was transformed and healed by his experiences among the Pentecostals, he was not certain that he wanted to become more officially involved. He could not say why. His doubt was small, but niggling. A few fellow churchgoers began pressuring him to join, while he began feeling guilty. He still had wonderful spiritual experiences in the meetings. As time went on, the minister began 'counseling' Patrick, quoting 'relevant' Scripture. Patrick remembers the pastor quoting Matthew 16:18: 'thou art Peter, and upon this rock I will build my church; and the gates of hell shall not prevail against it.' The pastor had been likening Patrick to Peter in recent months, when speaking both of Patrick's spiritual strengths and his wavering about joining, which the minister called his 'weakness.' Patrick, himself, now read Scripture daily. The minister followed with more Scripture. Patrick remembers, also, Matthew 16:24: 'Then Jesus said to His disciples, "if anyone wishes to come after Me, let him deny himself, and take up his cross, and follow Me."' The implications of this were that Patrick needed to deny himself, that he was being 'self-centered' in choosing not to get more officially involved.

After about a year of this kind of pressure, Patrick yielded and officially joined the Pentecostal movement. He had decided that his resistance was 'sinful.' And that he should simply override it. He felt that Christ was giving him the strength to see through the wiles of the devil (his resistance).

It is easy to see, here, that Patrick was in danger of losing his integrity, his inner sense of who he was, every bit as much as Loren had done, although in an entirely different context. He was losing his perspective, honesty, agency, point of view, and inner sense of direction. Patrick was piously coerced into giving all these up in the supposed name of God.

In fact, it took Patrick many years more of subordination to the minister's domination before he had a nervous breakdown that would not yield to prayer. Finally, he found the courage to seek therapy and was fortunate enough to find a counselor who understood the situation. Now at age thirty-five, and after five years of therapy, Patrick has left the Pentecostal movement, has married, and is in training to become a therapist himself. The hardest part for him is finding who or what God 'really is,' as he puts it. The fact that Scripture was used to piously coerce him has made him almost 'allergic' to Scripture—which he used to love. His search for the divine continues and is agonizing at times. The hardest part for Patrick is that he still sometimes wonders if he did the right thing in leaving, because 'the spirituality was so powerful.'

In general, like all abusers, spiritual abusers deny wrongdoing. Often, as we saw earlier, institutions support the abuser's denial, because institutions tend to protect those who are high in their hierarchies. By extension, they support the abusive behavior. Because perpetrators, and the institutions behind them, almost always deny wrongdoing, spiritual abuse disconfirms the wounded one's perceptions. This disconfirmation comes from a person, or an institution, who has been an authority in the person's life. If the abuser were to take responsibility for his or her behavior and apologize, much less harm would be done, but the confusion which follows upon the abuser's denial is traumatic.

Both Patrick's minister and Loren's therapist serve as examples of this. Patrick's minister insisted throughout that Patrick was neglecting to 'rightly divine the work of truth.' When Patrick finally found the courage to challenge the minister with having a self-serving point of view himself, he discovered why it had been so difficult to challenge this man earlier. The minister's face grew red with fury as he told Patrick that he had become 'Satan's ploy.' Loren's therapist, when Loren finally began withdrawing from her, acknowledged to others that she had hurt Loren somehow, but 'didn't know how.'

THE CONFUSION OF NICENESS WITH SPIRITUALITY

Spiritual abuse takes place in a spiritual context with a person who may be quite 'nice,' teaching spiritual principles. Perhaps the very niceness of the context, of the teacher and of the seeker, prevents the seeker from seeing what is going on. Many of us have grown up with niceness conflated with spirituality. White, middle-class, American women have been especially conditioned to be nice, although others, too, can be caught by the trap of niceness and compliance, and the confusion of these with genuine spirituality.

Projection is a psychological term, which refers to the human tendency to project images and experiences (as in a slide projector, projecting images upon a screen) onto other people. We then experience those images, along with the attendant emotions, as *belonging to the other*. We tend to do this most with rejected aspects of ourselves. This includes both positive, idealized aspects of ourselves, and negative, devalued aspects of ourselves. When we project either the ideal or the negative aspects onto others, we can remain simply nice.

In the early stages of a spiritual relationship, seekers often deify a spiritual teacher or healer, projecting images of the divine onto him or her. In other words, in a spiritual relationship, the initial projection tends to be highly idealized. It is a little like 'falling in love' in a spiritual context. For a time, this projection works. It fosters healing, spiritual growth, devotion, and discipleship. The person in power must know how to navigate projections skillfully, and not identify with them, or the outcome will be a lack of integrity and an inflation of the healer's ego. In the end, the healer must know how to hand the projections, the idealized images, back to the follower and then appear more fallible. Decidedly, this should not happen via manipulation or other forms of abuse at the hands of the healer, but rather by allowing the seeker some honest glimpses of the healer's humanity.

'Irene,' a former devotee of Gurumayi, the head of Siddha Yoga, was a member of a healing-from-abuse group that I co-led one year. That year she was getting in touch with sexual and emotional abuse that she had suffered as a child from both her parents. This she had repressed for many years. Irene had a tendency to dissociate when anything emotionally charged came up in group—and such things came up frequently! Irene loved her meditation practice, however. Meditating, which she had learned in Siddha Yoga, was a spiritual practice that felt completely safe to her. When she learned of the power and sexual abuses that had taken place in the Siddha Yoga community[4] she was devastated, especially because, as she put it, 'I had projected all my needs for mothering onto Gurumayi. She was the perfect Mother. I trusted her implicitly. I'd entrusted her with my soul.' Since trust was such a difficult issue for Irene anyway, the discovery that her beloved Gurumayi had been disingenuous with her followers was devastating. 'Is there no one out there who is trustworthy?' Irene wonders. She is presently working very hard with a therapist who is honest and skilled in working with transference and countertransference. Irene is doing the very difficult work of identifying and taking back projections. In so doing, she is experiencing a level of integrity heretofore unknown to her.

Projective identification is slightly different from projection. With projection, which is less complicated, the seeker is the initiator of the distorted perception (which projection is) when he or she projects onto the teacher, idealizing, or even deifying, him or her. Projective identification occurs when the recipient of the projection takes it in and *identifies* with it, acting it out. Projection exerts a kind of 'pull' on people to act the way they are being perceived. Projective identification refers to the process by which the 'pull' has been given in to, rather than resisted. This process takes place on an unconscious level, and becomes very painful and confusing.

Followers, as we have seen, generally project idealized images onto healers. In projective identification, wounding healers project their own inner conflicts unconsciously onto their followers, who take in and act out the projections. Wounding healers, in other words, are usually the initiators of the delusional perceptual system of a chronic projective identification, since they project their own issues onto their followers. Followers, who are susceptible to those projections, instead of being guided spiritually, receive projections which distort and divert them from their own issues. The healers' projections often take the form of criticism and blame, because wounding healers tend to project their own devalued, despised side onto their followers which is then hated and 'controlled.' Toxic projections from the healer reinforce a sense of inadequacy in the vulnerable seeker.

In a situation of equal power, projective identification might or might not be 'abusive.' It is always painful and confusing. On an unequal playing ground, followers are damaged spiritually, receiving a stone when they asked for bread. Unskillful healers do not take responsibility for their own needs and projections, and can be quite ruthless, both in projecting their unresolved issues onto their followers and in blaming the followers for being deficient in some way (usually in the very way in which the healer is deficient). When projective identification goes on for a long time, it is called chronic projective identification. The whole process resembles that of spouses or intimate partners who embody each other's deepest psychological issues and destructively play them out for each other.

The projective identification that we will examine here was complicated. It occurred when *both* people took in each other's projections and began acting them out. 'Anna,' a psychosynthesis leader, experienced her follower, 'Herb,' as abandoning her when he questioned whether or not he should remain in psychosynthesis. From what I have learned over the years, I suspect that Anna had experienced a great deal of abandonment in her life, and greatly feared it, and that she was unaware of the effect her past had on her. Herb now sees that he began to accept Anna's projection, even though his questions initially had nothing to do with Anna. As he put it, as Anna rejected his attempts to explain, he began to feel and to act abandoning. Anna now really felt abandoned and escalated her criticism, which Herb experienced as rejecting. Herb, it turned out, was quite sensitive to rejection, apt to feel it when it was not truly there. Now Herb began experiencing his worst fears. Anna and Herb became involved in a 'dance,' the dance of projective identification, where each took in the other's projection and acted it out. As in all relationships, an 'interactive field' was created between Herb and Anna. Eventually their interaction became as painful to Herb as it would have been had it occurred in a marriage. Unable to work it out, Herb eventually left psychosynthesis. He still feels confused about what happened. One of the most difficult aspects of this, for Herb, is that psychosynthesis had given him an identity, both personal and professional. But the level at which he had been caught in this painful 'dance' with Anna was undermining his integrity.

THE FALSE MIRROR

I use the term 'false mirror' to describe distortions in feedback to devotees, illustrated by all the above examples. We all need mirroring: an accurate reflection of ourselves back to ourselves. Young children need this kind of reflection in order to form a sense of self. The 'false mirror' substitutes distortions for more accurate mirroring, or feedback. Not realizing the feedback is distorted, the follower uses it to orient him or herself just as he or she would use more accurate reflecting. Seekers are especially apt to take on the projection if they are lacking in certainty about their own identity, such as Loren, or Patrick, both of whom were young when they became involved with their healers. Being uncertain in their own sense of identity, such people are ripe for someone else to define them.

Typically, wounding healers need a lot of mirroring themselves. Such healers often gather a crowd of admirers around them, using groupies to buttress their own ego and to shore up their faltering self-esteem. This, of course, is done without the healers' conscious awareness of their need. Spiritual healers like this end up using other people for their—the healers'—own narcissistic purposes, that is to make themselves feel better about themselves. There can be a predatory quality to healing relationships with deeply wounded healers. Followers end up unconsciously 'feeding,' sustaining, the wounding healer. This feeding seems to come right out of followers' own 'soul stuff.' The followers are engaged from the deepest level of themselves—and then find themselves exploited and damaged.

CONSEQUENCES OF SPIRITUAL ABUSE

As I mentioned earlier, all of the above dynamics end up being very confusing to the seeker, largely because they are invisible or denied. These dynamics are just the opposite of what the seeker expects from a healing context.

'Spiritual abuse is involved when a person in spiritual authority over someone induces the person to betray themselves. One of the most devastating consequences is that the person loses his or her own spiritual center.'[5] Dr Nancy Avery expanded this idea by saying that spiritual abusers use God in a way that creates compliance in the victim, and then elevate this compliance to the spiritual level. By 'using God,' Avery means that the spiritual abuser implicitly or explicitly suggests that God is in favor of the behavior the healer wants the seeker to engage in. Obviously, if God, or whatever is held to be sacred, desires or endorses this behavior, the abused one will comply, mistaking the behavior for God's will. At the same time, the abuser is creating a dependency in the seeker whose own inner sense of what is right (integrity) is becoming more deeply buried. With this kind of interaction, the seeker loses touch with his or her own spiritual center, and also with his or her own integrity.

In all forms of spiritual abuse, whether in psychotherapy or in church, the spirituality itself becomes contaminated with the abusive experience. Thus, eventually in the aftermath, spiritual abuse feels like a betrayal from God, or whatever is held to be sacred. Because the abused ones usually deified their spiritual teachers in the first place, the abuser and the divine are entangled with each other somewhere deep inside the abused psyches. This deep psychic place is where pain and trauma reside. Survivors of spiritual abuse sometimes suffer in some of the same ways that survivors of post-traumatic stress disorder suffer—with anxiety, flashbacks, hypervigilance, and difficulty trusting or relaxing.

The most troubling aspect of spiritual abuse is, therefore, that the seeker has been damaged spiritually. As a result, his or her relationship with God or with the sacred practice, as well as the psychic capacity for such a relationship, becomes damaged. The deepest consequence of spiritual abuse is that the seeker is traumatized with regard to the most central relationship of his or her life—that with God, or whatever is considered to be most sacred. Spiritually abused people now have a 'trigger' for traumatic, painful memories whenever they try to seek God or the sacred, whether it be by prayer, meditation, Scripture reading, or another avenue.

HEALING

Healing begins first of all by understanding what has happened. There are many avenues to healing from spiritual abuse. In order to accomplish it, some radical questions will need to be asked, and major shifts in perspective will probably be required. To ask such questions and make such shifts, most people find they need companions. A skilled therapist, a group of people who have had similar experiences, a new spiritual director, a new and different form of spirituality, can all be helpful on the path to healing. Journaling has also been found to help. All of these enable a survivor to become more honest, less self-deluded, reclaiming his or her integrity.

Many survivors seem to go through something like 'stages of recovery' after they realize that they have been abused spiritually. The stages are not chronological and may overlap. There may be blame—usually first self-blame, then blame of the wounding healer. There is almost always a stage of disillusionment, a time in the wilderness where nothing spiritual manages to comfort, even though comfort is desperately sought and wished for. During this period, spiritual words and concepts are stale; they turn to ashes in the mouth.

Sometimes there is disempowering anger, turned outward at the abuser or inward at the self. But there can also be empowering anger—an 'anger-in-the-service-of-self.' It can be likened to a mother bear's fierce protectiveness of her cub. Whereas fantasies of revenge, holding a sense of grievance, smoldering resentment, or blame and attack are disempowering, perpetuating an ongoing sense of powerlessness, 'anger-in-the-service-of-self' is a fierce sense of protectiveness towards the integrity of one's authentic perceptions and emotions. In other words, empowering anger is a fierce loyalty to and defense of one's stolen potential, one's derailed vocational goals, one's passions and joys. It is righteous indignation on behalf of one's integrity not only one's most deeply held values, but also one's wholeness which can only be actualized via *attunement* to one's own potential.

During the process of healing, many realizations come. For example, the wounded one may realize that he or she lacked a sense of identity or groundedness to begin with, and thus was ripe to take in someone else's projections. Many survivors feel that something very sacred—something like their soul—has been stolen.[6]

CONCLUSION

Non-pathological universal human yearnings, such as a longing for healing, love, liberation, guidance, wisdom, self-transcendence, and acceptance stand behind the search for spirituality. Our times are fraught with huge anxieties and problems. Our problem-laden world can in itself make us particularly needful of spirituality and especially vulnerable to spiritual abuse. Nonetheless, the spiritual search in itself is both fundamentally human and vitally contemporary. To be viable, it must be in accord with our truest values, our life goals, our developing sense of self, and our integrity.

NOTES

1. See J. Herman (1992) *Trauma and Recovery: The Aftermath of Violence—from Domestic Abuse to Political Terror* (New York: Basic Books) for an excellent discussion of the way in which trauma can be transmitted from a survivor to his or her caretaker. As my healer's role and my role reversed, I was cast in the role of caretaker. I ended up taking much of her trauma into my own psyche, without understanding what was happening. See esp. pp. 136–47, where Herman discusses traumatic transference and countertransference.
2. By 'feminist' I mean having an understanding of the influence of cultural factors in the shaping of women's (and men's) psyches; knowing the particular pitfalls that tend to plague each sex; being aware of the social construction of gender; being willing to advocate for the underdog; being aware of the effect of oppression in women's lives, especially the lives of women of color.
3. Although there are specific examples of healing paths in this chapter (Jungian psychotherapy, psychosynthesis, Pentecostalism, Siddya Yoga), I have struggled with myself about whether or not to identify them individually. It is all too easy, once certain paths are mentioned, for us to believe that the fault is with the particular path. Some people have pejoratively labeled these paths 'cults,' while others have vigorously defended them. In fact, cult-like dynamics—dynamics of manipulation, peer pressure, coercion, exploitation, domination, and fear mixed with promises for a better life and experiences of spiritual euphoria—exist inside and outside of what we officially like to call 'cults.' All of the above-mentioned paths have the potential to be 'cult-like,' but they need not be if they are in skilled hands. My focus is not on the particular organization, but rather on exploitative, dominating psychodynamics in a spiritual context. It is important to realize that these dynamics are found everywhere. When they are found in spiritual situations, they constitute spiritual abuse. See Arthur Deikman, MD (1990) *The Wrong Way Home: Uncovering the Patterns of Cult Behavior in American Society* (Boston: Beacon) for a cogent discussion of this point.
4. See Liz Harris 'O Guru, Guru, Guru,' *The New Yorker*, 14 November 1994.

5. Personal conversation with Nancy Avery, MD, at Episcopal Divinity School, 8 April 1996.
6. Shamanic literature suggests ways to retrieve one's soul, as if it had been stolen. See especially Sandra Ingerman (1991) *Soul Retrieval*, San Francisco: Harper San Francisco.

REFERENCES

Deikman, A. (1990) *The Wrong Way Home: Uncovering the Patterns of Cult Behavior in American Society*, Boston: Beacon Press.
Harris, L. (1994) 'O Guru, Guru, Guru,' *The New Yorker*, 14 November 1994.
Herman, J. (1992) *Trauma and Recovery: The Aftermath of Violence—From Domestic Abuse to Political Terror*, New York: Basic Books.
Ingerman, S. (1991) *Soul Retrieval: Mending the Fragmented Self*, San Francisco: Harper.
Johnson, D. and Von Vonderen, J. (1991) *Subtle Power of Spiritual Abuse: Recognizing and Escaping Spiritual Manipulation and False Spiritual Authority*, Minneapolis: Bethany House.
Kushner, H. S. (1981) *When Bad Things Happen to Good People*, New York: Schocken Books.
Nouwen, H. (1972) *The Wounded Healer: Ministry in Contemporary Society*, New York: Doubleday.

Chapter 5

Authenticity and integrity

A Heideggerian perspective

Charles Guignon

My interest in existentialism grew in the late Fifties as I looked for ways to deal with the illness and turmoil that pursued my family. Though I did not think of it this way at the time, I can now see that I was trying to find a center of stability and strength in what was for me a tumultuous and unpredictable world. Since Heidegger's notion of 'authenticity' appeared frequently in the secondary literature I was reading, I decided to sacrifice a week's lunch money to buy a copy of the English translation of *Being and Time* when it appeared in 1962. On a quiet evening I sat down with the book, carefully underlining what looked like important passages and jotting down notes in a notebook. After several hours of this, it finally dawned on me that I had not understood one word I had read. The book was totally incomprehensible.

It was nearly a decade later that, thanks to the lectures of Hubert Dreyfus at Berkeley, I began to get a glimmering of what Heidegger was saying. Ever since then, Heidegger's work has been central both to my teaching as a philosophy professor and to my life. My courses on existentialism and hermeneutics try to show students how Heidegger shakes up some of the most entrenched ideas in our Western way of thinking. Starting with the 'question of being'—the question, 'What is it for beings of various sorts to be what they are?'—his inquiry slowly opens up an exciting new way of looking at old things. Heidegger suggests that the intractable puzzles and conceptual logjams of Western thought arise because we uncritically buy into a particular conception of what things are. We assume that anything that exists—whether it be a familiar item in the world, a human being, an artwork, a number, or a text—must be regarded as a *substance* of some sort. The term 'substance' refers to the basic kind of stuff that makes things up; it is something which *lies under* (substance) the changing features of things. The idea of substance has its roots in ancient Greek and Roman thought, but its current form is determined by Descartes's philosophy as it influenced modern science. Our contemporary substantialist prejudice assumes that everything in the universe consists either of matter, or of mind, or of some combination of the two.[1]

This substance-metaphysics lies at the heart of almost all the problems of contemporary thought. It defines the well-known 'mind/body' problem. It generates the subject/object distinction and the problem of skepticism about the external world. It motivates the claim that humans cannot have free will. And it even provides the basis for contemporary claims that moral values are purely subjective, lacking any foundation in objective reality. When Heidegger sets out to formulate an alternative understanding of being of beings, then, he points to a way of radically rethinking the interminable squabbles that have dominated philosophy for the past 350 years. In particular, his alternative conception of human existence points to a richer and fuller sense of life's possibilities: the ideal of authenticity. Much of my teaching and writing in the past quarter-century has aimed at showing how Heidegger's conception of authentic existence can transform our ways of thinking in the human sciences, and especially in psychotherapy theory. I would like to sketch out the rough contours of this way of thinking in what follows.

THE CONTEMPORARY CONCEPTION OF HUMAN EXISTENCE

We can get a feel for Heidegger's view of human reality if we see how it contrasts with the dominant view of human agency in contemporary philosophy. The standard view of action makes a distinction between 'outer' behavior—physical motion—and an 'inner' realm of intentions, needs, interests, beliefs, and desires which are seen as causing the behavior. The physical event (e.g. the movement in the vocal chords and air when I speak) is regarded as only an external sign of inner intentions (e.g. conveying information). What makes action different from such inadvertent behavior as sneezing is that action is causally connected to mental intentions. This picture of human agency leads to a split between outer and inner, the physical and the mental, which is so deeply ingrained in our thinking that even strictly physicalist accounts of human phenomena assume that we must identify some physical correlate of the mental cause—namely, events in the brain—if we are to account for human agency.

The result is a picture of humans as consisting of two components: a physical body and a mind. As the philosopher Foucault (1984) and others have pointed out, the modern distinction between mind and body is bound up with a distinctive conception of the self, a conception of humans as essentially 'subjects of inwardness.' On this view, what is definitive of me is not my external deeds and connections to others, but what is going on deep within my mind, in my innermost self. 'I have that within which passeth show,' says Hamlet, and with this sharp distinction between outer show and the inner 'true self' comes our almost obsessive concern with getting in touch with the inner self, getting to know it, and expressing what we find (Trilling 1971: 3–4). The inner self is thought of as something unique, a 'center of experience and action' with a specific point of view. This picture makes it possible to conceive of humans as distinct individuals, as self-contained units with no definitive or essential relations to anything outside themselves. This modern view of the human might be called 'subjectivist individualism.' What is crucial to being a human, in the subjectivist individualist view, is that one have a unique field of consciousness, filled with a rich array of perceptions, beliefs, feelings, desires, memories, and needs, accompanied by an unconscious one can access through introspection under proper conditions.

A number of important consequences follow from this conception of the human. For one thing, there is a tendency to divide everything we encounter into categories of 'subjective' and 'objective.' Modern science tells us that we can give a purely objective, physicalist description of the world as a collection of quantifiable, causally interactive material objects in a space–time coordinate system. So regarded, the world is devoid of any inherent values or meanings. Correlatively, we suppose that values and meanings are subjective, projections of our desires and interests onto things, something we create rather than find. Another consequence is the modern view of humans as individuals who are, when all is said and done, ultimately self-contained and alone. This extreme 'ontological individualism' (Bellah et al. 1985) generates the contemporary ideal of the 'bounded, masterful self' (Cushman 1990), a self that sees all reality, including the social, as a value-neutral arena for means/ends calculations aimed at self-aggrandizement. Finally, the modern picture of the self paves the way to a particular conception of self-fulfillment or the good for humans. Genuine fulfillment is treated as a matter of being 'authentic,' where this means accessing and honestly expressing one's 'real,' innermost self—one's true feelings, needs, thoughts, and desires. As a result we draw a distinction between the 'true,' authentic self—one who is in touch with and faithful to the feelings, desires, and thoughts discovered within—and the 'false,' inauthentic self—the person who goes along with the crowd, acts out parts to please others, and generally is out of touch with his or her inner life.

Being and Time presents a sustained critique of the contemporary conception of human being while making a case for an older, more 'primordial' way of understanding our being as agents in the world. Only by 'retrieving' this older understanding and integrating it into the modern worldview can we move toward a mature and full understanding of ourselves as agents in the world.

HEIDEGGER ON BEING A SELF

Heidegger's 'phenomenological' approach to understanding the human starts by describing our lives as they unfold in familiar, everyday contexts of action, prior to theorizing and reflection. His description of *Dasein* (the ordinary German word for 'existence,' used by Heidegger to refer to the human) lights up dimensions of our existence usually concealed by traditional accounts. Heidegger conceives of human existence not as a thing or object, but rather as an *event*, the unfolding realization of a life story as a whole. Dasein is described as the entity for whom its 'being'—that is, its life as a whole—is *at issue* for it (1962: 32).[2] We are beings who *care* about what we are, and because we care about our lives, our identity as humans is something that is always *in question* for us.

Because our being is at issue for us in this way, we are always taking a stand on our lives in our actions in the world. I care about who and what I am, and I therefore have second-order desires about the sorts of first-order concerns that move me to action: I try to be decent or moderate or steadfast, for example. The stand I take on my life in turn gives me my sense of who I am: 'It is peculiar to this entity that with and through its being, this being is disclosed to it. *Understanding of being is itself a definite characteristic of Dasein's being*' (Heidegger 1962: 32). We all have some 'vague, average understanding' of what it is to be (p. 25) by virtue of the fact that we have grown up in an intelligible life-world and have come to master certain skills in that world. As a teacher, I understand a great deal about how school systems work, how I should relate to students, administrators, and other teachers, how classrooms are to be used, and so forth. Our understanding of what things are all about is embodied in the tacit know-how we pick up as we become adults in our cultural context. This tacit background grasp of things provides the basis for trying to articulate an understanding of being in general.

What must humans be like for there to be an understanding of this sort? To make sense of our capacities, Heidegger proposes that we think of human existence as a *happening* with a specific sort of structure. The first component of human life is called *thrownness*. We are always thrown into a world, already under way in realizing specific possibilities (e.g. being a teacher, being a parent) which give us a place in the surrounding social world. Our thrownness or 'facticity' becomes manifest to us not through cognition, but through feeling: we always find ourselves in some attitude (*Befindlichkeit*) or mood (where even the grayness of everyday life counts as a mood), and these moods disclose our situation in the world.

Heidegger's discussion of moods shows how his description of Dasein can avoid the inner/outer split. The German word for mood is also the word for 'tuning,' as in 'tuning a piano,' and so it conveys a sense of being *attuned* to things in our practical lives. At any particular time, we are *tuned* in to the world through our affective orientation: as blasé, irritable, anxious, enthusiastic, or some other way. Heidegger says that moods are neither inner nor subjective: 'We must dismiss the psychology of feelings, experiences and consciousness' and instead think of a mood as 'like an atmosphere in which we first immerse ourselves in each case and which then attunes us through and through' (Heidegger 1995: 67). Speaking of the mood of grief, Heidegger says,

> It is *not at all 'inside'* in some interiority, only to appear in the flash of an eye; but for this reason it is *not at all outside either*. Where and in what way is it then? Is this attunement, grief, something of which we may ask where it is and in what way it is? Attunement is not some being that appears in the soul as an experience, but the way of our being there with one another.
>
> (1995: 66)

Because moods define how things count for us, they provide the windows through which we first gain our sense of where we stand and how things are going. 'Attunements are the *"how"* [*Wie*] according to which one is in such and such a way' (Heidegger 1995: 66).

A second structural component of our lives is *projectedness* into the future. To be a human is to be constantly under way in accomplishing things. We are always 'ahead-of-ourselves' to the extent that, in each of our actions, we are moving toward the realization of possibilities that define us as agents of a particular sort: being a parent, a lawyer, a coward, and so on. This notion of projectedness is familiar to us from such everyday experiences as 'planning in the sense of the anticipatory regulating of human comportment' (Heidegger 1995: 362). But Heidegger is trying to get at something more basic than conscious goal-setting and planning with this concept. '"Projection" does not refer to some sequence of actions or to some process we might piece together from individual phases,' he writes, 'rather it is what refers to the unity of an action, but of an ordinary and properly unique kind of action' (1995: 363). This originary action is the defining feature of Dasein's being—taking a stand on one's life as a totality. Our projectedness toward the fulfillment of our lives is called 'being-toward-death,' where 'death' refers to the fact that we are finite beings, and so each of us stands before the possibility of having no more possibilities.

In existing as a movement toward our own completion (*Erganzung* [Heidegger 1995: 363]), we are at each moment making decisions about which possibilities we will assume and which we will let slide. For example, as a teacher and a parent, I find myself faced with a number of decisions about developing a personal style, balancing roles, and prioritizing goals. In resolving these issues—whether by careful deliberation or, what is more common, by simply drifting into certain patterns of action—I am defining my identity—my *being*—as a person of a particular sort. In this sense, each of my actions is contributing to shaping the totality of my being as a human being.

To say that life is a *thrown projection* is to say that, for the most part, humans just *are* what they *do*. I am what I make of myself in adopting roles and traits from the public world and realizing them in my own way. Humans are self-constituting or self-making beings: we are what we make of what we find in acting in the world. There are no 'essences' or fixed 'facts' about humans that determine what they must be or how they should act. This is Heidegger's point when he says, 'The "essence" of Dasien lies in its existence' (1962: 67). Since the characteristics we are born with and the traits we embody are defined and given shape by the ways we take them over in existing, there is nothing that compels us to be one way rather than another. Whether I realize it or not, my identity is something I am creating through my actions. My life is always *owned*, even if I usually don't own up to that fact. This owned quality of life is summed up in the claim that Dasein is 'in each case mine' (Heidegger 1962: 68). Actions are the actions of an 'I,' not an 'it,' even in those cases where what one is doing is what anyone in the same situation would do. But this talk of 'mineness' does not imply that there is a 'subject' who does the action, for the 'I' who acts just *is* the agency that unfolds over a lifetime.

BEING-IN-THE-WORLD

Our ongoing life course or life story never exists in isolation from the world. On the contrary, our everyday lives are always enmeshed in concrete situations in such a way that there is no way to draw a clear distinction between a 'self' component and a 'world' component. We can see this unified phenomenon of 'being-in-a-situation' if we consider what it is like to actually be caught up in a familiar situation. Suppose you have done something socially inappropriate—perhaps worn the wrong attire to a formal function. This situation has a particular significance: it is an embarrassing situation. Realizing you are improperly dressed, and feeling the gaze of others, you feel awkward and uncomfortable. Being in this situation is part of your thrownness at the moment; it determines what you can and cannot do in this social context. Yet, at the same time, the significance of the situation is something you shape and determine through your actions. You can worsen the situation by making a big deal of it, or you can defuse it by treating it lightly.

This example shows that there is such a tight reciprocal interaction between self and situation in ordinary contexts that what is normally given is an inextricable whole, not a mere coupling of two distinct items. This fundamental self–world unity Heidegger calls being-in-the-world (1962: 79). His claim is that, when everything is running its course in ordinary life, the distinction between self and world presupposed by the standard view simply does not show up. To use Heidegger's example, in hammering boards together in a workshop, what presents itself is a unified flow of agency that flows through the hammering into the carpentry project while forming the worker as someone who is building something in this context. The hammer can show up as a mere thing on hand only when there has been a *breakdown* in our familiar practical dealings in the workshop. In full flux of our everyday activities, there is simply no role to be played by the notion of objects set over against subjects.

The everyday practical world is always a shared, social world. As we are engaged in our ordinary involvements, we act according to the norms and conventions of the common world in such a way that there is no sharp distinction to be made between ourselves and others. The public world is the medium through which we first find ourselves and become agents. Heidegger says that 'this common world, which is there primarily and into which every maturing Dasein first grows, . . . governs every interpretation of the world and of Dasein' (1985: 249). Even working alone in a cubicle involves being attuned to the patterns and regularities that make possible the coordination of public life.

> It follows that, as agents, we are not so much 'centers of experience and action' as we are the 'they' or the 'one' as this is defined by our culture: We take pleasure and enjoy ourselves as *one* takes pleasure; we read, see, and judge about literature and art as *one* sees and judges; likewise we shrink back from the great mass as *one* shrinks back; we find shocking what *one* finds shocking. The one or they [*das Man*], which is nothing definite and which [we] all are, prescribes the kind of being of everydayness.
>
> (Heidegger 1962: 164, translation modified)

Social conformism of this sort should not be regarded as something entirely negative, however, for it is only through our inculturation into a community that we first pick up a grasp of the interpretations and assessments that give us a window onto the world.

The communal context of shared understanding is itself a product of history.

> Whatever the way of being it may have at the time, and thus with whatever understanding of being it might possess, Dasein has grown up both into and in a traditional way of interpreting itself: in terms of this it understands itself proximally and, within a certain range, constantly. By this understanding, the possibilities of its being are disclosed and regulated.
>
> (Heidegger 1962: 41)

We have all been initiated into the shared understanding of things that define the practices and sense of right and wrong of our historical culture.

As historical products, our possibilities of understanding and evaluation are drawn ultimately from history.

We are now in a position to see how Heidegger transforms our view of what is involved in making sense of human action. The standard picture of human action assumes that in order to understand a person's behavior as action we must identify or surmise the mental cause (beliefs, desires, intentions) behind that behavior. Understanding action is a matter of reading backward from external movements to their hidden, inner sources. In contrast, Heidegger's description of everyday life suggests that in most cases this distinction between physical display and hidden cause has no real role to play. As being-in-the-world, people usually do 'what one does' in the public world, and their actions are intelligible in terms of their place within the shared practices of the community. In ordinary contexts, there is generally no need to try to divine people's hidden intentions in order to understand their actions. We understand the smile of a passing acquaintance not by trying to figure out what is going on inside her head, but by understanding the role such greetings have in our life together. In a similar way, when someone blushes and averts her eyes in an embarrassing situation, we directly encounter this in relation to the socially determined meanings of the situation. We know, for example, that she is embarrassed not because she has dishonored her clan, but because her action is undignified by current social standards, and we know this not because we have some special sort of grasp of what is happening in her head, but because we have a tacit understanding of how things count in our historical culture.

This example helps clarify Heidegger's claim that even our *self-*understanding as agents is achieved not through introspection, but by grasping the meaning of the public contexts in which we act. I know that I feel embarrassed in a particular situation by grasping the social imports of the situation itself. Introspection here might reveal a burning, dysphoric sensation, but the only way I know that what I feel is embarrassment is by understanding the situation and my place in it. Without that understanding, I would have no way of distinguishing embarrassment from heartburn. Heidegger says that 'even one's *own* Dasein becomes something that it can itself proximally "come across" only when it *looks away* from "Experiences" and the "center of its actions," or does not yet "see" them all. Dasein finds "itself" proximally in *what* it does' (1962: 155).

Heidegger's account of human existence does not imply that there are no mental events or that the mental is never important in understanding others or ourselves. Instead, its aim is to deflate the uncritical assumption that every attempt to understand humans must take recourse to the mental. Heidegger's deflationary account of the mind shows us that we can pick out and identify the mental only through the medium of our being-in-the-world. In this sense, the mental is something secondary and derivative, not something simply 'given.' The picture of Dasein as being-in-the-world portrays human existence as an unfolding event that is inextricably enmeshed in the wider flow of a historical culture. Given such an account, there is generally no clear role to be played by the notions of 'mind' and 'matter.' The idea of a mental substance begins to look like a high-level abstraction, a by-product of detached theorizing, rather than something we actually encounter in life itself.

AUTHENTIC EXISTENCE

If Dasein is basically a place-holder in a social world, how does Heidegger account for our experience of *selfhood*, where this term is meant to capture the unity, integrity, and continuity we attribute to ourselves throughout our lives? The Christian doctrine of the soul and the modern conception of the thinking substance have led us to suppose that personal identity must be accounted for in terms of the enduring presence of a special sort of ghostly stuff we have within us: the mind. When Heidegger deflates the concept of mental substance, however, he rejects the standard view of personal identity. In fact, on his view, most of us for large parts of our lives are *not* selves at all. Although each of us has the *ability* to be a self, actually *being a self* is a task and a responsibility rather than a given. Selfhood is something we make, not something we find. We can understand this account of selfhood if we look at the distinction Heidegger draws between authentic and inauthentic existence.

The description of everydayness in *Being and Time* leads us to see that people generally live in a way that is inauthentic. The word for 'authentic' in German, *Eigentlich*, comes from the stem meaning 'own,' so an inauthentic life is one that is 'unowned.' We are inauthentic to the extent that we are distracted and dispersed in our everyday affairs, caught up in the busyness of humdrum preoccupations, with no overarching direction or coherence to our lives. We are what Gergen (1991) aptly calls 'saturated selves,' overloaded with information and entangled in multiple roles. Life seems to be a series of episodes, a matter of getting from one thing to the next, with no unifying thread running through it all. We act as 'one' does and trust that we are living well so long as we measure up to social norms. In this respect, our lives are not our own; they are owned by the public.

This condition of being adrift in a public world is more or less inevitable for us as inescapably social beings. Because we live as 'they-selves,' our possibilities for self-interpretation are 'already restricted . . . to what lies within the range of the familiar, the attainable, the respectable—that which is fitting and proper' (Heidegger 1962: 239). As a result, we tend to lose sight of the fact that what the social world offers is *possibilities*, not necessities. Falling into the 'they' leads to a 'leveling off of Dasein's possibilities to what is proximately at its everyday disposal,' and this 'results in a dimming down of the possible as such. The average every-dayness of concern becomes blind to its possibilities and tranquilizes itself with that which is merely "actual"' (Heidegger 1962: 239). We are blind to the fact that the forms of life we are assuming in our actions are just that: something we *assume*.

Seeing what we do as fixed and necessary leads us to *disown* our lives. Our existence is seen as a given that is 'out of our hands.' When this happens, nothing stands out as having any crucial importance any longer. Nothing seems to be genuinely *at issue* for us; we live as if 'everything is "in the best of order" and all doors are open' (Heidegger 1962: 222), and life becomes a matter of just going through the motions and getting by. Enacting innumerable public roles according to standardized performance criteria, we become effective means/ends calculators who, while possibly quite successful in our fields, are unable to get clear about the ends we are pursuing in our actions. The inauthentic individual is therefore prone to feelings of futility, purposelessness, and depression. For such a person, the question can arise: 'What is the point of it all?' and no answer presents itself.

The opposite of an inauthentic, disowned way of life is *owning up to* one's life—living in a way that is authentic. As authentic, Dasein's concrete way of living fulfills the 'ability-to-be' that is central to its existence. Instead of drifting aimlessly into various 'anyone' roles and doing 'what one does,' Dasein seizes on its 'mineness' and lives in a way that takes over the decisions it is already making as it takes up possibilities from the public world. Authenticity is a matter of 'choosing to choose,' that is, of making one's choices one's own and so being 'answerable' or 'responsible' (*verant-wortlich*) for one's life (Heidegger 1962: 313, 334).

What makes it possible for us to take ownership of our own lives? The experience of anxiety. In anxiety, we are faced with the ultimate contin-gency of the 'they' possibilities we pick up from the public world. Anxiety brings us before our 'being-toward-death,' where 'death' refers not to 'demise,' but to the fact that our own existence is contingent. In anxiety, I recognize that I stand constantly before the possibility of no more possi-bilities, and that each day of my actions contributes to the composing of my life story, a story that could be complete at any moment.

The confrontation with death leads you to live every moment as if it were your last. This imparts a degree of intensity and earnestness to life it normally lacks. Facing up to the finitude of life, I realize that not every-thing is possible for me and that I need to decide what form my life is taking and will take overall, from birth to death. To take a stand on my own death, then, is to live in such a way that, in each of my actions, I express a lucid understanding of where my life is going—of how things are adding up as a whole. A life lived in this way becomes focused and coherent in its future-directedness: 'one is liberated from one's lostness in those possibilities which may accidentally thrust themselves upon one; and one is liberated in such a way that for the first time one can authentically understand and choose among those factical possibilities lying before' one's death (Heidegger 1962: 308). We see possibilities *as* possibilities,' something we choose, and so we see our lives as something we are knitting together in our own way.

It should be obvious that this conception of authenticity has nothing to do with getting in touch with your inner feelings. Instead, authenticity is a matter of living in such a way that your life has cumulativeness and purposiveness as a whole. Authentic self-focusing is achieved by 'simplifying' one's life so that one 'becomes free from the entertaining "incidentals" with which busy curiosity keeps providing itself' (Heidegger 1962: 226, 358). By achieving 'a sober understanding of what are factically the basic possibilities for Dasein' (Heidegger 1962: 358), one can center in on what is truly worth pursuing in one's life. Only through such a decisive appropriation of possibilities does Dasein first become 'individuated' and hence a true 'self.'

Becoming authentic is not a matter of rising above the herd or becoming a 'free spirit' in any sense. The authentic person does not necessarily take up new possibilities or sever ties with the familiar world (see Heidegger 1962: 344). But authenticity does change the way a person lives. In our ordinary lives, our actions generally have an instrumentalist 'means/ends' structure. We do things in order to win the rewards that come from having performed in a socially acceptable way. These rewards are thought of as something external to the action itself: for example, the cocktail at the end of the day, the two-week vacation each year, a comfortable retirement in one's old age. We then live as strategic calculators, trying to figure out the most cost-efficient means to our obtaining the ends we desire, and life is experienced as a zero-sum game where others show up as potential aids or obstacles to be manipulated and controlled.

In contrast, the authentic individual experiences actions as contributing to the formation of a life story as a whole. Life then has a 'constituent/whole' structure: when I act *for the sake of being* a person of a particular sort, my actions present themselves as constituents of a complete life that I am realizing in all I do. In this sort of life, the ends of acting are not external rewards that might be obtained in some other way than by performing this action. They are instead *internal* to the action and hence define the meaning of that action. Thus, although both the 'means/ends' and 'constituent/whole' styles of life may consist of the same actions, there is an important qualitative difference in the actions themselves. There is an obvious difference between helping others *in order to* feel good and helping others *for the sake of being* a caring, decent person. And there is an important difference between telling someone the truth in order to gain their trust and telling the truth as part of being a truthful person. In each example, the action is the same, but the quality of life expressed in the action is different. In the authentic way of living, I take responsibility for the character I am forming through my actions, and I assume my identity by being answerable for the kind of person I am. To be authentic, on this view, is to satisfy the old injunction: 'Become what you are' (Heidegger 1962: 186).

What is it that imparts connectedness and continuity to the experiences that make up a life? What makes it possible for the totality of experiences to form a unity? For much of the Western tradition, this question was answered by the idea of an immortal soul or psyche—an enduring, nonphysical substance in which experiences inhere. As the concept of the soul or mind falls away, however, it is increasingly hard to account for the unity of experience and the integrity of the self. The same holds for the idea of a 'meaning' in life. We normally assume that our lives can have a meaning, but it is hard to see how the disjointed one-after-another nature of a string of experiences can come to form a meaningful unity. So we can ask: How can the experiences that make up a life have a meaning?

On Heidegger's view, it is only by becoming authentic that we can begin to achieve the focused and integrated way of living that constitutes selfhood and a meaningful life. The unfolding of an authentic existence is characterized by a form of 'historicity' that gives it connectedness and coherence. As authentic, we understand ourselves as thrown into a historically shaped 'heritage' from which we draw our possible ways of understanding ourselves. In authentically facing death, we come to see this historical field in a new way. An authentic individual 'retrieves' or 'repeats' the possibilities he or she has inherited in undertaking the projects definitive of his or her own life.

The concept of authentic existence therefore provides the basis for understanding the connectedness, continuity and coherence of life. The integrity of a life history is grounded not in some enduring spiritual stuff that detaches us from our worldly being, but in what we do in the world. Action is a matter of resolutely drawing on the pool of possibilities opened by one's historical culture and remaining true to them in what one does. Such a life has a narrative structure (Ricoeur 1984–88; Guignon 1998). Just as a narrative gains its meaning from the direction the course of events is going 'as a whole,' so an authentic life gains its meaning from the way the events and actions are focused on realizing something as a totality—'right up to death.' Only by living in this way can one be an 'individual' in any meaningful sense of the word.

NOTES

1. Descartes thought that 'mind,' 'spirit,' and 'soul' refer to the same thing—a ghostly, nonmaterial substance found in the world only in humans.

2. Where the translators of *Being and Time* translate the German noun *Sein* with the upper case as 'Being,' I use the lower case 'b.' The use of the upper case creates the misleading impression that this ordinary word for what things are has some special, mysterious significance.

REFERENCES

Bellah, R. N., R. Madsen, W. M. Sullivan, A. Swidler, and S. M. Tipton (1985) *Habits of the Heart: Individualism and Commitment in American Life*, New York: Harper & Row.

Cushman, P. (1990) 'Why the self is empty,' *American Psychologist*, 45: 599–611.

Foucault, M. (1984) *The History of Sexuality*, vol. 1, trans. R. Hurley, New York: Vintage.

Gergen, K. J. (1991) *The Saturated Self: Dilemmas of Identity in Contemporary Life*, New York: Basic Books.

Guignon, C. (1998) 'Narrative explanation in psychotherapy,' *American Behavioral Scientist*, 41: 558–77.

Heidegger, M. (1962) *Being and Time* (orig. 1927), trans. J. Macquarrie and E. Robinson, New York: Harper & Row.

Heidegger, M. (1985) *History of the Concept of Time* (orig. 1925), trans. T. Kisiel, Bloomington: Indiana University Press.

Heidegger, M. (1995) *The Fundamental Concepts of Metaphysics: World, Finitude, Solitude* (orig. 1929/30), trans. W. McNeill and N. Walker, Bloomington: Indiana University Press.

Ricoeur, P. (1984–88) *Time and Narrative*, 3 vols, trans. K. Blarney and D. Pellauer, Chicago: University of Chicago Press.

Trilling, L. (1971) *Sincerity and Authenticity*, Cambridge, MA: Harvard University Press.

PART II

Wisdom

is one of the ways that this recontextualization and learning takes place (Winson 1985; Stevens 1995). The fact that the brain is capable of creating new synaptic connections through its evolving experience gives a scientific basis for my empirical observations as a practicing analyst: that part of the wisdom of the unconscious resides in the psyche's ability to recreate the subjective inner world, and to create new meaning out of old experiences.

So on the one hand, the unconscious is seen as embodying wisdom because it is the seat of the deepest levels of information-processing in the service of developing better ways in which to meet the future. This deep level of processing is particularly related to the recontextualization of affects and emotionally laden experience. On the other hand, the unconscious is felt to be wise because it partakes of the 'two-million-year-old' person (Stevens 1993), reaching backwards to the instinctual, genetically hard-wired codes that make up a human being, hailing from the ancient plains of the African savannah or from present-day New York City. This is the part of the psyche which just 'knows' what to do, because it is adapted to act on instincts which are (or were) in harmony with the environment in which they evolved.

This archaic wisdom is often personified in dreams by figures of animals. Animals in dreams can be understood to personify various traits which are instinct-bound: animals live absolutely 'true' to their natures, and indeed they cannot do otherwise. This animal grounding in unreflective consciousness is considered sacred in numerous cultures. All tribal cultures have their totemic animals, and the ancient Greeks and Egyptians, one branch of Western psychological ancestry, included theriomorphic representations of their gods, such as the wolf of Apollo, the owl of Athena, falcon-headed Horus, and the lioness Sekmet. The sacred wisdom of animals and instincts, while it can easily be romanticized, is also vitally important because it can reconnect our disembodied ego-consciousness to emotional and instinctual sources that provide important direction in life. For example, a woman falling headlong into a difficult relationship dreamt that as she came up the path to her lover's house, the door was barred by a barking, but friendly dog. In working with the dream she came to feel that the dog was protecting her. The dog represented an instinctual sense of boundaries, something she tended to discount in waking life. As this entered into ego awareness, she was able to maintain her integrity in the midst of her interpersonal difficulty.

Another inherent wisdom of the psyche is personified by numerous wise human figures who appear in dreams, visions, and fantasies. Jung (1963) himself maintained a long relationship with such an inner figure named 'Philemon,' which gave rise to his formulation of the importance of 'Wise Old Man' and 'Wise Old Woman' archetypal images. Such charismatic images convey a sense of supernatural power, vitality, and wisdom characteristic of timeless intuitions about the deeper meaning of human life.

When these figures appear in dreams or fantasies, they often signal a developing potential for both healing and increased consciousness, hence their 'wisdom.' Jung (1966a) remarked that such inspiring figures symbolize the

> desired mid-point of the personality, an ineffable something betwixt the opposites, or else which unites them, or the result of conflict, or the product of energic tension: the coming to birth of personality, a profound individual step forward, the next stage.
>
> (p. 382)

Such figures may signal the end of a depression, or the resolution of internal or interpersonal conflict. Elsewhere (Salman 1999) I discuss the meaning of such a dream figure in the psychology of a middle-aged woman struggling in analysis with feelings of paranoia, persecution, and dependency. In the dream she and her analyst were in an uncomfortable analytic session, as was usual at that period of time. But she is amazed to see another woman in the room as well, a mysterious magical figure who, in her hands, is holding out a small, shiny sphere that reflected both patient and analyst, and was obviously intended for them.

The figure of the mysterious woman is an inspiring inner companion, offering something helpful in the form of a reflecting stone. This reflecting stone introduced something new into the tension of the transference field. It was, psychologically speaking, an invitation to look for a different way of understanding and experiencing the meaning of what appeared to be an insoluble state of internal and external tension. The dreamer, shocked by this image, began to feel that there was 'something bigger going on here,' a method behind the madness of her disturbing feelings.

THE SELF AND TOTALITY

The dream figure described above could also be understood as a symbol for what analytical psychologists refer to as the 'Self.' Such images of the Self are distinct from the 'self' of ego awareness, and personify the goal of psychological totality and wholeness, the inclusion in one's awareness of all the contrasting features of one's own complexes and conflicts. This goal includes the discovery or creation of meaning from what had previously been meaningless. Totality or wholeness, as imaged in symbols of the Self, is very different from what is generally considered 'perfection' and is another factor in what constitutes the realization of wisdom.

Totality of personality includes unconscious factors, all of one's disagreeable traits sometimes called 'shadow' elements, such as envy, rage, or hopelessness. Wholeness also necessitates a conscious and ethical relationship to the irredeemable and damaged or destructive aspects of the personality, including evil, suffering, and meaninglessness. For example, it is a hallmark of psychological wisdom, mature development, and therapeutic cure when an individual who suffered abuse in childhood moves through blame, recrimination, and victimization toward acceptance of the effects and meaning of the experience, and an evolving relationship with the difficult and painful factors that ensue.

According to this form of psychological wisdom, perfection is a state of psychological one-sidedness (being a 'wise-ass'), no matter how smart, clever, or brilliant the perfected one has become. The wisdom imaged in the symbol of the Self, by contrast, contains a living acknowledgment of suffering and woundedness. The marriage of these 'darker' elements of human life with lighter and brighter factors forms a totality, allowing mature wisdom to shine through whatever ego identity the individual has developed. Jung (1966b) comments:

> The ancient and long obsolete idea of man as a microcosm contains a supreme psychological truth which has yet to be discovered. In former times this truth was projected upon the body, just as alchemy projected the unconscious psyche upon chemical substances. But it is altogether different when the microcosm is understood as that interior world whose inward nature is fleetingly glimpsed in the unconscious. And just as the cosmos is not a dissolving mass of particles, but rests in the unity of God's embrace, so man must not dissolve into a whirl of warring possibilities and tendencies imposed on him by the unconscious, but must become the unity that embraces them all.
>
> (p. 196)

This unity or Self, at the beginning of one's life, is like a seed or genetic blueprint that develops and comes into being through time and lived experience. This potential for unity or coherence (holding together) acts as an ordering factor behind all development. This perspective on the Self has been elaborated by Jung and Jungians through interpretations from medieval alchemy in the image of the 'stone' that begins its journey as a chaotic *massa confusa*, and passes through innumerable alchemical procedures, until it becomes the *lapis* or *Philosopher's Stone*, the *elixir* of immortality. This is a symbol of ideal wholeness. What was there at the beginning is still there at the end, but the Stone is no longer just a stone.

Symbols of the Self, however, are also thought to express the unfolding and development of what is *not* given, what transcends the given and is acquired through psychological process alone. This wisdom is an 'opus contra naturam,' a work *against* nature, human consciousness becoming aware of itself. Symbols of this process include the god-imago and other religious mythologems of transcendence and divinity.

And finally, symbols of the Self are thought to express an essential 'mystery' that is fundamentally unknowable. In an interview with Miguel Serrano (1966: 50) Jung refers to the Self as a 'dream of totality,' acknowledging that he has never found a definite center in the unconscious, and that he doesn't believe such a thing exists. Recent theoretical developments (Salman 1999) suggest that the Self is neither a reified structural entity, actual or potential, nor is it symbolic of a deified redemptive god-imago. Symbols of the Self may express psychological process alone, be part and parcel of the psyche's acts of creation or the creation of psychological ground and meaning out of an affective and interpersonal wilderness.

In all cases, however, these visions of the Self speak to what constitutes wisdom, psychologically understood: the capacity to see, understand, and live-out what has been given, the ability to reach for what is not given and transcend the boundaries of fate, and the mysterious process of creating meaning and new experience where there had been none before.

FATE AND INDIVIDUATION

The Indo-European root of the word wisdom is 'weid,' meaning 'to see.' But what is it that wisdom sees? And how are we to see wisely? As was mentioned at the beginning of this chapter, *amor fati*, or love of one's fate, is intimately related to wisdom. Making what fate intended one's own intention, participating willingly in what one's life provides, both in terms of possibilities and of limitations, involves waking up to the Self within. Consciously choosing and actively struggling with the imperatives of one's fate, and recognizing that the choice to do so as the ultimate expression of 'free will' is the real goal.

The resolution of this paradox, the transformation of fate or *heimarmene* (compulsion by the stars) into a conscious life which both rests in the containment of its boundaries and transcends them at the same time, is also the real goal of depth psychotherapy. All past history, even the most damaging traumatic experience, both seeks this transformation and is essential for the development and growth of creativity. Depth psychotherapy works to engage the psyche in what is essentially the creative process of its own transformation. From the perspective of analytical psychology the conscious engagement in this process is called *individuation*, and one of its fruits is wisdom.

Individuation does not mean just becoming 'an individual,' although it includes this, but also involves the development of a relationship to society and the larger culture, and most importantly an ego function in the service of wholeness. Individuation is not attained once and for all and forever, although once the path is opened it appears that there is no going back. Individuation is a psychological process, and the process itself is the goal. It happens in large part through a journey of differentiation and assimilation of psychological 'opposites.' Its yield is an eternal and ever-increasing consciousness, a wisdom of the wholeness of life, and the loving embrace of one's fate.

It will be apparent at this juncture that, from a psychological perspective, wisdom is realized through a subjective process akin to the suggestion of the Delphic oracle to 'know thyself.' There are really no gurus, no teachers, and not even a step-by-step method that can bring us wisdom. God, gods, truths, and doctrines may be met along the way, but in the end psychology has a subjective slant on what constitutes wisdom, a slant grounded in the individuation of one's fate.

Fully arrived subjectivity appears to open up into a shared objective awareness, personified in such mythological figures as Apollo, Dionysus, and the Divine Sophia, to name but a few. These archetypal figures represent different, but universal modes of knowing. To Apollo belong the wisdom-attributes of discrimination, insight, and the understanding and expression of illumination. The figure of Dionysus symbolizes the qualities of intoxicating intense experience, suffering, yielding, and the mysterious transformation through submission. The Sophia, spirit and breath of God, is the image of the loving spirit of creation and the building of the world. Discriminative understanding, emotional depth, and a loving spirit all partake of the individual and universal character we call wisdom.

THE PROCESS AND THE DIALOGUE

One of depth psychology's contributions to the understanding of wisdom is the articulation of the aforementioned subjective paths to various dimensions of objective awareness. Through the process of psychotherapy and spiritual transformation, the individual travels a subjective path that follows and then reveals a creative dialogue with unconscious material. The remainder of this chapter describes one version of this path.

As was mentioned earlier, unconscious material moves forward toward something, as much as it emerges from the past. This material expresses numerous potentials and probabilities in what the ancients considered 'prophetic' language. The problem for psychotherapists has always been how to understand these expressions. First off, this understanding involves an appreciation of our psychological self-regulating mechanisms, foremost among which are *regression* and *symbolization.*

When the natural flow of psychic energy is stopped, as in the case of a neurosis or a personal loss, for example, it appears to regress both to infantile longings and to forgotten, half-remembered, discarded, or never-realized potentials and capacities. This kind of regression is quite powerful and expresses both our vision of psychological illness and its cure. For example, when libido regresses during illness, symbols emerge from the unconscious which represent both 'infantile' material and 'new' untapped potential. These symbols appear to be capable of bringing unconscious psychic energy into the sphere of conscious awareness making it more available. Both the facilitation of regression and the unearthing of psychic energy, expressed in various symbolic forms, are the nuts-and-bolts work of depth psychotherapy. With each successful regression, more psychic energy is brought forward enlarging the sphere of psychological awareness and experience.

Regression appears to be a self-regulating capacity, since it usually stops when new psychic energy is generated. Both regression and its fruits, symbolization, are part of the process by which the psyche comes to know itself. 'Solve et coagula,' 'dissolve and coagulate', said the alchemists, and this process of breakdown and rebuilding is one of the ways the wisdom of totality is achieved.

Another phenomenon encountered during regression is the experience and *tension of opposites*. Whatever is in our ego consciousness appears to have its mirror opposite in the unconscious. This is both good and bad news: for example, someone who is compulsive and perfectionistic usually experiences a rigidity in the ability to meet the demands of life in a creative way. This may precipitate a regression, which is expressed in dreaming or waking life as images of people or animals who are helpless, damaged, far from 'perfect.' I understand these to be encounters with a dissociated and wounded secondary personality. The ego-ideal is one of perfection, but the shadow image is of damaged goods, its opposite. From a Jungian perspective the feeling of being 'damaged goods' is important because it not only opposes, but compensates or corrects, the perfectionistic personality and provides the first step towards living more fully and creatively, recognizing the inevitable feelings of inferiority and helplessness.

No person is a homogeneous entity. Complexes and shadows abound in all of us, and these 'work' to create wholeness. It is important to bring psychological opposites into conscious awareness for the sake of psychic health and vitality. Without holding the tension of opposites in awareness there is little chance for resolution of impasses and losses. For the sake of wisdom, including and acknowledging both sides of the tension of opposites is a *sine qua non*, nothing short of an ethical imperative. Without it the wisdom of wholeness is impossible, one's behavior toward others lacks understanding and compassion, and there can be no embodied connection to the universal aspects of human reality and experience.

But in addition, analytical psychologists postulate a further process related to the opposites called the *transcendent function*. This function is the psyche's capacity to create symbols that express resolution of seemingly insoluble opposites. When it is exercised this function transcends both ordinary ego awareness and unconscious complexes to arrive at a 'third' position different from the initial polarity. The creative holding of the tension of opposites and the consequent activation of the transcendent function are the mature work of psychotherapy. The third position of the transcendent function is often expressed in paradoxical images such as the 'wounded healer,' the person who heals others through the strength of her own resilience, or in a poignant dream image of a little dog who had a serviceable braid of ribbons attached to the stump of his mutilated tail.

The varieties of resolution via activation of the transcendent function are endless in their subjective expression, but all point to the creativity of the psyche and its capacity to handle paradox and ambivalence. Wisdom may even be defined as the human capacity to resolve paradox through creativity and to generate an ever-evolving consciousness capable of change and transformation. I would call this realization of wisdom the *marriage between rational thought and the mythopoetic non-rational images of unconscious perception.* As in any dynamic marriage, sometimes one partner 'knows better' and sometimes the other, but usually they both work toward the resolution of problems and conflicts in the service of mutual growth.

When the instincts, desires, affects, wounds, and perceptions in unconscious processes and symbols are married to the reflective rationality and feeling of conscious awareness, we discover a vision of an interpenetrating world. 'As above, so below,' said the old alchemists, and we may now add 'as within, so without.' This vision of an interdependent world includes the ongoing resolution of dichotomies such as subject/object, psyche/matter, and self/other through an altered perception of their connections. The glue that holds together and unites what had previously been separate and divided is the experience of *meaning.* Thus, the realization of wisdom is also dependent on the acceptance of a further dimension of psychological experience, that of new *meaning* developed through the transcendent function.

Harkening back to the example of perfectionist/wounded opposites and their resolution expressed through dream images, we are left asking a question about meaning. Does a symbol need to be understood consciously in order to be meaningful? Can it benefit a person equally well remaining unconscious, as in dreams or enactments that are never understood? This remains a subjective issue for each individual, but unless reflective awareness is joined to unconscious expression in some way, that expression usually remains dissociated and somewhat inert. For example, the common image of a child in dreams which often appears during the process of therapeutic regression, usually personifies the paradox that in order to live life anew with the spontaneity of a child, to see things as a child, one must give up being childish and impulsive. In order to benefit from this insight, the child-image must be consciously understood.

Wisdom is conventionally, and appropriately, understood as the ability to know what things mean on the most profound level. From the perspective of analytical psychology, the discernment, discovery, or creation of meaning is a quintessentially psychological process. Wisdom is one of the flowers of individuation gained through a conscious life of conflict; it is the outcome of the work of psychological creativity which resolves paradox and ambivalence. It arises from the loving embrace of fate.

REFERENCES

Charet, F. X. (1993) *Spiritualism and the Foundations of C. G. Jung's Psychology*, Albany: State University of New York Press.

Edelman, G. (1992) *Bright Air, Brilliant Fire: On the Matter of the Mind*, New York: Basic Books.

Jung, C. G. (1956) *Symbols of Transformation* (1912/1916), *Collected Works*, vol. 5, Princeton, NJ: Princeton University Press.

Jung, C. G. (1963) *Memories, Dreams, Reflections*, ed. Aniela Jaffe, New York: Pantheon.

Jung C. G. (1966a) *Two Essays on Analytical Psychology* (1935/1953), *Collected Works*, vol. 7, Princeton, NJ: Princeton University Press.

Jung, C. G. (1966b) *The Practice of Psychotherapy* (1954) *Collected Works*, vol. 16, Princeton, NJ: Princeton University Press.

May, R. M. (1991) *Cosmic Consciousness Revisited: The Modern Origins of a Western Spiritual Psychology*, Rockport, MA: John Knox Press.

Salman, S. (1997) 'The creative psyche: Jung's major contributions,' in *The Cambridge Companion to Jung*, eds Young-Eisendrath and Dawson, Cambridge: Cambridge University Press.

Salman, S. (1999) 'Dissociation and the Self in the magical pre-Oedipal field,' *Journal of Analytical Psychology*, 44: 69–85.

Serrano, M. (1966) *C. G. Jung and Herman Hesse: A Record of Two Friendships*, New York: Schocken Books.

Stevens, A. (1993) *The Two-Million-Year-Old Self*, College Station: Texas A. & M. University Press.

Stevens, A. (1995) *Private Myths*, Cambridge, MA: Harvard University Press.

Tresan, D. (1996) 'Jungian metapsychology and neurobiological theory,' *Journal of Analytical Psychology*, 41: 3.

Whitmont, E. C. (1969) 'The destiny concept in psychotherapy,' *Spring*, New York: Analytical Psychology Club.

Winson, J. (1985) *Brain and Psyche: The Biology of the Unconscious*, Garden City, NY: Anchor Press/Doubleday.

Chapter 7

Relationship as a path to integrity, wisdom, and meaning

Ruthellen Josselson

> How deeply worried self-made man is in his need to feel safe in his man-made world can be seen from the deep inroad which an unconscious identification with the machine . . . has made on the Western concept of human nature . . . The desperate need to function smoothly and cleanly, without friction, sputtering, or smoke, has attached itself to the ideas of personal happiness, of governmental perfection and even of salvation.
>
> (Erikson 1968: 84)

What is it that adult women learn that leads them to a sense of integrity and wisdom at midlife? How are we social scientists equipped to study that process?

Of the final stage of his epigenetic model of human development, 'Integrity vs. Despair,' Erikson (1950) had this to say: 'Only in him who in some way has taken care of things and people and has adapted himself to the triumphs and disappointments adherent to being the originator of others or the generator of products and ideas only in him may gradually ripen the fruit of these seven stages. I know no better word for it than ego integrity' (p. 268). Erikson, however, went on to say that he could not define this sense, but could only point to its markers, which include a sense of world order and spirituality, an acceptance of one's one and only life cycle as being something that had to be, and the readiness to defend the dignity of one's life against all physical and economic threats. Later, he adds that the 'favorable ratio' derived from the integrity stage is wisdom.

Late in his life, Erik, in collaboration with his wife, Joan Erikson, devoted much of his energy to working out the ways in which integrity and despair are balanced at the close of the life cycle (Erikson and Erikson, 1997; Erikson, Erikson and Kivnick 1986). Increasingly, they emphasized the accretion of wisdom as the hallmark of this stage.

The crisis of integrity versus despair is initiated by the realization that there is not time remaining to correct the life course or to realize unfulfilled dreams. Thus meaning must be sought only through reflection. But Erikson's epigenetic model includes the recognition that each life stage has precursors in the ones before as 'the individual is increasingly engaged in the anticipation of tensions that have yet to become focal' (Erikson et al. 1986: 39). This would imply that a reaching for integrity (and a con-comitant escape from despair) is in the shadows of the earlier stages and becomes more prominent in its influence as one draws closer to death.

From the Identity stage onwards, each new stage has as a subtext issues of integrity and wisdom, phrased differently and of different import as life moves forward. Identity, for example, the hallmark of the late adolescent phase, always has as its subtext a sense of meaningfulness. What might I do or be that would matter in this life? wonders the young person. How can I join the world as I find it in a way that would feel meaningful? Similarly, in the generativity stage, the adult makes efforts to invest his or her efforts in products, be they children or projects, that would offer to the world something that seems purposeful. Particularly at midlife, the adult wonders, Is this a worthwhile way to be spending my time? Generativity is the effort to do something productive (Bradley and Marcia 1998; Bradley 1997; McAdams and de St Aubin 1998). Integrity is the sense that what one is doing has larger meaning.

Elsewhere I have asserted that for women the development of identity and intimacy stages appears to be conflated (Josselson 1987). The sense of meaningful engagement in the world is inextricably tangled with the sense of meaningful connection to others—not just spouse and children, but also parents, friends, colleagues, neighbors, and those to whom her work is devoted: patients, students, clients. Similarly, the experience of generativity is also bound up with the experience of intimacy: what a woman produces is interwoven with her sense of connection to those to whom her efforts are directed.

Here I intend to explore the way in which for women at midlife—in America at this Millennium—the sense of integrity, wisdom, and meaning develops on a path of intimacy and relatedness. Traditional concepts of wisdom lead to abstract principles and disembodied ideals (Chandler and Holliday 1990), far from the pulse of emotional knowledge. The Eriksons, however, tracing the roots of the words 'integrity' and 'wisdom,' locate them in the earthbound strengths of seeing, knowing, and touching. 'It is in actuality that we live and move and share the earth with one another. Without contact there is no growth' (Erikson and Erikson 1997: 8). The contemporary American woman, embedded in a culture that both valorizes and denigrates relatedness, does not simply 'have' relationships, but invests them with her spirit (Miller 1999), grows through them, and derives her sense of meaningfulness from them.

The intersection of relationship and wisdom for women is to be found in two separate but related processes: deepening the understanding of relationships and enlarging the meaning of care. Before exploring these processes, however, I want to first reflect on how we, as social scientists, can learn about others' meaning-making.

THE STUDY OF MEANING-MAKING

Meaning-making relies on forms of knowing that are not easily captured in linear representation. Such understanding is experienced as an inner knowledge, an awareness of insight, and an enlargement of the sense of self and, because of its affective and intuitive base, is often difficult to express in language. Labouvie-Vief (1990) asserts that adult development and wisdom consist of integrating what she terms *logos*, or rational thought with *mythos*, a subjective sense of union with some larger principle. In mythos, 'truth is psychological rather than logical and validation is by intuitive criteria of "felt sense"' (p. 55). While logos can be defined and demonstrated with precision and agreement, mythos refers to what Clinchy (1996) has called 'connected knowing,' where knowledge derives from empathy and intuition, as well as consensually validated phenomena.

Labouvie-Vief (1990) argues that social pressures of human development privilege logos in Western society. The child learns that imagination and inner states have no objective existence, and must find ways to suppress these experiences in terms of the external, conventional world. In other words, the task of development in pre-adult life is to 'fit in' through learning the symbol systems, skills, and value systems of the culture and society in which the young person is growing. But in adulthood, once worldly competence has been reasonably mastered and the claim to identity has been staked, the cognitive and emotional turn is inward, once again valuing the truths of the heart. The integration of the emotions and even irrationality itself lends richness to adult experience and forms the core of adult psychological development.

But these forms of development are resistant to research endeavors which are framed in paradigmatic modes (Bruner 1986) that favor logos, deduction, and prediction. Narrative knowledge, by contrast, privileges human intentionality and meaning-making, finding truth hermeneutically in experience rather than in what is externally verifiable. Surveying contemporary research on wisdom, Robinson (1990) and Birren and Fisher (1990) suggest that the hegemony of the late nineteenth-century scientific method has led to a Dark Ages in our knowledge of wisdom which may only be accessible through phenomenological forms of inquiry.

Interview methods are necessary to access mythos and narrative forms of knowing, but even with these it is difficult to transcend the interviewee's overlearned habits of speaking about their knowledge in terms of logos. Because we live in a culture which so privileges the rational, the demonstrable, and the externally justified, there is a fair amount of shame attached to publicly airing emotions that lie close to a deeply valued core of self. Even with the most skillful interviewer, all interviewees want to sound 'normal,' 'healthy,' and acceptable. Thus, those of us who do research interviews must learn to read between the words for underlying meaning and to hear in tones or emphases what moves another person, what grounds his or her existence.

When I was asked to write this chapter—based on the long-term research I have done on development in women, having followed with intensive interviews a group of thirty women from the time they graduated from college in 1970 until they were forty-three (Josselson 1996)—I felt immediately that I knew these women's paths to wisdom. The paths are lined with experiences of relationships. I 'know' this on the basis of mythos, a connected form of knowing that grows out of having known these women deeply over twenty-two years. In order to write it, however, I must translate this knowledge into some logical form in order to try to share with my readers what it is I believe I know. And then I must try to integrate that with other analyses of adult development in a way that does not obliterate the very mythos that is fundamental to their (and my) meaning-making.

As I review the interviews that I have conducted over all these years, I am aware that the women I have been following have been trying to tell me how they have been making meaning. But as they do this, they are also trying to translate an inner, complex, emotional process into stark language which often won't absorb and transmit the hard-won knowledge they so prize. These are not especially spiritual women, at least not in the religious sense—only two of the thirty are devoutly religious; most disclaim any but the most superficial religious affiliation. They do not move in communities which offer them a language of transcendent growth, unless one were to count self-help books. Nearly all are employed; half are mothers. Most would be considered either Generative or Communal according to the generativity status classification devised by Bradley and Marcia (1998). Leading ordinary lives, they are not exemplars of 'wise' people, yet each experiences a growth in wisdom and insight as she ages. Each tries to speak of what she has 'seen' and 'known' and what she has touched and been touched by—and how she feels part of something larger than herself.

THE CENTRALITY OF RELATIONSHIPS

I asked these 30 women when they were forty-three years old to imagine they were eighty years old, looking back over their lives (inviting them to project themselves into Erikson's integrity stage)—what would they be most satisfied to have accomplished or experienced in their lives? I asked this question at the end of a 4–5-hour interview and they were tired; yet, this was an easy question for them. Nearly all spoke immediately to their relationships:

Brenda—married with no children: I would love to leave some kind of eternal legacy, but without any artistic talent, creativity, or inventiveness, I don't feel that I can leave much behind me except friends who love me, whose life I made more pleasant in some way. Maybe, if I advance in my career I can leave some legacy, but the accomplishment of rising in industry won't be as satisfying as friendships and love would be.

Nancy—married with no children: To look back and feel the relationships I've been in have been deep and meaningful and I helped make that happen.

Helen—married, two children: I will be satisfied to be married fifty-nine years at that point. I will be proud of my children and of my career. I will be proud of all the students that I was able to help.

Leslie—unmarried, no children: I will be satisfied in knowing that I had an opportunity to love someone deeply and be loved back; that my own little corner of the world was better off for my having been there.

Regina—married, two children: If my life had to end right now, I would say that I've covered all the important bases for myself already. I have friends who I think truly love me, I have maintained good family relationships, and I have a husband who really loves me. I have retained the relationship with him through some daunting ups and downs in recent years. I have begun to raise two children, who are exuberant and happy children. I think I've made a genuine difference in some people's lives—clients who had new life directions with my support, students who refer to me as teaching them everything they knew. I've had a rich inner life, a life I've been able to share with other people from time to time.[1]

Written on a page or even heard on the tape recorder, these answers sound pat, superficial, hardly wise. They name relational connections, point to roles these women have taken with others (mother, wife, teacher, doctor, etc.), but the substance of their experiences is only implied. Only by listening carefully and often between the lines of a woman's interview does the wisdom about relationship emerge.

WISDOM IN RELATIONSHIP

Until recently, we have understood relationship in terms of social roles. The developmental story of relationship that has dominated our understanding of a woman is that her fate lies in her choice of a life partner.[2] The rise of the novel concretized this construction, giving prominence to the 'marriage plot' in which a woman's destiny is sealed by the man she marries. But we never know what happens after—how she continues to create meaning in her life (Heilbrun 1988).

A woman may be a spouse or partner to one other person, but the question is what kind of partner *she* will be; a woman may be a mother or a nurturer to the next generation, but she now has many choices about the ways in which *she* will nurture. Friendship is beginning to receive the recognition it deserves as a source of meaning in adult life, and a woman has many different forms of friendship (Apter and Josselson 1998). Work and career, too, are often experienced and expressed in relational terms (Josselson 1996). Relationships become the site at which individual identity and social commitment are melded and form the arena of meaning and integrity.

If wisdom and integrity are traceable to experience in relationships, just what is it that is 'seen' and 'known' that we might say are indicative of these attributes? One problem in taking up this question is that the discourse about knowledge in relationships has largely been muted in our individualistic society (Swidler 1980). A second problem is that knowledge about relationships is not primarily cognitive (although it may have a cognitive component). Rather, it is visceral, empathic, a kind of knowing that fundamentally alters one's experience of Otherness and hence one's experience of self in the world.

Even with interview methods, this experience of insight about relationships is hard to put into language. Grappling for words, Clara, an otherwise highly articulate woman, said, 'With time, I just *understand so much more about people*.' Again, we might ask, but what does she understand? In what lies her wisdom? And can we ever hope to get this into psychological language?

In late childhood, as friends begin to take on emotional significance beyond companionship, girls begin to grapple with the complexity of being intimate with another person outside the family. This is the introduction to the problems of bringing oneself to others and taking them in as who they are. A friend may be unresponsive, may not understand one's deeply felt emotions, may betray confidences in ways that shame, or may reject in favor of another friend. The growing girl must learn to come to terms with the tension between what she really feels in relationships and what she learns she must be and how she must act to gain approval[3]—and therefore connection—from others. How can you say what you think when it may hurt someone else's feelings and then they may abandon you? But what is friendship if you can't say what you think? In all these experiences, the growing girl must try to make sense of human unpredictability, of the complexities of trust and of the difficulties that inevitably accompany being with and relying on others.

As she passes into late adolescence, the young woman must again confront these dilemmas as she explores the possibilities for deep intimacy with someone who may be a life partner. Most young women have ideals for intimate relationships. Women in midlife speak of intimate relationships—and of friendship—differently. They have learned that relationships are difficult processes: People won't be what you want them to be and being with others is a constant state of rethinking who one is and who they are.

Part of what accompanies the experience of wisdom in relationship lies in a growing and changing appreciation of otherness which moves beyond categorization and projection. Development involves learning first to define the self in contrast to others: I am like this, others are like that. With time, however, one becomes reified in these descriptors and begins to question them. I am white, but what does whiteness really mean? I am female, but what is gender? I am caring, but also have my hostile and selfish sides. Adult development involves moving out of those identity categories that one was at such pains to solidify earlier moving to a more relativistic position, not just cognitively, but emotionally, recognizing the shared humanity and other shared attributes in all of us. This is perhaps what Jung was trying to elucidate in his concept of individuation.

Within psychoanalytic theory, there has been increasing focus on subject–subject relations as opposed to object relations (Mitchell 1988, Stolorow and Atwood 1992). The more problematic and challenging aspects of psychological and emotional development concern the articulation of self with others who are also selves. In this view, the experience of self is intertwined with an intersubjective context which forms, sustains, and allows expression of self.

The development of intersubjectivity is a complex matter which brings to the forefront the murky borderland of human interconnection. Others are in part a product of our own construal while we are in part an amalgam of what others have made of us. And yet we must form ongoing relationships with the others who retain a reality independent of our mutual representations and misrepresentations. Buber (1965) suggests that true 'I–thou' relations are possible through 'making the other present,' through our empathic capacity to 'imagine the real.' And these processes, to Buber, are at the heart of human development.

Intersubjectivity is a developmental process in which increasing knowledge of others exists in tandem and in tension with knowledge of the self, interactively, recursively, and, often, paradoxically. The higher levels of moral development (Kohlberg 1976), ego development (Loevinger 1976), and self development (Kegan 1982) all involve greater tolerance for the individuality of the other and a complex experience of interpersonal life in which one's separateness and connection are multilayered and shifting. Wisdom may develop out of relationships which challenge our views of ourselves and others, both cognitively and affectively (Kramer 1990). The hallmark of increasing intersubjectivity is the capacity for recognition of another's subjectivity (Benjamin 1992), fully allowing others to be who they are as we are who we are, and to feel recognized by them. Separateness is transcended even as individual distinctiveness is confirmed (Erikson et al. 1986).

Throughout life, other people may be experienced in four different ways: The Other may be not be differentiated at all, as in merger; the Other may be experienced as a need-satisfier—an object who may or may not be internalized as part of the self; the Other may be felt as a selfobject (Kohut 1977)—separate but still part of the self; or the Other may be represented as fully a subject—related to oneself but operating from a separate center. Recognition of the Other as subject is an unevenly realized task of development. At times, we may recognize someone as a separate subject—only in the next moment to experience him as a selfobject. Or, we may acknowledge the subjectivity of some people but treat others as need-gratifiers. As development progresses (optimally), there is an increase in intersubjective awareness, but this does not eliminate the other processes. With intersubjective functioning and the capacity to enjoy mutual recognition with another subject come the concomitant capacities for empathy, responsiveness, and concern.

Intersubjectivity does not imply a state of interpersonal harmony; that would be a sterile form of conformism. Processes of projection, introjection, projective identification, and other forms of distortion occur throughout life, leaving us always with the task of sifting through and reworking our inner experience of others and self. Living is a process of breakdown and repair in relationships, discord followed by increases in understanding. To the extent that we can accomplish this, we grow wise and integrated.

The confrontation with otherness takes place in small ways in an adult life—although these moments may feel quite dramatic to the individual. Rarely do we as psychologists have an opportunity to witness them *in situ* unless we are therapists who see in our patients the dawning and then flowering ability to more fully take in another person. A recent example from my teaching, however, comes to mind.

In a graduate seminar on depth interviewing for research at the Hebrew University of Jerusalem, Dafna, a 35-year-old woman doing doctoral research on attitudes toward the Holocaust, interviewed Abdul, an Israeli Arab man, also a student in the class. This young man was quite candid and forthright in his responses and related to her in detail his efforts to make sense of the Holocaust. But his views were so far from anything she expected or had ever heard before—so utterly shocking—that she came to me after the interview in tears, filled with outrage and despair that anyone—ANYONE—could assert that the Holocaust never happened and was merely a Zionist hoax. I tried to empathize with her distress and attempted to help her see that this presented an excellent opportunity for her to try to understand someone who looks at the world differently from the way she—and everyone she knows—looks at it. But she couldn't move out of her fury and was now beginning to include me as someone who, in not joining her in her outrage, must be one who could condone such a despicable view. I asked her to transcribe the tape so that we could listen to it together.

Once she did this, Dafna realized that what her interviewee had to say was far more complex than a simple-minded assertion that the Holocaust didn't happen. In fact, he never said this at all. Rather, he was trying to explain the particular meaning the Holocaust had for the Palestinian people and how he, as an Arab, had to integrate that with the dominant Jewish society in which he lived and studied. After much work and discussion, Dafna wrote her final summary of what she learned from the interview:

> the feelings that I felt whilst listening to the interviewee were very strong. I was hurt and offended by his opinions. I did not believe what he was actually saying—not the content so much but that he was saying it.
>
> I also feel that what he said was very strong and on a certain level, it was essentially an antisemitic viewpoint. I do not believe that he would have thought so. I believe that some of the shock that I experienced was that his views did not seem to me to 'suit him.' He appeared before and still appears to be an open, sensitive soul, and his words did jar me.
>
> I believe that the interviewee had a script, according to the demands of his beliefs and ideology . . . I believe that he is firm in his convictions and completely loyal to his beliefs, yet he was very stuck in his rhetoric and did not appear to even want to budge, to try and examine some of the things he said. When he experienced moments of reflection regarding what he said, he immediately gave another statement which suited his script. (I suppose that these moments, even if moments, are the windows.)
>
> The interviewee displayed two very strong, yet contradictory 'feelings.' He was angry at the Israelis, the Zionists and the State of Israel, yet he felt a curiosity about Jews and the Holocaust. He claimed to be part of their world, a world which he was open to examine. Yet he was opposed to the institutions of the State and of Zionism: Yad Vashem, the army, etc.
>
> I tried to correct him, rather than try to understand how he got to the information he had . . . I feel that the whole feeling of shock that I experienced, inhibited me from telling about the 'other' moments, moments of dialogue that he had with himself and some of the more gentle moments of the interview.

I quote this write-up at length to demonstrate the multi-layeredness of this growth-producing moment as Dafna is poised between her 'projecting' style—i.e. it is the interviewee who is stuck in a rigid script—and her genuine efforts to integrate his difference and his wholeness even in the face of her disgust with him. She hasn't yet arrived; she teeters between wanting to reject and dismiss him and wanting to embrace and empathize with him. If (when) she succeeds with this, she will have moved ahead in wisdom— and, when she reflects on it, to an experience of integrity. These are the turning points of adult growth in wisdom and integrity and what constitute the experience of greater knowledge about relationships. Later, Abdul was able to tell Dafna, in a kind way, that he was aware of her shock and she was able to acknowledge this to him. It seemed to be an important encounter for them both. They were able to acknowledge and continue to be who they were with a greater understanding and empathy across difference.

The capacity to embrace difference in relationship enlarges the self, expanding the repertoire of representations that we carry of people who inhabit the world we share, both sharpening the boundaries of the self and connecting the self in deeper ways to others. Wisdom in relationship involves accepting difference without either assimilating the self to the other (through identification) or reducing difference to sameness (see Benjamin 1994; Sampson 1993). Wink and Helson (1997) regard wisdom as insight and knowledge about oneself and the world that deals with matters that are uncertain, entailing sensitivity to context, relativism, and paradox. This is a soulful knowing in which one feels a deeper and more meaningful con-nection to others, who are experienced in their contradictory—and often frustrating—wholeness.

The women who I have been following for twenty-two years have all had similar moments that led to increases in their understanding of others and therefore in wisdom. Amanda, for example, increased in her sense of wisdom after her husband was diagnosed with a brain aneurysm.

> The critical decision with my husband was that I let him make the decision about what had to be done. Even though I was a nurse and knew more about it. They had told him that without the surgery he would most likely die within six months but with the surgery he faced a high chance of having major brain damage. I felt that was something I couldn't decide for him. Had he chosen not to have the surgery, I would have supported him in that. I think he went into surgery thinking that he would be all right after surgery. He never really believed it would happen to him. I knew it probably would and what that meant. I felt that it was such a decision I couldn't make it for him. I told him I would stand by whatever. That was tough to do. I knew that if he did have major damage afterwards what that meant in terms of recovery. But he had major determination that I'm not sure I would

have had in that situation. He has had a lot of fight from the beginning and has exceeded anyone's expectations in terms of his recovery.

. . . With what he went through, there is a newfound respect for him for the strength that he has. Most men are babies about illness, but I think the stamina he had and the will that he had—I have such respect for him—how he would never accept the limitations that others kept putting on him. And I think he also saw a strength in me. I held things together. I worked. I took care of the kids, visited him every day. It brought us closer. We found each other. We care about each other. We've been through some rough times together and I can see where this could drive people apart. One thing we're struggling with right now is that he wants to keep reliving what he'd been through and my daughter and I want to say, Aren't you over it yet? But we've really come through it stronger.

Still, it has been hard for Amanda to adjust to his cognitive impairments:

I feel like I need to help him and be a teacher almost and there are times that I resent it   not resent it but I forget it and then realize, Oh my God he didn't catch what I said. Or I do something quickly and think he should be right there with me but he's not. And its frustrating. But then I think, what if it were me and how would I want someone to treat me? The kids, too have been very good with him. People can say, its horrible and I hate it, but . . .

We note here that Amanda is struggling to acknowledge and find a place for her resentment about her own loss. Logically, she knows it is irrational to resent her husband for what he is physically incapable of doing, and yet this is what she feels—but quickly retracts. She ends her statement by projecting her despairing feelings on nameless others, and we recognize that this is exactly what she is trying so hard to integrate. When she accomplishes this, she will be adding to the considerable wisdom and integrity that she has already created.

Erikson (1968) says that the mature ego 'through the constant interaction of maturational forces and environmental influences, [develops a] certain duality between higher levels of integration, which permits a greater tolerance of tension and of diversity, and lower levels of order where totalities and conformities must help to preserve a sense of security' (pp. 81–2). The higher order, Erikson calls 'wholeness;' the lower, 'totality.' It is this movement toward wholeness that the individual experiences as wisdom, the affective sense of being able to tolerate the tension of difference. Wholeness and wisdom thus contradict the mechanistic model of humanity Erikson deplores in the quotation cited in the epigraph—neither can exist without friction, sputtering, or smoke. Integrity consists in the sense that contradictions coexist, that one's mistakes in life were necessary, that one's life course is multidetermined and contains irrational as well as rational elements—and that these insights are true for all the significant others in one's life as well. And the project of knowing others is, as Spelman (1988) puts it, 'strenuous.' As we begin the twenty-first century, wisdom about relationships is the greatest challenge as we recognize the diversity of the world in which we live. How do we know those who are other from us without stereotyping them or denying their difference? How can we build a world where we can honor our differences and live together? These are the questions most in need of everyone's wisdom.

THE ENLARGEMENT OF CARE

A second major path toward wisdom and integrity in adulthood is the enlargement of the meaning of care. Most of the women I have studied, as we saw above, locate their sense of pride and meaningfulness in their capacity to care for others. Without much reflection, they ground their sense of integrity in their ability to have provided valued emotional resources for others. Actively engaged in professional work, these women also ground the meaning they find in their work in terms of feeling that they had some positive impact on the lives of others. They wondered about what their work really meant, whether it was essential. It wasn't enough to be 'good at' their jobs. They wanted their work to have effect, to mean something.[4]

In Erikson's developmental model, care is the virtue of generativity, the project of adulthood where one seeks to provide for the growth of others, to 'pass it on' in Vaillant's phrase. The activities of caring are those of generativity—taking care of children, mentoring others, serving the community. Yet, reflection on the meaning of these activities—understanding their impact in the larger scheme of things—belongs to the growing sense of integrity (versus despair).

Care is found at all developmental levels, but it evolves into an ethical system (Noddings 1984) and a core of morality (Gilligan 1982). Never, however, does care lose its base in affect: emotion and thought are integrated in care, experienced as deriving from the heart as well as the mind. Thus, the experience of caring, in the mature adult, is accompanied by self-reflective appraisals as having integrity and finding meaning. Care can be experienced as transcendent, as a form of connection to others in the world where the self has reached past its own boundaries to draw on what is outside.

The experience and integration of care changes and develops across the life cycle—from the idealism of late adolescence to the realism of the mature adult, who recognizes the limitations and still continues to try to offer the resources of the self in the interest of tending some aspects of the world. The personal quest to be a 'good enough' carer often evolves into the crises of adult integrity.[5]

Care involves the effort to balance the interests of the self and the interests of a differentiated other. We offer our help and sustenance in momentary as well as grand ways. We visit a sick or bereaved friend or bring a funny gift to someone we like. And we care by taking on the cares of those we love (Gilligan 1990), worrying with them, intervening for them. We tend relationships as well as particular others, by enacting dozens of small practical rituals that strengthen our bonds—looking after the home, taking charge of the neighborhood get-together, and so on (Bateson 1989). These myriad acts, taken together, are apt to be where midlife women locate their sense of integrity when they refer to locating their value in the world in the hearts of those whom they have touched.

Beyond our generative wish to care we learn much as adults about the limits of our caring. Our perception of need may be faulty and the intention to care may be experienced by the Other as suffocating, controlling, or patronizing ('But I meant well'). What we offer as care may not be regarded as such by those towards whom we extend it. I want my nineteen-year-old daughter to call me every night while she is on a road trip because I worry about her and want to be sure she is safe. But she regards this request as intrusive and confining; she wants to be in charge of her own safety. My growth then involves finding other ways to express my love for her while I manage my worry.

These lessons are by no means confined to life at home. The workplace daily provides challenges to care. Marlene, one of the women in my longitudinal study, made personal sacrifices to train as a nurse-midwife and work to promote women's health in the inner city. Initially, she had high hopes for how much change she could effect, hopes that were quickly subjected to disappointments. At the time of the interview, she had integrated a clearer vision of what she could and could not accomplish, but this came after a long process of inner struggle.

As our knowledge about care expands, we become more aware of its complexities. We learn the fatuousness of the ease with which we can mindlessly regard ourselves as caring people and instead come to search out ways that we are hardened, oblivious to the plight of others—or perhaps incapacitated in terms of response. Racists regard themselves as moral, loving people. A mature effort at a sense of integrity is to learn to identify the racism in oneself—in all of us. I remain haunted by the Nazi doctors who in the name of science tortured people all day, then went home to be loving fathers and husbands to their families at night, regarding themselves on balance as ethical and caring human beings (Lifton 1986).

Mindfulness about care forms a formidable path of integrity for women in middle adulthood. Care can hurt as well as help. Caring for people in the larger society engages us in political realities that confound the simple impulse to help. And care for people in other societies, care for the world environment, elude most of us, even as we sigh in despair over the morning newspaper.

The experience of integrity and the accretion of wisdom in middle adulthood is created when one's intimate relationships and generative activities evoke a sense of transcendent meaning. Understanding more about others and finding ways to care for them in welcome and useful ways enlarge the self and lead to enlightenment which may transform a woman's view of the world and her place in it. Through reflection on their experiences in relationships, women come to find new significance in old truths, knowing what they always in some sense knew, but knowing it in a new, deeper sense.

NOTES

1. These responses are very similar to what Erikson et al. (1986) heard from the elders they interviewed about their experience of meaningfulness in their old-age life review.
2. Even Erikson gave voice to this position by asserting that 'much of a young woman's identity is already defined in her kind of attractiveness and in the selective nature of her search for the man (or men) by whom she wishes to be sought' (1968: 263). This has been much quoted and much maligned. But Erikson later said that this is determined by the 'role possibilities of her time.'
3. See Gilligan (1990).
4. Helson and McCabe (1994) also found that women in search of new identity in midlife most wanted to achieve a status where they had something valuable to give to others.
5. Speaking from a feminist point of view, Luepnitz (1988) suggests that the discussion of nurturance has been a taboo topic under patriarchy, which is contemptuous and frightened of mothering.

REFERENCES

Apter, T., and Josselson, R. (1998) *Best Friends: The Pleasures and Perils of Girls' and Women's Friendships*, New York: Crown.

Ballou, M. (1995) 'Women and spirit: two nonfits in psychology,' *Women & Therapy*, 16/2–3: 9–20.

Bateson, M. C. (1989) *Composing a Life*, New York: Atlantic Monthly Press.

Benjamin, J. (1992) 'Recognition and destruction,' in N. J. Skolnick, and S. C. Warshaw (eds), *Relational Perspectives in Psychoanalysis*, Hillsdale, NJ: Analytic Press.

Benjamin, J. (1994) 'The shadow of the other (subject): intersubjectivity and feminist theory,' *Constellations*, 1: 231–54.

Birren, J. E., and Fisher, L. M. (1990) 'The elements of wisdom: overview and integration,' in R. J. Sternberg (ed.), *Wisdom: Its Nature, Origins, and Develop-ment*, Cambridge: Cambridge University Press.

Bradley, C. L. (1997) 'Generativity-stagnation: development of a status model,' *Developmental Review*, 17: 262–90.

Bradley, C. L. and Marcia, J. E. (1998) 'Generativity-stagnation: a five category model,' *Journal of Personality*, 66/1. 40–64.

Bruner, J. (1986) *Actual Minds, Possible Worlds*, Cambridge, MA: Harvard University Press.

Buber, M. (1965) *The Knowledge of Man*, New York: HarperCollins.

Chandler, M. J. and Holliday, S. (1990) 'Wisdom in a postapocalyptic age,' in R. J. Sternberg (ed.), *Wisdom: Its Nature, Origins, and Development*, Cambridge: Cambridge University Press.

Clinchy, B. M. (1996) 'Connected and separate knowing: toward a marriage of two minds,' in N. Goldberg, J. Tarule, B. Clinchy, and M. Belenky (eds), *Knowledge, Difference and Power*, New York: Basic Books.

Erikson, E. H. (1950) *Childhood and Society*, New York: Norton.

Erikson, E. H. (1968) *Identity, Youth and Crisis*, New York: Norton.

Erikson, E. H. and Erikson, J. M. (1997) *The Life Cycle Completed*, New York: Norton.

Erikson, E. H., Erikson, J. M., and Kivnick, H. Q. (1986) *Vital Involvement in Old Age*, New York: Norton.

Gilligan, C. (1982) *In A Different Voice*, Cambridge, MA: Harvard University Press.

Gilligan, C. (1990) 'Joining the resistance: psychology, politics, girls and women,' *Michigan Quarterly Review*, 29: 501–36.

Heilbrun, C. G. (1988) *Writing a Woman's Life*, New York: Ballantine.

Helson, R. and McCabe, L. (1994) The social clock project in middle age. In B. Turner and L. Troll (eds) *Growing Older Female: Theoretical Perspectives in the Psychology of Aging*. Newbury Park. Sage, 68–93.

Jordan, J. (1986) 'The meaning of mutuality,' in *Work in Progress*, Wellesley, MA: The Stone Center.

Josselson, R. (1978) *Finding Herself: Pathways to Identity Development in Women*, San Francisco: Jossey-Bass.

Josselson, R. (1992) *The Space Between Us: Exploring the Dimensions of Human Relationship*, San Francisco: Jossey-Bass.

Josselson, R. (1996) *Revising Herself: The Story of Women's Identity from College to Midlife*, New York: Oxford University Press.

Kegan, R. (1982) *The Evolving Self*, Cambridge, MA: Harvard University Press.

Kohlberg, L. (1976) *Collected Papers on Moral Development and Moral Education*, Cambridge, MA: Center for Moral Education.

Kohut, H. (1977) *The Restoration of the Self*, New York: International Universities Press.

Kramer, D. A. (1990) 'Conceptualizing wisdom: the primacy of affect-cognition relations,' in R. J. Sternberg (ed.), *Wisdom: Its Nature, Origins, and Development*, Cambridge: Cambridge University Press.

Labouvie-Vief, G. (1990) 'Wisdom as integrated thought: historical and develop-mental perspectives', in R. J. Sternberg (ed.), *Wisdom: Its Nature, Origins, and Development*, Cambridge: Cambridge University Press.

Lifton, R. J. (1986) *The Nazi Doctors: Medical Killing and the Psychology of Genocide*, New York: Basic Books.

Loevinger, J. (1976) *Ego Development*, San Francisco: Jossey-Bass.

Luepnitz, D. A. (1988) *The Family Interpreted: Feminist Theory in Clinical Practice.* New York: Basic Books.

McAdams, D. P., and de St Aubin, E. (1998) *Generativity and Adult Development*, Washington, DC: APA Books.

Miller, J. B. (1976) *Toward a New Psychology of Women*, Boston: Beacon Press.

Miller, M. (1999) 'Religious and ethical strivings in the later years: three paths to spiritual maturity and integrity,' in L. E. Thomas and S. A. Eisenhandler (eds), *Religion, Belief and Spirituality in Late Life*, New York: Springer.

Mitchell, S. A. (1988) *Relational Concepts in Psychoanalysis*, Cambridge, MA: Harvard University Press.

Noddings, N. (1984) *Caring*, Berkeley: University of California Press.

Robinson, D. N. (1990) 'Wisdom through the ages', in R. J. Sternberg (ed.), *Wisdom: Its Nature, Origins, and Development*, Cambridge: Cambridge University Press.

Ruddick, S. (1989) *Maternal Thinking: Towards A Politics of Peace*, Boston: Beacon Press.

Sampson, E. (1993) *Celebrating the Other: A Dialogic Account of Human Nature*, Boulder, CO: Westview.

Spelman, E. V. (1988) *Inessential Woman: Problems of Exclusion in Feminist Thought*, Boston: Beacon Press.

Stolorow, R., and Atwood, G. E. (1992) *Contexts of Being: The Intersubjective Foundations of Psychological Life*, Hillsdale, NJ: Analytic Press.

Swidler, A. (1980) 'Love and adulthood in American culture,' in N. J. Smelser, and E. H. Erikson (eds), *Themes of Love and Work in Adulthood*, Cambridge, MA: Harvard University Press.

Wink, P., and Helson, R. (1997) 'Practical and transcendent wisdom: their nature and some longitudinal findings,' *Journal of Adult Development*, 4: 1–15.

Chapter 8

Affect complexity and views of the transcendent

Gisela Labouvie-Vief

In Euripides' tragedy *The Bacchae*, the god Dionysus comes to Thebes disguised as a stranger. He is outraged by king Pentheus' refusal to honor his divinity, and his outrage is worsened when the king denounces and imprisons him. Dionysus escapes, but devises a revengeful plan. The king is to behold the mysteries of the women worshiping Dionysus. But in their frenzied and ecstatic fury, the women dismember the king.

Euripides' play is a parable of the relationship between emotion and reason. The frenzied women and the god Dionysus represent an emotionality unbridled by, and hostile to, the rational. In a similar way, the king's rigid rationality and contempt for Dionysus suggest that he is cut off from the realm of emotions. Thus the play admonishes that without a balance of these two domains, fragmentation and destruction take over.

This poetic wisdom of the dangers of polarizing reason and emotion rarely has guided our views of these domains. Whether in art or science, there often exists a tension between the two domains, and two views have prevailed. One of them reflects a traditional epistemological stance that depicts men as rational and women as irrational. According to this view, it is a uniquely human/male capacity to orient our images, actions, and thoughts away from the ongoing moment, and then to exist in realms that transcend the here and now. The second view instead holds that much of human experience cannot be encompassed by such elevation over the emotions. In contrast, it is at its fullest when we live in the realm of emotions and deeply felt experience.

Not all traditions, however, have epitomized one of these contrary views. Many philosophers, writers, scientists, artists, or religious people suggest that the highest level of human experience is found not in either of these views, but rather in some transaction between them. It was, indeed, a unique development of the twentieth century that integration has become a guiding principle for a range of disciplines. In a similar vein, the search for integration of these two modes has come to describe many recent theories of development. These theories no longer view as the ideal of humanity either the self that lives disembodied in a transcendent abstract space, or the self driven by emotional impulse. Instead, a view is evolving that has begun to marry reason and emotion in experiences that unite both rational restraint and the ability to encompass deep personal meaning and emotional expression.

In this chapter, I suggest that in theories of individual development across the lifespan, wide-ranging interest in integrated transcendence is a relatively recent historical development. This is true even though there have existed, throughout the course of history, individuals and traditions that displayed such integrated forms of being and thinking. However, only in the twentieth century did we begin to think of a balanced relationship of reason–emotion as a new norm of development. While our classical theories of development tended to see maturity as the ascent of reason and logic over the realm of mythos, more recent reformulation of these classical views are likely to emphasize a dialectical balance between logos (the rational and abstract) and mythos (the concrete, deeply felt here-and-now) (Labouvie-Vief 1994). This is particularly true for conceptions of mature and later adulthood, where individuals may leave behind more dualistic conceptions of reality that are rooted in conventional laws and norms, and move towards conceptions that reach spiritual dimensions.

In my own work over the years, I have elaborated a view of such integration in my research and writing of mind, self, and emotions (see Labouvie-Vief 1994). In this work I show how, in our individual development, most of us move through periods or levels in which reason and emotion participate in a polarized and conflicting relationship. Relying on either of these capacities is a source of conflict and even pathology. Indeed, some individuals are able to move to more integrated levels in which they develop a more cooperative relationship between reason and emotion, imparting personal meaning and deeply felt experience to one, and enriching the second with order and discipline.

In this chapter, I suggest that conceptions of spirituality and transcendence follow a similar pattern. On one hand, for many individuals the notion of spirituality or transcendence involves a dualistic view of the dictates of reason, rule, and law pinned against a realm of emotions that is considered problematic and inferior. In contrast, another view of spirituality and transcendence maintains that in their most evolved and 'enlightened' forms, these concepts imply a marriage between our rational inclinations and our emotional faculties. Indeed, I suggest that more integrated forms of spirituality and transcendence can offer individuals a set of unique gifts that are usually referred to as 'wisdom': the ability to open our hearts to the suffering of self and others, with a sense of hope that springs out of encompassing the full range of the human condition.

TRANSCENDENCE IN DUALISTIC TRADITIONS

In traditional dualistic views of reality, transcendence is often identified with the control of reason over the passions. This view has predominated in Western ways of thinking, and was first formulated in Plato's philosophy around the fifth century BCE. With some variations, this view of reality has dominated discourses about the nature of the transcendent. This traditional discourse is deeply embedded in the cultural practices and folklores of many societies.

How such views of reason evolved out of mythic and folkloric views of reality is well exemplified in the concept of reason in Greek philosophy. Early Greek philosophers attempted to develop a new language of reality, one that was to replace more mythic and nature-based views of the past (see Cassirer 1944; Donald 1991; Labouvie-Vief 1994). These efforts found a first culmination in Plato's work, which proposed a two-layer view of human nature. Plato argued that a layer of mind, abstract thought, spirit, or ideals is 'better' or more 'advanced' than a more concrete, sensory, and bodily layer. Thus, the faculty of logos was declared to be a higher and more developed faculty than that of mythos.

In what ways, specifically, did this more abstract layer transcend the more concrete one? Cassirer (1944) suggested that one aspect of transcendence is reflected in a transformation of the concept of space. For pre-Platonic thinkers, space was a sensuous space—an experienced, concrete space with unique textures of concrete sensations, physical movements, and psychological associations. That space gradually became transformed by abstracting those concrete features to create a purely abstract or mathematical space, such as the space of idealized lines and angles that was defined by Euclidian geometry.

In this abstract space, an individual's thinking was believed to transcend the social and interactive dimensions of thinking. For example in the *Odyssey*, thoughts are usually displayed as inherently dialogical. They take place between people and are not primarily inner processes. However, for Plato thinking was an inner process, an internal dialogue that the self carried out with itself. And so, thinking was able to remove itself from the senses, the emotions, and the body. Thus, the highest form of thinking was thinking that concerned itself with pure abstractions. In contrast, thinking that was permeated by the emotions, such as art, poetry, or music, was considered less valuable than that concerned with such abstractions as philosophy and mathematics.

These layers, then, were arranged hierarchically: mind–spirit formed the superior pole, body and senses the inferior one. Thus, the mind became that part of the self that was able to transcend those parts that were 'merely' body—parts that enslaved us to the demands of context, time, and matter.

To be sure, the notion of transcendence as the ability to live in abstract realms was not unique to the Greeks. It appears to have emerged at about the same time in other world philosophies and religions. And until recently, it continued to characterize, in one version or another, mainstream Western philosophy. However, its claims to superiority over the excluded realm of mythos became a matter of animated debate, especially in the twentieth century, when many disciplines began to thoroughly deconstruct the traditional concept of transcendence.

In retrospect, despite claims to the contrary, the traditional concept of transcendence was, in actuality, permeated through and through with specific mythic images that hinted at the relations between reason and embodied emotion. In music, art, and religion, transcendence and immanence took on specific cultural garb, especially the depictions of gender. The masculine was associated with gold, airy heights and light, and reason, while the feminine was associated with darkness, nature and earth, and the emotions.

In the *Symposium*, Plato discussed the nature of love and assigned different values to different forms of love. On the one hand, there are physical and material forms of love involving women and children; on the other, forms of love that have to do with spirit and idea—and with soul. Says Plato:

> Those whose creative instinct is physical have recourse to women, and show their love in this way, believing that by begetting children they can secure for themselves an immortal and blessed memory hereafter forever; but there are those whose creative desire is of the soul, and who long to beget spiritually, not physically, the progeny which it is the nature of the soul to create and bring to birth . . . If you ask what that progeny is, it is wisdom and virtue in general.
>
> (quoted in Keller 1985: 24)

The equation drawn here uses the specific metaphor of sexual reproduction. Plato's model (and more generally, the Greek view; see Foucault 1986) implied a strong valuation of forms of desire, parallel to the hierarchy of forms of knowledge. This association of the masculine with transcendence (mind and spirit), and of the feminine with the immanent (body and matter) remained relatively implicit in Plato's theory. It became much more explicit in his student Aristotle, who incorporated it into his theory of reproductive processes. Aristotle argued in *De Generatione Animalium* that this hierarchy was evident in processes of sexual reproduction. He theorized that the woman contributed the more primitive, material principle to the embryo, and he denied that the man's contribution was of a material sort. Instead, he held that the masculine contribution was more spiritual or 'divine.' This superiority was derived from the belief that the masculine principle is active while the feminine principle is passive.

The transcendence of the masculine over the feminine principle of creation is reflected in many religions across the world. For example, in the *Theogony* Hesiod (1983) tells of the primordial creator couple, Gaia and Uranus, who are personified as earth and sky. Uranus bent over Gaia and the couple produced the Titans. That the spatial sub- and superordination of earth and sky is to be taken seriously as a hierarchical arrangement was one of the concerns of Hesiod, who told of the gradual disempowerment of the female principle. More generally, Lerner (1986) has argued that in the mythology and religions of the Occident, such imagery often occurs as the theme of the overthrow of original female divine figures by the male godheads or heroes who become the true creators, creating the world not organically but conceptually, through pronouncing words.

Indeed, in most conventional interpretations of major world religions, divinity is represented as masculine while the feminine principle occupies an inferior position not considered divine, per se. These religious interpretations also are associated with a devaluation of those functions that are considered 'feminine,' especially the body with its emotions and autonomous organismic processes. A frequent spiritual or religious goal is to drive out these processes through oppressive and ascetic practices that are based on guilt, shame, and penance.

DIALECTICAL VIEWS OF TRANSCENDENCE

Dualistic views of transcendence characterized Western thought until recently. However, in the twentieth century, there has been a thorough deconstruction of the notion that the dualistic mind is a transcendent mind. Instead, major traditions within philosophy and the sciences began to propose more relational solutions to the mind–body problem. In those solutions, context, matter, and emotion are part and parcel of a theory of mind and self, redefining the mind, self, and transcendence as dialectical interactions.

TRANSCENDENCE IN THE PSYCHODYNAMIC TRADITION

Within psychology, the first vision of the mind as an integration of opposite poles arose out of critiques of the two grand developmental theories born of Freud and Piaget. Freudian psychoanalysis argued that all of human behavior, including advanced forms of rationality, ultimately is to be placed in the context of important emotional systems. For Freud (e.g. Freud 1911/ 1957), development is based on the tension and balance between two modes of being and defining reality. One is primary process, an organic mode in which an inner world of desires and wishes prevails. The other is secondary process, a conceptual mode no longer directed by the inner reality of wish fulfillment and fantasy. Secondary process allows us to find out what is objectively true or what holds in the outer world.

Even though Freud's aim was to liberate the realm of mythos from its devalued position, he nonetheless maintained a traditional, classical view of the mind. This conflict is also evident in the work of Piaget, where the ideal of a balance between the rational and the organismic was also a basic tenet (e.g. Piaget 1967). Paradoxically, neither theorist carried that notion to its logical conclusion. Freud's theory, for example, is aimed less at a harmonious balance between inner and outer reality, and more at a fairly complete victory of secondary process over primary process. Indeed, the former is called 'reality principle,' while the latter is termed 'pleasure principle.' Thus, Freud defines education 'as an incitement to the conquest of the pleasure principle, and to its replacement by the reality-principle. The ideal of the adapted individual is the scientist who 'comes nearest to this conquest' (Freud 1911/1957: 43–4). In a similar fashion, Piaget's theory was based on a duality of organismic and rational processes, but maintained the rationalist bias.

From a psychodynamic perspective, one major theorist to define a new way of looking at adulthood was Jung (e.g. Jung 1933; see also Fordham 1966; Jacobi 1962; Whitmont 1969). Jung's famous break from Freud was motivated out of his belief that Freud, though in one sense liberating primary process from its devalued position, in another sense had continued to imprison it in a rationalist perspective. For Jung, the broad organismic heritage expressed in story, myth, and visual symbol was not merely a primitive mode of processing displaced by the ascent of reason, but potentially a rich and highly advanced mode of processing in its own right. Beyond the capacities of reason, it revealed a larger context that constrains reason, a context of universal biological heritage and of the enduring emotional patterns related to birth, death, sexuality, love, and generational succession.

Jung's major contribution (e.g. 1933) was to emphasize that functions of the ego might play different roles at different points in the lifespan. Early, in the process of forming a primary adaptation based on conscious ego control, the individual disowns many emotional experiences that are not congruent with the ideals of culture. Nevertheless, these rejected self aspects strive for expression in distorted ways, as in processes of dissociation and splitting. Jung believed that the unique potential of adult development consisted in healing these splits and in forming a more integrated structure. In that process, there is also a reevaluation of the ego and rational processes, with the realization that they are undergirded by powerful archetypal patterns.

Confronting the dialectical tension between these two systems—ones I refer to as logos and mythos in *Psyche and Eros* (1994)—the individual can eventually form a new structure—the Self—that transcends either system, yet blends both within higher-order forms of experience. This transcendent way of relating, according to Jung, reconceptualizes the world from an ordinary sense of objective reality to one in which the opposites of reason and emotion, self and other, or masculine and feminine, are blended into a new experience of reality.

This new reality is defined by universal aspects of the human condition as it is experienced through times and cultures. This view is essentially a spiritual one, repeated in many religious traditions, and often represented by the union of two contrasexual figures in a 'divine marriage' (Fordham 1966; Jacobi 1962). The self represented by this marriage, then, transcends the processes that were formative in the early years: internalization of parental behaviors and standards, the rules and norms of conventional culture, and the dualisms these create.

Jung's view of positive development in later life has influenced several writers. Among the first to put them to the test were Gould (1981) and Levinson et al. (1978). Both of these authors reported that their empirical studies reflected the kinds of changes Jung had proposed as part of midlife development: an inward turn and heightened interest in the non-rational, an increasing openness to life's negative and disappointing aspects, a greater tolerance of paradoxical oppositions such as good and evil, young and old, masculine and feminine.

More recently, Chinen (1985) suggested that these same themes are mirrored in fairy tales around the world, especially those that address later-life issues. While fairy tales of early life often stress the importance of forming a *persona* or social role, adjusting to a reality defined by the existing social system, those about mid- and late life reveal a turning away from conventional roles, a blending of gender possibilities, and the emergence of an inner-oriented self. Such tales help define a unique story of the older individual that differs from those of youth. The older individual is seen as a spiritual leader, and as an expert in the realm of emotion rather than technique. Older women often fulfill heroic roles reserved for men in the younger tales, while older men are challenged to suffer, empathize, and nurture.

In a similar vein, research by Adams and Labouvie-Vief (e.g. Adams 1991; Adams et al. 1990; Jepson and Labouvie-Vief 1992) suggests that mature and older individuals may interpret myths and stories differently from younger people. College-age people often interpret stories in terms of their overt detail and the sequence of actions and events, but older individuals are more likely to focus on the psychological meaning of the information: what it reveals about the general condition of being human, or about transcendent principles that allow us to accept misfortune and injustice.

Findings such as these also are reminiscent of Erikson's (e.g. 1984) view that later life is a period in which issues of integrity come to the fore. Faced with approaching limitations and decline, the elderly person needs to re-examine his or her life with its positive and negative dimensions. He or she needs to accept it as a structure that, overall, is meaningful and coherent. Following Erikson, several authors (e.g. Tornstam 1989) proposed that this process requires a shift of focus away from preoccupations with body, ego, or personal self, and towards the general human condition. Tornstam (1989) has referred to this process as one of 'gerotranscendence.'

VIEWS OF TRANSCENDENCE IN COGNITIVE THEORIES OF DEVELOPMENT

Jung's influence has been only indirectly felt in academic psychology. Yet the notion that mature development brings a transcendence of objectively based views of reality, and includes a more general vision of what life could and should be, also arose out of more cognitively based accounts, such as Piaget's. As already noted, Piaget's theory was based on a duality of organismic and rational processes, and, like Freud's theory, it maintained the rationalist bias of early psychoanalysis.

As a consequence, one major impetus to searching for continued growth in later life has come from the cognitive-developmental expansions of Piagetian notions, such as those of Loevinger and Kohlberg (for a review, see Labouvie-Vief 1990; 1994). These theorists described how, as individuals acquire cognitive structures that are more complex and powerful, they move beyond conventional and institutional interpretations, rules, and roles. At advanced levels, individuals develop modes of thinking that expose both a more differentiated and a more individuated self. They attempt to locate that self within broader, supra-individual structures. Thus, the notion of 'postconventional' forms of thinking has a decidedly Jungian ring! Nevertheless, these post-conventional or post-conformist forms still can remain rooted in rational principles, in contrast to Jung's emphasis on mythos. This is especially true of Kohlberg (1984), who remained committed to rational principles of justification that motivate the search for post-conventional principles.

The last two decades have seen a plethora of attempts to extend Piagetian structures of youthful thinking to cover the whole span of adulthood. Proponents of this approach suggest that formal operations are not the final stage of cognitive development, but that a qualitatively new form of thinking emerges during adulthood which is often referred to as 'post-formal' or 'dialectical' thinking (Riegel 1973). This new form of thinking goes beyond the decontextualized, abstract formal reasoning observed during adolescence and young adulthood, and involves a higher use of reflection and integration of contextual, relativistic, and subjective knowledge. This approach has resulted in an array of studies concerned with post-formal or wisdom-related aspects of knowledge (King and Kitchener 1994; Kitchener and King 1981; Kramer and Woodruff 1986)—important real-life knowledge such as the processing and decision-making in conflict situations (Kitchener and King 1991; Kuhn et al. 1983), or the representation of and reflection on self, emotions, and values (Commons et al. 1984; Labouvie-Vief et al. 1989).

All of the above proposals indicate that rational processes on the one hand, and processes related to self and emotions on the other, are profoundly interconnected. Even though this is true at all stages of development, only at advanced levels are individuals able to represent and understand these interactions and integrate them within single, non-conflicting systems. This ability to bridge the tensions between the universal and the contextual, the theoretical and the pragmatic, and the rational and emotional is often referred to as wisdom (Baltes and Staudinger 1993; Clayton and Birren 1980; Labouvie-Vief 1990).

While all of the work discussed addresses aspects of 'wisdom' (see Sternberg 1990), the most detailed research project that thus far has attempted to provide a specific operational definition of 'wisdom' is that of Baltes and his colleagues (Baltes and Staudinger 1993). In the view of these researchers, wisdom is defined as expert knowledge with regard to important but uncertain matters of life, and can be characterized by several components. Individuals receive ratings on each of these components, and an overall 'wisdom score' is derived. As is true of the studies reported earlier in this section, Baltes and collaborators found that although age itself was not a sufficient condition for the development of wisdom, older adults were somewhat more likely to be nominated as wise, and those nominated in fact produced the highest wisdom scores. In general, there was no evidence for a strong link between age and wisdom.

This lack of association between age and wisdom may be due to the particular criterion of wisdom used in Baltes' research project: that wisdom is primarily cognitive and emphasizes relativism and differentiation. This approach does not emphasize a central aspect that is proposed by advanced spiritual traditions: *integration*—which springs from the understanding that there are general principles that structure both emotional and cognitive realities. That principle has been suggested in Jung's work, and is expressed in other research. For example, my own work suggests that the essence of wisdom lies in the integration of cognitive understanding and the knowledge of emotional and interpersonal regularities (Labouvie-Vief 1994). In a similar vein, Kitchener and King (1981) proposed that the wise person realizes that the search for truth is not merely a cognitive enterprise, but is embedded in communal and relational processes. Thus individuals committed to more integrated notions of truth and objectivity commit themselves to a *process* of critical inquiry in which notions of 'objectivity' are relocated into the intersubjective domain. In my own work, I refer to this form of thinking as 'hermeneutical thinking' (Labouvie-Vief 1994). In its most objective and evolved form, individuals realize that truth can only arise out of the interaction of individuals that are committed to shared inquiry, free of such coercive constraints as differentials in status, power, or gender.

For example, we (Labouvie-Vief et al. 1989) demonstrated that younger individuals described emotions in terms of outer appearance, conventional standards, relatively static impulse-monitoring, and an emphasis on control and ideals. In contrast, those older or of higher ego level (as assessed by Loevinger's sentence-completion test) conveyed a more keen sense of differentiation of self from norms; of vivid felt experience; of an individuality that is distinct, historically formed, and subject to change and transformation; of complex psychological trans-actions both within the self and between self and others. Similar changes also were evident in individuals' descriptions of themselves and their parents (Labouvie-Vief et al. 1995a, b). This work is also consistent with other writings on emotion (e.g. Blanchard-Fields 1997) and the self (e.g. Kegan 1982; Noam 1988).

What does this work say about early notions that these types of changes might reveal late-life structures of thinking? In actuality, our data suggest that the apex of thinking in terms of complex integrations is not in late life, but rather around midlife. Individuals past the age of sixty may have a high degree of emotional integration, but this does not appear to imply a complex cognitive view. For example, in Adams' study on text processing, the elderly summarized the text in terms of its emotional significance, but had difficulty remembering specific actions and events from the narrative. Similarly, my work on emotions and self showed that older adults were more likely to describe emotions in simple, conventional, undifferentiated terms. However, more recent analyses (Labouvie-Vief and Medler 1998) have demonstrated that the elderly—or any other age group for that matter—are not a homogeneous group. In our research, about 30 per cent fell into a subgroup that was characterized by high cognitive complexity and emotional well-being. However, another 20 per cent, while scoring high in emotional well-being, also were low in complexity and indicated a high degree of denial and repression and low levels of tolerance of ambiguity and emotional exploration. Overall, this group appeared emotionally con-stricted and defensively closed.

Thus it is becoming apparent that we should not make overall gener-alizations about older individuals, but rather look for those factors that are related to high levels of emotional complexity. Our research consistently shows that apart from emotional well-being, education, cognitive com-plexity—including ego development and self complexity—and tolerance of ambiguity, and regression in service of the ego, are strong predictors of cognitive-emotional integration.

DIALECTICAL TRANSCENDENCE IN SPIRITUAL TRADITIONS

Earlier I noted that many major world religions adhere to strongly dualistic views of transcendence. However, within those world traditions exist views that demonstrate how processes of emotional complexity can play a role in spiritual development. Such views are often out of the mainstream and considered esoteric or even heretical. Yet, as Fowler (1981) suggests, they attest to the fact that some individuals proceed beyond dualistic thinking to a view of faith and religion as dialectical, integrated, and universal. In this section, I briefly discuss how such dialectical visions of faith and spirituality are exemplified in three major world religions: Buddhism, Islam (specifically, its 'esoteric' version of Sufism), and Christianity.

Buddhism

While sometimes associated with an otherworldly withdrawal from the senses, many forms of Buddhism are examples of disciplines that foster cognitive-emotional integration. To be sure, Buddhism exists in many variations, each with its own different interpretations. Yet some of Buddhism's core tenets throughout the ages overlap with principles that recent psychological science is elaborating. The basic problem posed by Buddhism is how we can live amidst suffering and yet continue with a sense of hope. This problem is addressed by the Buddha in the Four Noble Truths (Brazier 1997).

According to the first and most basic Noble Truth, suffering is an important fact of life. To talk about suffering to the novice reader on Buddhism can have a rather austere connotation, as if the purpose of life was to immerse oneself in suffering. However, Buddhism merely maintains that some sources of suffering are part of the human condition and cannot be avoided. For example, we experience losses, we are the victims of catastrophes, we grow old, we face our own process of dying, and so forth. In addition, much of our suffering is created because we hold onto the notion that we can escape the inevitability of suffering if we accept certain internalized standards. For example, we may seek stimulation, power, ambition, and acknowledgment because it seems to buffer us from the unavoidable difficulties of existence.

According to legend, Siddartha Gotama, the prince who was to become the future Buddha, confronted human suffering as a young adult who had led a very sheltered life until that point. At first, he tried to master this suffering by consulting masters who taught him that the source of all our suffering is the body. Therefore, to stop suffering he was advised to subject the body to ascetic spiritual practices. These practices only exhausted Siddartha, and eventually he had an insight: neither ascetic practices to deny the body, nor pleasure-seeking, can release us from suffering. From that moment he practiced a way of living and meditating that came to be known as the Middle Way, the way between the extremes of pleasures and pain. Using this method, eventually the young prince came to full enlight-enment. From this experience, he proposed the First Noble Truth:

> birth, old age, sickness, death, grief, lamentation, pain, depressions, and agitation are dukkha (afflictions). Dukkha is being associated with what you do not like, being separated from what you do like, and not being able to get what you want.
>
> (Brazier 1997: 285)

The Second Noble Truth states that, rather than separating ourselves from these experiences, we allow ourselves to experience a continual flow of feelings. These, like hunger or thirst, are part of the human condition. In other words, this implies that if we suffer, it 'doesn't mean that something is wrong. What a relief . . . Suffering is part of life, and we don't have to feel that it's happening because we personally made the wrong move. In reality, however, when we feel suffering, we think that something *is* wrong' (Chödrön 1997: 40). Instead, when we accept that to suffer is simply to be human, there is no blame or shame involved, and hence less suffering ensues.

The ultimate goal in Buddhism, then, is not to be emotionless. Rather, we are encouraged to accept all emotions without putting up resistances and barriers and to let them flow through the self naturally like water flows through a lake. In Freudian language, we might say we no longer experi-ence the blaming and shaming commands of the Superego. Instead, we naturally confront our suffering, and, in so doing, we often realize that it is not entirely negative, but also can have positive consequences. Being able to suffer is said to open the ability to have compassion and to accept all of reality with a loving and open heart.

The Third and Fourth Noble Truths state that we can contain our suffering by decoupling our desire from the object of our desire. For example, we do not necessarily act on our anger towards the person at whom we are angry, but we merely become aware of the anger as our own feeling. More generally, we do not give up our desires, but rather we stop acting on them automatically and reflect on and become conscious of them. Being able to do so keeps us on the Middle Path, living within the para-doxical nature of human existence.

The differentiation between non-truths and the Noble Truths is not unlike Jung's differentiation between the persona and the Self, or Loevinger's and

Kohlberg's differentiation between conventional and post-conventional thinking. For example, according to Chödrön (1997), in Tibetan Buddhism this differentiation is made by referring to different aspects of the 'mind.' There are two words for 'mind.' One is the self-image we carry of ourselves. In Tibetan Buddhism, this is *sem*, and it is contrasted with the other form of mind, *rikpa*. 'Sem is what we experience as discursive thoughts, a stream of chatter that's always reinforcing an image of ourselves. Rikpa literally means "intelligence" or "brightness." It is thinking that is oriented at getting ground under our feet, by holding on, not letting go and open exploration. Behind all the planning and worrying, behind all the wishing and wanting, picking and choosing, the unfabricated, wisdom mind of rikpa is always here. Whenever we stop talking to ourselves, rikpa is continually here' (p. 27).

How do we move from sem to rikpa? The answer is to come to observe our emotions with care and discipline, and to turn away from the chatter of sem: in the empty spaces when sem stops, rikpa automatically emerges. In that space, feelings and thoughts come and go, emotions do not have the usual valences. They are merely part of human existence. 'It is just the same kind of human experience that's been happening to everyday people from the beginning of time. Thought, emotions, moods, and memories come and they go, and basic nowness is always there' (pp. 26–7).

Sufism

In a somewhat different language, a very similar message is also conveyed by Sufism, a sub-discipline of Islam. The Sufis make a differentiation between two kinds of self as well. One of those is called the 'Commanding Self'—the self that arises out of unreflective desires and unenlightened socialization practices (Shah 1994). The Commanding Self is that part of ourselves that has been shaped by 'conditioning, brain-washing, and attitude-engineering' (Shah 1994: 2). As a result, we tend to think of many of our emotions as 'bad.' For example, Shah suggests, many familiar religions and philosophies have censored emotions as 'bad.' In so doing, they have oversimplified things. In fact, the censoring only results in channeling emotions into what the respective traditions decided is 'good.'

Both Buddhism and Sufism advocate the transcendence of the conventional self in spiritual development. Both traditions assume that spiritual development is no automatic outgrowth of aging. Rather, education and practice are extremely important to spiritual advancement. However, education is not merely a formal process and involves more than information accumulation; it is a guiding relationship between an initiated teacher and a novice. The stimuli for advancement must be closely tailored to the individual situation, fitting a person's understanding and ability. The teacher 'intervenes to provide the stimulus at the right time for the right person' (Shah, 1994: 3).

'Examine your assumptions; avoid mechanicality; distinguish faith from fixation' (p. 2). Indeed, suggests Shah, traditional and conventional forms of religion are not truly spiritual at all. As a result, the Sufi way of teaching places high demand on the integrity and advanced development of the teacher. 'The Sufi teacher . . . has to be someone who has experienced all the stages of the Way along which he will conduct his disciples. Outward observers are not able to comment upon Sufism, only upon its externals.' Thus, knowledge is not merely external, it is also an inner process. In fact, Sufism declared the inherent subjectivity of knowledge before it became a twentieth-century movement. Accordingly, knowledge is a deeply subjective yet disciplined process that cannot be explained to non-initiates: they lack both the experience and the capacity to discriminate between real and degenerate forms. 'Who tastes, knows,' is a Sufi saying. Equally, whoever does not taste, does not know (Shah 1994: 2).

In this way, Sufism stresses the complete interpenetration of discipline and spontaneity, abstract knowledge and concrete experience. Thus, the spiritually advanced person is able to engage in dialectical thinking, bridging the opposites in a coherent way of living in the moment.

Christianity

In Western Christianity, the teachings of advanced spirituality are part of mystical and esoteric traditions. One example is the writing of the great sixteenth-century mystic St John of the Cross, who in *The Dark Night*, described the transition from a more conventional form of spirituality to an advanced dialectical form. In fact, the writings of John of the Cross are often quoted in Jungian literature as an example of the process of the integration of the Self.

Jung believed that midlife often included a depressive challenge to the individual. This was a challenge to the youthful idealisms and conventional knowledge of early adulthood. Similarly, John of the Cross suggests that spiritual transformation begins with a 'dark night of the senses.' This is a time when the individual attempts to take hold of his or her spiritual quest and to live by conscious submission to the divine by means of ritual, obedience, penance, and devotion. At that point, spiritual forces take over and begin to dismantle the power of the ego. First, the individual withdraws from the world as 'the senses and desires are dulled, interior faculties are deactivated, and in general the ego is disempowered' (Washburn 1994: 223). This initiates a period during which 'the ego is assailed and engulfed by dark forces, agonizingly purged of all defenses, disabused of the last vestiges of self-importance, and gradually prepared for union with the divine' (p. 223).

This process is one of regression in the service of transcendence in which original structures of self and object relations are dismantled and reconstructed. This period of de-idealization only gradually leads to a period of

decreased ambivalence and spiritual awakening—a period no longer dominated by ego-based demands but rather by an integration that transcends
the personal ego.

The outcome of this process is a self that is stripped of self-importance
and all the defenses of grandiosity and omnipotence over others. One no
longer feels in control of one's destiny. Instead, one feels moved by forces
and laws we experience as supra-individual. One has become part of a
universal human condition and experience.

CONCLUSIONS

In this chapter, I have suggested parallels between views of the transcendent
and psychological views of cognition–affect integration in adulthood. The
notion that some individuals move beyond a family- and culture-based
construction of the self, in terms of conventional categories, ties both of
these traditions together. In such cases, a self-organization emerges that
focuses on more universal issues, such as the meaning of human life, of
suffering and death, and of the self within a broad supra-individual scheme.
Both traditions suggest that there are commonalities to this process of self-
reconstruction: a confrontation with forces that at first are experienced as
dark and dangerous, but that ultimately are understood to be no more than
the result of our earlier idealized structures that were based on conformity
and the conventions and rules of family and culture.

The outcome of this process is progressive and constructive rather than
regressive and destructive. The individual who has freed the self from its
early identifications, and reconstructed it along spiritual lines, no longer
promotes the interests of the self only. His or her emotions no longer are
driven by self-interest. Rather, she or he is able to invest self and feelings in
all of humanity, since all human creatures are understood to share the same
condition, regardless of more transient criteria such as social power, gender,
or other socially based classifications.

ACKNOWLEDGMENT

Preparation of this chapter was facilitated by National Institute of Aging
Grant AG09203.

REFERENCES

Adams, C. (1991) 'Qualitative age differences in memory for text: a life-span
developmental perspective', *Psychology and Aging*, 6/3: 323–36.

Adams, C., Labouvie-Vief, G., Hobart, C. J., and Dorosz, M. (1990) 'Adult age group differences in story recall style', *Journal of Gerontology*, 25: 17–27.

Baltes, P. B., and Staudinger, U. M. (1993) 'The search for a psychology of wisdom,' *Current Directions in Psychological Science*, 2: 75–80.

Blanchard-Fields, F. (1997) 'The role of emotion in social cognition across the adult life span,' in K. W. Schaie, and M. P. Lawton (eds), *Annual Review of Gerontology and Geriatrics*, vol. 17, New York: Springer, 238–65.

Brazier, D. (1997) *The Feeling Buddha*, New York: Fromm International.

Cassirer, E. (1944) *An Essay on Man*, New Haven, CN: Yale University Press.

Chinen, A. B. (1985) 'Fairy tales and transpersonal development in later life,' *Journal of Transpersonal Psychology*, 17: 99–122.

Chödrön, P. (1991) *The Wisdom of No Escape*, Boston, MA: Shambhala.

Chödrön, P. (1997) *When Things Fall Apart*, Boston, MA: Shambhala.

Clayton, V. P., and Birren, J. E. (1980) 'The development of wisdom across the life span: a Reexamination of an ancient topic,' in P. B. Baltes, and O. B. Brim, Jr (eds), *Life-span Development and Behavior*, vol. 3, New York: Academic Press, 103–35.

Commons, M. L., Richards, F. A., and Armon, C. (1984) *Beyond Formal Operations: Late Adolescent and Adult Cognitive Development*, New York: Praeger.

Donald, M. (1991) *Origins of the Modern Mind: Three Stages in the Evolution of Culture and Cognition*, Cambridge, MA: Harvard University Press.

Erikson, E. H. (1984) *The Life Cycle Completed*, Boston, MA: Norton.

Fordham, F. (1966) *An Introduction to Jung's Psychology*, New York: Pelikan.

Foucault, M. (1986) *The Care of the Self*, New York: Pantheon.

Fowler, J. W. (1981) *Stages of Faith: The Psychology of Human Development and the Quest for Meaning*, San Francisco: Harper & Row.

Freud, S. (1911/1957) 'Formulations regarding the two principles in mental functioning,' in J. Rickman (ed.), *A General Selection from the Works of Sigmund Freud*, Garden City, NY: Doubleday, 43–4.

Gould, S. J. (1981) *The Mismeasure of Man*, New York: Norton.

Helson, R., and Moane, G. (1987) 'Personality change in women from college to midlife,' *Journal of Personality and Social Psychology*, 53: 176–86.

Hesiod (1983) *Theogony* 590–601, in A. N. Athanassakis, *Hesiod: Theogony, Works and Days, Shield*, Baltimore, MD: Johns Hopkins University Press.

Jacobi, J. (1962) *The Psychology of C. G. Jung*, New Haven, CT: Yale University Press.

Jepson, K. and Labouvie-Vief, G. (1992) 'Symbolic processing in youth and elders,' in R. West and J. Sinnot (eds), *Everyday Memory*, Hillsdale, NJ: Erlbaum.

Jung, C. G. (1933) *Modern Man in Search of a Soul*, trans. W. S. Dell and C. F. Baynes, New York: Harcourt, Brace & World.

Kegan, R. (1982) *The Evolving Self*, Cambridge, MA: Harvard University Press.

Keller, E. F. (1985) *Reflections on Gender and Science*, New Haven, CT: Yale University Press.

King, P. M., & Kitchener, K. S. (1994) *Developing Reflective Judgement*, San Francisco: Jossey Bass.

Kitchener, K. S., and King, P. M. (1981) 'Reflective judgement: concepts of justification and their relationship to age and education,' *Journal of Applied Developmental Psychology*, 2: 89–116.

Kohlberg, L. (1984) *Essays on Moral Development*, vol. 2. *The Psychology of Moral Development*, San Francisco: Harper & Row.

Kramer, D. A., and Woodruff, D. (1986) 'Relativistic and dialectical thought in three adult age-groups,' *Human Development*, 29: 280–90.

Kuhn, D., Pennington, N., and Leadbeater, B. (1983) 'Adult thinking in developmental perspective,' in P. B. Baltes and O. G. Brim, Jr. (eds), *Life-span Development and Behavior*, vol. 5, New York: Academic Press, 158–95.

Labouvie-Vief, G. (1990) 'Wisdom as integrated thought: historical and developmental perspectives,' in R. J. Sternberg (ed.), *Wisdom: Its Nature, Origins and Development*, Cambridge: Cambridge University Press.

Labouvie-Vief, G. (1994) *Psyche and Eros: Mind and Gender in the Life Course*, New York: Cambridge University Press.

Labouvie-Vief, G. (1997) 'Emotional integration in later life,' in P. M. Lawton and K. W. Schaie (eds), *Emotions in Adult Development*, New York: Springer.

Labouvie-Vief, G. (1998) 'Emotions in later life,' in V. Bengston (ed.), *Theories of Adult Development and Aging*, New York: Springer.

Labouvie-Vief, G., and Medler, S. M. (1998, November) 'Positive, negative, and complex affect: their roles in life span development,' paper presented at the Annual Meeting of the Gerontological Society of America, Philadelphia.

Labouvie-Vief, G., Devoe, M., and Bulka, D. (1989) 'Speaking about feelings: conceptions of emotion across the life span,' *Psychology and Aging*, 4: 425–37.

Labouvie-Vief, G., Chiodo, L. M., Goguen, L. A., Diehl, M., and Orwoll, L. (1995a) 'Representations of self across the life span,' *Psychology and Aging*, 10: 404–15.

Labouvie-Vief, G., Diehl, M., Chiodo, L. M. and Coyle, N. (1995b) 'Representations of self and parents across the life span,' *Journal of Adult Development*, 2: 207–22.

Lerner, G. (1986) *The Creation of Patriarchy*, New York: Oxford University Press.

Levinson, D. J., Darrow, C. N., Klein, E. B., Levinson, M. H., and McKee, B. (1978) *The Seasons of a Man's Life*, New York: Ballantine.

Loevinger, J. (1993) 'Measurement of personality: True or False,' *Psychological Inquiry*, 4: 1–16.

Noam, G. G. (1988) 'The self, adult development, and the theory of biography and transformation,' in D. K. Lapsley and F. L. Power (eds), *Self, Ego and Identity: Integrative Approaches*, New York: Springer.

Piaget, J. (1967) *Six Psychological Studies*, New York: Random House.

Riegel, K. F. (1973) 'Dialectical operations: the final period of cognitive development,' *Human Development*, 16: 346–70.

Shah, I. (1994) *The Commanding Self*, London: Octagon Press.

Sternberg, R. J. (ed.) (1990) *Wisdom: Its Nature, Origins, and Development*, Cambridge: Cambridge University Press.

Tornstam, L. (1989) 'Gerotranscendence: a reformulation of the disengagement theory,' *Aging: Clinical and Experimental Research*, 1: 55–63.

Washburn, M. (1994) *Transpersonal Psychology in Psychoanalytic Perspective*, Albany, NY: State University of New York Press.

Whitmont, E. C. (1969) *The Symbolic Quest: Basic Concepts of Analytical Psychology*, Princeton, NJ: Princeton University Press.

Chapter 9

The Tao of wisdom

Integration of Taoism and the psychologies of Jung, Erikson, and Maslow

David H. Rosen and Ellen M. Crouse

The metamorphosis of one's false (non-genuine) self into one's true (genuine) self is a central aspect of Taoism and the psychologies of Jung, Erikson, and Maslow. Through the transformation of the inauthentic into the authentic self, one attains integrity (wholeness) and wisdom (spiritual knowledge). While transcendence is a vital step in the process, it is not the place to remain, because only continual acts of transformation lead to real personality change. In this chapter, we focus on the lifelong development towards wholeness as described in Taoism and the psychologies of Jung, Erikson, and Maslow. In the end, death completes the cycle of development, returning us to the state of wholeness from which we emerged at birth.

How does wisdom develop? From infancy through adulthood, we come to learn about the varying aspects of wisdom through art (symbols and images), fairy tales, parables, and human experience. Stories of judicious kings and wise sages appeal to listeners of all ages, because of the multiple levels at which they convey meanings that are at once pragmatic, empathic, intuitive, and just. These multiple levels are interpreted here as corresponding to the stages of human development from various theoretical perspectives. Viewing wisdom through the lens of developmental theory provides a means of clarifying our understanding of this attribute, because as we grow, each new stage of development opens onto yet another facet of wisdom's diverse and complicated nature. Here we combine individuation (process towards wholeness) together with the Tao (the Way) and the te (integrity) in a developmental view of self-actualization, and consider Taoism and the major theoretical perspectives of Jung, Erikson, and Maslow as the most important theoretical models for understanding the evolution of wisdom. In the final analysis, human experience is the great teacher which yields seeds of wisdom that grow and develop throughout a lifetime.

Jung's theory is similar to Taoism in that the ego, or sense of personal self, emerges from a background of Self or Tao (Rosen 1997: 4). The Self is Jung's concept of the Universal Being that contrasts with the self of

Table 9.1   Erikson's eight stages of human development

Stage	Age	Essential strength	Psychological issue	Basic virtue
1. Infancy	0–2	Drive	Trust vs. mistrust	Hope
2. Early childhood	2–3	Self-control	Autonomy vs. shame and doubt	Will
3. Play age	3–6	Direction	Initiative vs. guilt	Purpose
4. School age	6–13	Method	Industry vs. inferiority	Competence
5. Adolescence	13–19	Devotion	Identity vs. identity diffusion	Fidelity
6. Young adulthood	19–30	Affiliation	Intimacy vs. isolation	Love
7. Adulthood	30–60	Production	Generativity vs. self-absorption and stagnation	Care
8. Old age	60+	Renunciation	Integrity vs. disgust and despair	Wisdom

Source: Adapted from Erikson 1982: 32–3.

personal being. From the beginning a split develops in the human being (outer and inner, conscious and unconscious, false self and true self, persona and shadow) which takes a lifetime to heal or to make whole again. Jung describes a state of wholeness at birth, from which the ego emerges into a 'dualistic phase,' becoming cognizant of the division between itself and the outer world (Jung 1933: 100). In Taoism *t'ai chi* (yin and yang) mirrors Jung's concept of the divided self which yearns to return to *wu chi* or its natural state of wholeness. We shall see that Jung's psychology and Taoism both advocate transcendence of the opposites as a step toward an individual's transformation into an authentic self. Both proceed towards wholeness, which in Jung's psychology is achieved through the process of individuation.

Jung's concept of individuation is virtually the same as Maslow's concept of self-actualization. Likewise in Erikson's developmental psychology, one proceeds towards wholeness or integrity, which he defines as the resolution of eight tasks: a series of eight inner and outer conflicts or crises of each developmental period. He also outlines eight essential strengths that help the individual resolve these conflicts and develop eight virtues (see Table 9.1).

Erikson defines wisdom as the 'informed and detached concern with life itself in the face of death itself' (1982: 61). Ego can be viewed as the self-protectiveness or separateness that creates anxiety and isolation. For Erikson, wisdom is the result of the renunciation of ego that allows spiritual wholeness or integrity to develop. It is also the result of a lifetime of resolutions of antecedent stages that begin with birth. Erikson's stages cannot be viewed as a simple linear progression, however. Instead they are a continual process, in which the individual frequently returns to earlier stages, at later points in life, to rework and refine the resolution of each.

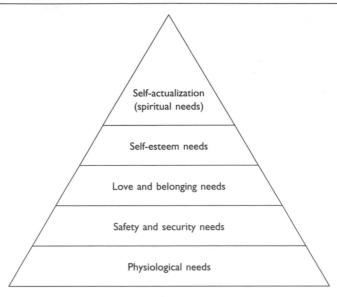

Figure 9.1   Maslow's hierarchy of needs. (Adapted from Maslow 1943.)

Each of Erikson's stages contributes its own unique component to the development of wisdom in old age.

Although Maslow's 'Hierarchy of needs' (1943) does not fall into distinctly defined chronological stages, his theories align well with Jung's and Erikson's. When resources are available to satisfy human needs, the normal progress for most individuals moves from Maslow's lower physiological and security needs toward the higher self and its spiritual needs. Taoism also posits a goal of spiritual wholeness, integrity, or wisdom as the final attainment in a psychologically healthy and satisfying life. In Taoism, one goal in old age is to become like a child who exhibits intuitive wisdom. Jung also underscores the value of the child's world of symbols and creative imagination when he states, 'there is a thinking in primordial images–in symbols. . . . It is only possible to live the fullest life when we are in harmony with these symbols; wisdom is a return to them' (1933: 113). Erikson's renunciation of ego in old age ushers in wisdom and harkens back to the symbolic play stage of childhood, where the divine gifts of creativity and humor originate.

THE SEEDS OF WISDOM

In Erikson's schema, the first conflict facing the infant is *basic trust versus mistrust*, which, when successfully resolved, develops the virtue of *hope* (Erikson 1982: 56). The development of hope and trust in the infant forms an integral step in the birth of wisdom in the adult in that it incorporates the view that the world and its inhabitants are basically good. How can we become wise to the ways of the world unless we have attained a basic level of trust in the consistency and order of the universe? The baby girl who learns that her mother or father will come to her and hold her when she cries, and the baby boy who discovers that when he smiles, his father and mother smile back, have both achieved a bit of understanding about the world. The world makes sense and can be trusted. Similarly, in Maslow's hierarchy, when the *basic physiological needs* of food and shelter are met, the infant learns that there is order in the universe and can begin to focus its energy elsewhere (Maslow 1943: 375). The positive resolution of Erikson's first stage promotes the aspect of wisdom that relies on optimism and hope for the future, trusting and believing there is an underlying order to the universe even when it is not apparent. The seeds of this basic hope and trust encourage the child's sense of the 'numinous' (Erikson 1982: 56).

The second tier of Maslow's hierarchy, *safety and security needs*, is a support for subsequent stages, as it is in Erikson's theory. For Maslow, when a person's safety needs are met, that individual is free to explore relationships with others and the world (Maslow 1943: 378). Jung echoes this sentiment when he describes the *presexual stage* (birth to age six) as one in which the child is dependent, like the caterpillar, which must rely on a safe and nurturing environment for its survival (Jung 1970b: 105–17). Similarly, Erikson posits that an environment that is safe and consistent promotes trust in the world, encouraging the child's ability to test his or her own potentiality. In Erikson's second stage, *autonomy versus shame and doubt*, a central focus for the toddler is the development of the virtue of *will* (Erikson 1982: 56). Children who successfully negotiate this stage discover that individuals can impact and change their environment. When they are allowed to explore the world within the context of a secure and consistent family system, they also learn that there are reliable and logical consequences to their actions. With successful resolution of Erikson's second stage, the toddler can begin to understand the nature of right and wrong.

THE ROOTS OF WISDOM IN CHILDHOOD

The next stage of Erikson's schema relates to the roles of play, humor, and empathy as aspects of wisdom. In the preschool years, or Erikson's *play age*, the central conflict is *initiative versus guilt*, which finds its resolution in the development of a sense of *purpose* (Erikson 1982: 56). Children at this stage, utilizing symbols and images, learn to pretend and to imitate the world around them. The boundless world of fantasy, when contained securely in a loving and reliable adult world, provides fertile ground for the child to test his or her strengths and abilities. Erikson also describes a transcendent function of the third stage: the binding together of the numinous and the judicial into the dramatic (1977: 101). Erikson describes this stage as the basis for children's confidence in their creativity, adding, 'In playfulness is grounded, also, all sense of humor, [including] man's specific gift to laugh at himself' (1982: 77). The child who successfully attains the basic virtue of purpose has the ability to imagine himself or herself in a variety of roles. From this new 'What if?' perspective springs the ability to find surprise and humor in the world. From the preschooler's early fantasy and experimentation with different roles, the wise adult gleans the primitive beginnings of empathy. In the young child's first, crude attempts at humor, wisdom finds the divine roots of its appreciation for laughing with the spectacle and miracle of life.

The central conflict of Erikson's fourth stage, which spans the elementary school years until puberty, is *industry versus inferiority* (Erikson 1982: 57). The virtue that develops with successful resolution of this stage is *competence*. Children at this age are focused on learning and cultivating experiential knowledge of the world around them. The facet of wisdom that takes root at this stage is discernment. Erikson refers to the growing understanding of the 'factuality' of the world as a major focus for the school-aged child (1982: 76). Jung views the *prepubertal* stage as a time of incubation or germination, when the dependent child is slowly developing a sense of independence, like the caterpillar during the pupal or cocoon phase (1970b: 105–17). In the late adult years, wisdom incorporates pragmatism and experiential knowledge, which have their beginnings in this stage, as vital components in its manifold nature.

By comparison, the third level in Maslow's hierarchy, *love and belonging needs*, is centered around finding friendship, love, and a sense of one's place in the world (Maslow 1943: 381). The ability to love and accept the love of others is a necessary component of wisdom. Reviewing the third and fourth stages in Erikson, we see how the needs in Maslow's third level are prominent. The preschooler who is play-acting and the eight-year-old who is negotiating the rules at school are both seeking a place in their worlds where they will be loved and accepted. The same holds true for the adolescent and young adult.

SENDING UP SHOOTS

For Erikson, the central conflict of adolescence is *identity versus identity diffusion* and a positive resolution results in the virtue of *fidelity* (Erikson 1982: 72). Adolescence is a time when an individual's attention shifts from the pragmatic factuality of the previous stage to ideological concerns (Erikson 1982: 32–3). Teenagers frequently try out new positions and belief systems as a means of reviewing their own from a different perspective.

Erikson notes that fidelity 'maintains a strong relationship both to infantile trust and to mature faith' (1982: 73). The secure center of the self that develops with trust and hope in early life is maintained even as the adolescent searches the outside world for new ideas and beliefs. Erikson points out the need for the process of exploration, with the support and acceptance of the family and society, as an integral step in the 'evolving configuration' of the individual in the process towards wholeness (1982: 74). The positive resolution of Erikson's identity conflict promotes a strong internal system of views about oneself and the world to which one remains true, even in the face of adverse or changing circumstances. The development of fidelity is related to one's genuine self and thus forms a crucial aspect of the growth towards wisdom in maturity. Similarly, Jung saw *adolescence* as a metamorphosis, that is, the psychological birth of the true self, separate from one's parents and independent like the butterfly (unique, beautiful, and free) (Jung 1970b: 105–17).

In Maslow's hierarchy, another level comes into play at this stage of development, where *self-esteem needs* form the fourth tier. Adolescence is a time when one is intensely concerned with both *love and belonging* and with the need to be acknowledged as a separate and worthy individual. With the security of loving relationships, the adolescent is freed to explore avenues for achievement (Maslow 1943: 381). Maslow felt that many individuals never progress past the fourth tier of his hierarchy, but that those who venture into the highest level, that of *self-actualization*, have a chance at concluding their lives with a sense of meaning, wisdom, and serenity (1943: 383).

BRANCHING OUT

In Erikson's sixth stage of development, the central conflict centers around *intimacy versus isolation*, with the virtue of *love* emerging from its successful resolution (Erikson 1982: 32–3). The desire for intimacy can be viewed as a need to merge with that which is not one's self. The capacity for love is not present until a strong fidelity to one's own identity has been established. Love is also an aspect of wisdom that Erikson relates to the essential strength of *affiliation*. As a facet of wisdom, affiliation expresses itself in genuine warmth and regard for one's friends, lovers, family, and humanity at large. Affiliation acknowledges the underlying connection between all of life. Jung characterizes this phase as an inner marriage—an internal love of the contrasexual aspect of one's psyche (for a man his *anima*, or feminine side, and for a woman her *animus*, or masculine side), which provides a template and potential for the realization of a successful outer marriage (1970: 189–201). Maslow views this type of non-possessive affiliative love as one manifestation of *self-actualization* (1955: 1–30). Similarly, Jung believed that individuation included selfless altruistic service. *Self-actualization* forms the uppermost tier of Maslow's hierarchy, but it is a level that Maslow felt few people achieved and maintained on a consistent basis. Given the dependence of each stage of both Maslow's and Erikson's models on prior stages, every individual must reassess the needs and rework each of the conflicts to some degree with each new phase of life. The chronic inability to meet basic needs or failure to resolve early conflicts can impair an individual's ability to successfully negotiate future conflicts. Nevertheless, the successful resolution of the psychological issues and development of the virtues of each of the eight stages of Erikson's life cycle can enhance one's opportunities to become a self-actualized, individuated, and wise person.

BLOOMING

Adulthood is characterized by a struggle between *generativity versus self-absorption and stagnation*, which can be positively resolved with the virtue of *care* (Erikson 1982: 67). For Erikson, generativity encompasses *procreativity*, the bearing and nurturing of children, *productivity*, the developing of one's own and others' intellect and abilities, and *creativity*, the exploration of one's intuition and inner resources (1982: 32–3; see Tables 9.1 and 9.2). Erikson describes this stage as the 'store' for future generations, and in this description we see a hint of our traditional concept of the wise old man or woman. As Erikson's description implies, however, this is not the stage of hoarding things or passively doling out knowledge. It is the time at which many people are at the peak of their productivity and creativity. The central conflict of this stage, generativity versus self-absorption and stagnation, is expressed as the difficulty of embracing the sum of one's experiential knowledge and intuitive understanding of the world in benefiting the world, while deepening one's own storehouse of wisdom. Again, the form of active service and care of others is the essence of Jung's concept of successful individuation and Maslow's self-actualization.

FRUITION

It is in Erikson's final phase of the life cycle, *integrity versus disgust and despair*, that one is most likely to become a Taoist-like sage and also realize Jung's objective of individuation and Maslow's goal of self-actualization. The struggle is to let go of one's persona and ego identity, which is made possible on the one hand by shedding one's work and parental roles, and on the other hand through developing a connection with an inner spiritual meaning. In addition, it is the stage for which the positive resolution is the

Table 9.2   Relationships between Maslow's hierarchy, Erikson's stages, and the development of wisdom

Maslow's level in hierarchy	Erikson's psychosocial stage and virtue	Aspect of wisdom developed
Physiological needs	Trust vs. mistrust Hope	Experience of goodness and seeds of faith
Safety and security needs	Autonomy vs. shame and doubt Will	Judiciousness
	Initiative vs. guilt Purpose	Empathy and humor
Love and belonging needs	Industry vs. inferiority Competence	Experiential knowledge (pragmatism), discernment
	Identity vs. identity confusion Fidelity	Commitment to one's own philosophy and true self
Self-esteem needs	Intimacy vs. isolation Love	Understanding the unity of the universe and drive towards wholeness
	Generativity vs. self-absorption and stagnation Care	Intuition, exploration of one's own internal resources
Self-actualization	Integrity vs. disgust and despair Wisdom	Mature faith and experience of spiritual wholeness

attainment of the virtue of *wisdom*, thereby opening the way to integrity (Erikson 1982: 67). Wisdom consists of all of the essential strengths and virtues of the preceding stages combined into one whole (see Tables 9.1 and 9.2). Interestingly, it is also the point at which one integrates the entirety of one's spiritual philosophy into a mature faith in the world and its underlying sense of order, harkening back to the basic sense of trust and the virtue of hope that were developed in the first stage of life. For Jung, wisdom is attained through the renunciation of ego and contact with one's divine center (Jung's concept of the Self, similar to the apex of Maslow's hierarchy). Jung has compared this successful integration to the aesthetic balance achieved in great works of art, noting that 'the art of life is the most distinguished and rarest of all the arts' (1933: 110).

As Jung has underscored, the symbol of the circle is an apt one for the Self and the Tao (Jung 1968: 355–84). It has no beginning or end and its center point is not the ego, but something larger than the self (personal being), which Jung called the Self, the same as Universal Being. In the final stage of development there is both an acceptance of the return to the source (the Self or Tao) and a sense of peace and harmony.

Erikson points out that the antithesis of integrity is disgust and despair over one's life and the mistakes one has made along the way when he states that the concept of despair in Spanish (*desesperanza*) is also the opposite of hope (*esperanza*) (Erikson 1982: 67). When one becomes truly *integrated* one has hope and the circle is completed. Spiritual wholeness or integrity is the embodiment of Tao. It is also realizing one's true self with a connection to the Self, the divine center and totality of all.

CONCLUSION

The Tao has been described as the Way, Supreme Being, Primary Essence, Eternity, Wholeness, Mystery, Meaning, and Ultimate Being and Non-Being (Rosen 1997: 23). The supreme task of Taoism is to realize the Tao through *te* or virtue, which yields integrity. One is born out of the Tao, experiences ego in *t'ai chi* (duality of yin and yang) but proceeds towards wholeness (*wu chi*) to return to a child-like state, rejoining the Tao in death. As Jung maintained, 'Tao is the right way. . . . The middle road between opposites, freed from them and yet uniting them in itself' (1971: 120).

Jung's psychological perspective is very similar to that of Taoism (Rosen 1997: 4). One emerges out of the Self or Tao to develop persona and ego and a divided self (true self/false self). The process of individuation is to let go of the false self, transcend the opposites, undergo a transformation, and realize one's true self, secondary to a force beyond the personal being (self), that is, the Self or Tao. The process of transcendence includes the recognition by the individual not only of one's higher abilities but also of one's less noble impulses and desires, and the ability to embrace and incorporate one's weaknesses and frailties into the whole of the psyche. This process leads to the embodiment of one's genuine self, generativity, creativity, and service, which is related to finding meaning and peace. The end result (as in a successful realization of Erikson's and Maslow's psychologies) is an integrity-full person who has wisdom.

REFERENCES

Erikson, E. (1977) *Toys and Reasons: Stages in the Ritualization of Experience*, New York: Norton.
Erikson, E. (1982) *The Life Cycle Completed: A Review*, New York: Norton.

Jung, C. G. (1933) *Modern Man in Search of a Soul*, New York: Harcourt Brace & Company.

Jung, C. G. (1968) 'Concerning mandala symbolism,' in H. Read, M. Fordham, G. Adler, and W. McGuire (eds), *The Archetypes and the Collective Unconscious* (*Collected Works*, vol. 9, pt. 1), Princeton, NJ: Princeton University Press.

Jung, C. G. (1970a) 'Marriage as a psychological relationship', in H. Read, M. Fordham, G. Adler, and W. McGuire (eds), *The Development of Personality* (*Collected Works*, vol. 17), Princeton, NJ: Princeton University Press.

Jung, C. G. (1970b) 'The theory of psychoanalysis,' in H. Read, M. Fordham, G. Adler, and W. McGuire (eds), *Freud and Psychoanalysis* (*Collected Works*, vol. 4), Princeton, NJ: Princeton University Press.

Jung, C. G. (1971) 'Schiller's ideas on the type problem,' in H. Read, M. Fordham, G. Adler, and W. McGuire (eds), *Psychological Types* (*Collected Works*, vol. 6), Princeton, NJ: Princeton University Press.

Maslow, A. H. (1943) 'A theory of human motivation,' *Psychological Review*, 50: 370–96.

Maslow, A. H. (1955) 'Deficiency motivation and growth motivation,' in M.R. Jones (ed.), *Nebraska Symposium on Motivation*, Lincoln, NB: University of Nebraska Press

Rosen, D. H. (1997) *The Tao of Jung: The Way of Integrity*, New York: Penguin.

PART III

Transcendence

Chapter 10

Psychotherapy as ordinary transcendence

The unspeakable and the unspoken

Polly Young-Eisendrath

If pushed, I might say that psychotherapy is a great spiritual practice that awakens us to how and why we create suffering and shows us a path toward compassion and interdependence. But I would rather not. I would rather talk about psychotherapy as its own practice: a practice of ordinary transcendence. This kind of transcendence provides evidence and insight that being human means being dependent, and that the life space we inhabit is one of interdependence, not independence. It also shows us that self-protectiveness, isolation, and the ubiquitous human desire for omnipotence produce great suffering. This type of transcendence carries no special labels such as 'mystical' or 'spiritual.' It frequently goes unnoticed outside of psychotherapy or other practices designed to reveal it, because it goes against the grain of our culture of individualism.

In effective psychotherapy, ordinary transcendence becomes focal and conscious through a process in which the participants sustain their respect and regard for each other in the midst of dangerous affective dynamics that are expressed and understood as part of a search for new insight and meaning. Specific individual knowledge about the patient increases while both parties learn a lot about what it means to be human. They repeatedly encounter limitations of their own power and knowledge while they discover their interdependence and mutual playfulness in expanding a shared purpose.

ORDINARY TRANSCENDENCE IN CONTEXT

In my clinical practice of psychotherapy, I see individuals in psychoanalytic psychotherapy in face to face encounters at the frequency of one or two (fifty-minute) sessions per week. I also work with individuals in more intensive psychoanalysis, sometimes using the analytic couch at the frequency of three or four sessions per week. Additionally, my husband Ed Epstein and I work together as a team seeing couples in a form of psychotherapy that we originated, called Dialogue Therapy, which uses psychodynamic principles and psychodramatic methods to help couples improve their abilities for intimate communication and partnership. And finally, I supervise psychologists, social workers, and psychiatric residents in the practice of psychodynamic psychotherapy.

In all of these settings, I witness the process of transcendence that I describe in this chapter. My professional preparation includes a background in developmental psychology which I taught at the graduate level for a long time, and a wide variety of different trainings in psychoanalytic approaches (such as object relations and self psychology). Additionally, I have for many years been a practitioner of Zen Buddhism, Jung's analytical psychology, and feminism.

As a Jungian analyst, I find myself uncomfortable with the habit among many Jungians of labeling certain experiences as 'numinous' or 'soulful' because of the dichotomy between spiritual and secular that is implied. Thinking and theorizing along the lines of a secular–spiritual dichotomy can, in my view, lead to overlooking spiritual yearnings that naturally arise through exploring ordinary problems. Urgent longings to understand why we are here and why we die may be revealed, for example, in discovering the meaning of being 'workaholic' or seeing what is being communicated through the habit of being late for appointments. Without elevating or redeeming these troubles, they can unveil a profound search for life's meaning. So, I want to stand clear of calling certain states of mind or ways of seeing more extraordinary than others; I prefer not to predict what is, or where I or anyone might find, a moment of transcendence.

Can we speak of the spiritual value of our psychotherapeutic work and hold it lightly, without sounding like it is akin to meditation or religion? On one hand, we have the problem of not speaking too much about something that takes form and shape according to the needs and being of each individual. Although there are conditions within the therapeutic set-up that increase the possibilities for what I am calling ordinary transcendence, there are no guarantees that any particular therapist–patient dyad will reach this goal. The elusive spiritual quality of psychotherapy is—I believe—fundamentally 'unspeakable' because it is hurt or even spoiled by too much theorizing or commercializing. Later I will say more about this unspeakable quality in terms of its unknowable character.

On the other hand, psychotherapy has certain transformative aspects that derive their strength precisely from putting into words that which has been 'unspoken.' These include not only the interpretation of transference and dreams, but especially the interpretation of *projective identification*. This latter experience is an unconscious communication of affective meaning for which language may never have been available. As an unintentional attempt to communicate unconscious emotional memories through perceiving their frightening or stimulating implications in another's being, words or actions, this kind of projection tends to evoke an enactment of what is projected. The other person feels emotionally kidnapped by, and appears to identify with, the projection that the sender is unconsciously making. There are both 'subject' and 'object' poles in such a communication, and the person who receives and plays out the projected dynamic will be an actor in the other's inner theatre.

When the unspoken aspects of our hidden emotional intentions are revealed to us, they show us how we create a world through our projected meanings and fantasies. Witnessing this with a trusted therapist, in the moment it is happening, reveals the roots of our suffering. Perhaps the most widely read Buddhist text, *The Dhammapada*, begins with these lines: 'We are what we think. All that we are arises with our thought. With our thoughts we make the world' (Byrom 1993: 1). Effective psychotherapy shows us exactly this.

When I began my training to be a Jungian psychoanalyst in 1978, I was already a formal student of Zen Buddhism. Therefore, I have always practiced and understood depth psychology from a Buddhist perspective. Buddhism has assisted me in interpreting, revising, and practicing analysis and psychotherapy from a 'non-essentialist' perspective that typifies all Buddhist practices. Essentialism—like substantialism (see Guignon's chapter, this volume)   is a philosophical position that presumes that certain permanent, unchanging essences underlie human experience and perception. These essences are believed to determine aspects of our world that fall completely outside our subjectivity—are not matters of our own interpretation or perception. For example, a current popular form of essentialism is a belief that our moods, actions, and other characteristics come from permanent or given physical or biological traits—genes or brain chemistry. In earlier periods of time, essentialist beliefs were cast as ideal forms (Plato) or mental categories (Kant) that determined human agency and experience. Non-essentialism rejects the notion of an unchanging essence or substance at the foundation of our experiences. Instead it assumes that nothing is permanent and unchanging. Even the very world that we perceive as solid and stable is constructed or created from our own perceptions and interpretations.

In Jung's later years, after 1944 (he died in 1961), he moved away from essentialist reasoning about archetype and complex, and the collective and personal unconscious. He unsystematically revised many of the principles of his theory to fit the prevailing new ideas about innate releasing mechanisms, predispositions to certain emotional enactments, and the role of interpersonal situations in emotional adaptation. Many later psychoanalysts (including most Jungians themselves) have overlooked this major change in his thinking. It is this *ethological* process-oriented approach that I have embraced in Jung, have further developed in my own writings and practice, and find consonant with Buddhism, and with contemporary constructivism. Psychological and biological constructivism—distinct from social constructivism—is a branch of postmodern theorizing that claims that our phenomenal world (the physical, emotional, and psychological) arises from the constraints of our embodied consciousness imposed on an environment in flux that we can never know directly. What I write here exemplifies a dialogue between Buddhism and analytical psychology, but also sketches out a constructivist psychology for understanding transcendence through effective psychoanalytic psychotherapy.

TRANSCENDENCE THROUGH MULTIPLE REALITIES

I often think of the famous anecdote about the Zen patriarch Bodhidharma, who is said to have brought Buddhism to China. The eminent Chinese emperor Wu asked the great master Bodhidharma, 'What is the highest meaning of the holy truths?' Bodhidharma said, 'Empty, without holiness.' The emperor said, 'Who is facing me?' and Bodhidharma replied 'I don't know.' Here 'empty' means without an essential nature. The answer cautions us not to elevate and separate out certain things as holy while assuming that other elements of our experience are inferior. The reply to the question of identity (Who is facing me?) is yet another reminder not to foreclose on meaning, and name just one identity when our identities are fluid and always changing.

Psychotherapy is a relationship founded on human suffering, attempting to alleviate it through an awakening—awakening to how we create worlds through our thoughts and intentions. When this drama is fully engaged, it always leads to the great spiritual questions—Why are we here? Who are we, as humans? Why do we die?—but it cannot provide answers to these questions because it is not designed to function at such a universal level. When spiritual questions arise in a therapy session—not defensively but earnestly—I respond with interest. I show by my manner that the questions merit further inquiry. If an individual has an established spiritual context, a religion or practice, I direct the questions into that context. If the patient is confused and uninformed, I may suggest some extra-therapeutic reading or going to a center to pursue spiritual inquiry, but I clarify that I am a not a spiritual expert or teacher. Answering the great spiritual questions requires, in my view, a religious or spiritual practice or method that has been developed specifically to answer spiritual questions.

Psychotherapy was not designed to answer the great spiritual questions, but rather to deal with necessity, often in the face of pain and suffering. The ordinary transcendence that can emerge in psychotherapy arises from the *necessity* of dealing with overwhelming affective states—erotic, fearful, hateful, idealizing—in the context of respect and a search for personal understanding. Like taking out the garbage, mopping the floor, or feeding the dog, making use of overwhelming affective states is something we 'have to do' in effective psychotherapy. Making use of these states takes us by surprise. Most people seek therapy not because they want to, but because they have to. Psychotherapy is only moderately desired at best by the people who have to pay for it. The negative affective states of patients are only ambivalently desired, at best, by the therapists who are responsible for containing and transforming them. Consequently, people are really surprised when they suddenly feel deeply appreciative of their dependence on each other and the compassion that arises from it.

Effective therapy is transformative on a level beyond talk or interpretation. I have come to see its core process of transformation as an interaction between the patient's (and sometimes the therapist's) projections and the *transcendent function*—Jung's term for our ability to hold onto psychological and emotional openness in the face of pressure and impulses. The transcendent function, as a back-and-forth dialectic between different sides or images of a demanding conflict, permits the discovery of something new and unexpected, a creative solution that transcends the original conflict.

The transformation of troubling emotional patterns, through the transcendent function of psychotherapy, depends on the paradoxical and unknown, although it is guided by theory, knowledge, and expertise. The therapeutic set-up is paradoxical itself. By the set-up, I mean the frame around psychotherapy that defines and protects it as confidential, (relatively) anonymous on the therapist's part, business-like, ethical, non-retaliatory, and exclusive of other relationships (such as sex, friendship, supervision, mentoring and the like) with the patient. The therapeutic set-up renders the therapeutic relationship to be impersonally personal, empathically non-gratifying, erotically non-sexual, provocatively non-aggressive, and welcoming of spontaneous communications within a strongly bound time–fee–space limit.

A person coming for help, already in distress, is likely to want to create an order—an old emotional order—in such a paradoxical environment. The analyst or therapist, in response to what the patient imposes on the therapeutic relationship, is also likely to impose an old order in terms of theory, authority, and/or her or his own unconscious emotional habits. But, the *effective* therapeutic process is like a Zen koan for both participants: it invites and defies old orders and known interpretations.

What permits psychotherapy to be transformative is the gradual ability on the part of the participants to penetrate the multiple layers of the therapeutic relationship and process. These multiple layers are explained by Modell (1991), who describes three 'realities' in which patient and therapist are engaged.

We can envision Modell's three realities as concentric or nested frames that characterize different worlds existing simultaneously. Each new frame encompasses and reorganizes those within so that the same experience can be felt to mean something different at each level. At the center is the *projective transference*. This is the transference of unconscious emotional memories in the form of psychological complexes. These complexes—from a Jungian perspective—are the tendencies to repeat unknown or partly known emotional memories through enacting them with others as though those others were predominantly the same as the significant others of childhood. At the core of each complex is a predisposition to experience a particular affectively charged image—for example, of a weak and ineffectual mother—as though it were a present reality when it was actually a reality of one's early powerless existence as an infant and young child. The image is an amalgam of sight, sound, smell, kinesthetic, and other cues that are triggered in such a way that one believes that danger, threat, or stimulation is present *again* as it was before. Within the dynamics of the projective transference, the therapist may identify with some aspect that is projected by the patient. In a projective identification, the therapist inescapably and unconsciously plays out the patient's projections through an enactment that keeps the projections going, giving the patient 'evidence' of being once again treated as badly as she or he had been as a powerless child. Projective identifications of this kind will have already troubled the patient in many other relationships, although the patient may be unaware of it. Within the projective transference, the patient and therapist experience highly charged emotional moments in which it seems to both parties that the underlying meanings and images are dangerous and overwhelming. This is the realm of sexual and aggressive longings, of demonic and intrusive fantasies, and of supernatural and idealistic images of all kinds.

Surrounding this projective swamp, within the layered model that I'm using here, is the *ordinary human connection* of two people who are limited by their knowledge and embodiment, attempting to accomplish a task together: helping the patient ameliorate suffering through seeing how he or she creates it, and becoming free enough to stop. This is sometimes called the 'real relationship,' but in fact all the realities of psychotherapy are 'real' and this one is no more so than the others. Jung called it 'kinship libido,' by which he meant that the two people are united in the sense of being human and fallible, both of them having to cope with the pain and miseries of human life. An important fact to note in this ordinary connection between therapist and patient is that the patient has hired the therapist and acts as an employer, free to fire her or him.

The power of the patient to fire the therapist counterbalances the projective transference. But the third therapeutic reality, the outer frame of the nested model, creates an effect that can hold sway over the other two layers. Through the influence of Kohut's self psychology, I call it the unobjectionable *idealizing transference*; Modell (1991) dubbed it the 'dependent-containing transference.' This frame around the other realities of psychotherapy sets therapy apart from life by insuring that it is an interpersonal space in which the patient is safe to experience all affective dynamics without risk to life outside of therapy. This frame absolutely depends on the therapist's ethical conduct, emotional stability, professional training, and personal self-knowledge. For in order for the therapist to contain the multiple meanings of the paradoxical set-up I have been describing, she or he must be capable of tolerating and working with the full range of her or his own subjective experiences, as well as the patient's, without putting the patient at any risk of retaliation. Within the unobjectionable idealizing transference, the patient experiences the therapist as a very potent figure. The therapist must be trusted to defeat the patient's symptoms and to understand the patient's suffering, as well as knowing how to ameliorate it. If this trust is betrayed, the patient may fall into a serious psychological illness, come to hate the therapist, or even commit suicide.

UNSPEAKABLE TRANSCENDENCE

In my view, the idealizing transference provides the foundation for effective psychotherapy. In its absence, there is *no* psychotherapy. The other two realities present in therapy—projective transference and ordinary human connection—are the stuff of life outside of therapy. The idealizing transference provides a unique environment in which two people can discover the particular meanings of a subjective life. The power of this transference, monitored by a genuinely ethical and interested therapist, allows psychological changes to occur because it is completely safe to express and examine what would otherwise endanger one emotionally or physically in the presence of others or in the isolation of oneself alone.

Moreover, the experience of the idealizing transference is an awakening of inchoate spiritual yearnings in the patient—yearnings for compassion and wisdom. Those yearnings are known to the patient at first through the hope and belief that this psychotherapist can be (could be) helpful with things that no one else has ever seemed to help with. This hopeful belief is a direct by-product of a well-maintained therapeutic set-up, a good-enough therapist *and* the patient's (sometimes unconscious) feeling of coherence or unity of self and world. It is a conviction that suffering will someday make sense and that life has a purpose that goes beyond one's own identity.

Jung describes this transference as a yearning for the *transcendent function*: the capacity to hold the tensions of conflict and struggle without collapsing prematurely into a judgment that 'this is bad' or 'this is good.' In 1916, Jung (1916/1969) wrote of this kind of transference,

> The patient clings by means of the transference to the person who seems to promise him a renewal of attitude; through it he seeks this change, which is vital to him, even though he may not be conscious of

doing so. For the patient, therefore, the analyst has the character of an indispensable figure absolutely necessary for life. However infantile this dependence may appear to be, it expresses an extremely important demand which, if disappointed, often turns to bitter hatred of the analyst.

(p. 74)

Jung recognized that the idealizing transference has a purpose that cannot be reduced to childish longings or primitive impulses. It expresses the unconscious striving for spiritual development in the patient. Sometimes, maybe often, it is the patient's first authentic and sustained experience of the 'unspeakable' unity of existence—the unnameable that is called God, the Tao, Buddha Nature, True Nature, and the like.

The effective treatment relationship is one in which the patient feels safely held and securely known so that she or he can encounter dangerous and troubling feelings in a safe environment in which both interdependence and compassion are discovered. Effectiveness can be disrupted and even permanently betrayed through a break in the idealizing transference. Of course, this can happen through an ethical violation by the therapist or through a gross mismanagement (for example, the therapist missing appointments or showing up late) of the therapy. On a more subtle and more common level, effectiveness can be breached through the collapse of the idealizing transference into a chronic projective identification in which the therapist is experienced as yet another inadequate, uninformed, or unempathic caregiver. Under these conditions, the therapist will seem to the patient to be still another caregiver who is not capable of helping, who has failed to treat the patient fairly and/or see the patient clearly. In my view, this kind of failure can also block the natural spiritual yearnings of the patient through a kind of hopelessness about ever being known or helped by an ideal figure.

Effectiveness can also be diminished through the therapist's (conscious or unconscious) unwillingness to admit to mistakes and/or to see his or her own failings. If a therapist cannot tolerate being seen in a negative light, she or he will avoid the patient's most dangerous affective dynamics in order not to make a mistake. Sometimes the patient actually improves, all the same, and feels entirely accepted and understood without encountering the frightening aspects of his or her emotional life, but the transcendent function will not be engaged because the conflict of opposites is not encountered. Under these circumstances, the patient will also feel a keen need to protect the therapist from dangerous affects. This too will be a repeat of childhood tendencies to protect one's parents, but will not be made known within the therapy.

More harmful than avoiding negative feelings is a therapist's longing for idealizing projections. If a therapist cannot tolerate being seen in a critical or negative light, she or he will have problems maintaining the constraints of the therapeutic set-up and will engage in excessive lowering of fees and granting special favors to the patient, and/or will give premature reassurances and support. Avoidance of negative emotions and images will rob psychotherapy of its heart through eliminating the possibility of transcending the patient's most troubling complexes.

While the projective transference is diminished or dissolved through mutative interpretation, the idealizing transference is enhanced and strengthened. The more the patient experiences the transformation of suffering, the more the patient will respect and even revere the analyst/therapist who seems to embody this means of understanding and developing. After an effective psychotherapy has come to an end, the idealizing transference continues to develop. News about one's therapist, years after therapy (especially shocking news like an ethical violation), can change the effects of the therapy. Protecting this frame around the realities of psychotherapy is a lifelong ethical and compassionate task of any psychotherapist.

On the other hand, the power of the idealizing transference is not a *personal* matter, except as the therapist would protect the therapeutic set-up and be effective on all levels. The therapeutic set-up itself—with the ritual of time–fee–space regularity, and the anonymity of the therapist—opens the door to the patient's beliefs that the effective therapist somehow magically transcends ordinary life circumstances. Psychotherapists who become well-known for their abilities are especially at risk for identifying with projections of power in the idealizing transference. Some charismatic and flawed leaders of psychotherapy movements—from Freud and Jung on down to Fritz Perls and R. D. Laing—have mistakenly identified themselves or their methods with special powers. Then they may demand adherence to their particular ideas and/or become capricious in their influence because they believe that they *personally* have discovered something unique, rather than crediting the ritual and the human universal longing for a 'renewal of attitude' (as Jung says above). The charismatic leader may also ignore certain ethical or social codes of decency in believing that he or she is beyond criticism. In the end, identification with the unspeakable transcendence of psychotherapy brings about some kind of collapse or failure because people can never identify with this power without harmful effects of grandiosity.

When a patient momentarily experiences me as embodying this idealized state, I breathe deeply and thank her or him (bowing inside to the transcendent nature in each of us)—knowing that I am grateful that the process of psychotherapy or analysis is working. In a brief psychotherapy, the idealizing transference may never be spoken; it may only be felt as something very potent, very helpful. Near the conclusion of a more extended treatment, when the patient speaks of me in reverent tones, I name the agent as psychotherapy itself, reminding us how it allows us to witness our capacity to transform suffering and develop compassion. I express gratitude for having experienced psychotherapy with this particular patient, and point out that it was not me personally who brought about the transformation.

SPEAKING THE UNSPOKEN

What I regard as the goal of an effective psychotherapy or psychoanalysis is to have fairly reliable access to the transcendent function, especially in the midst of psychological complexes being triggered. This means an openness in one's attitude towards oneself and an interest in genuine dialogue between oneself and others. Experientially this is a willingness to be accountable for both conscious and unconscious intentions, moods, and impulses—as they become known to oneself—and to recognize how one creates suffering through imposing old emotional habits, and wanting or wishing the world and others to conform to one's desires and ideals.

In my view, patient and therapist move unevenly toward this goal through repeated encounters with the patient's psychological complexes, presented in dreams and the projective transference, and understood and transformed through effective interpretations. As I said earlier, such interpretations are transformative beyond words: they allow both patient and therapist to witness our interdependence in the discovery of emotional meaning and confront us with the multiple levels of reality in our affective lives. Effective interpretations emerge from the therapist's openness to uncertainty and new discoveries. In the midst of a patient's negative complex, this is a challenging task. A brief example follows, from my own clinical work.

An attractive middle-aged woman, divorced and living alone, sought therapy with me because she wanted a 'more exciting life.' At the start of therapy, she made a point of saying how she hoped that I would challenge her to grow and not just be supportive. About four months into her once-per-week sessions, she accused me of repeatedly 'wanting too much' from her. My encouragements of her making casual conversations with acquaintances or meeting new people and going out socially were received and heard as pressures and demands. She vehemently stated that I misunderstood her and that I did not fully appreciate the wisdom of her introversion, the value of the few friends she had, and the necessity of the lifestyle she had developed—working late evenings at her demanding job and staying at home on weekends with her dog and bird.

The patient's mother had had very low self-esteem regarding her own physical attractiveness, and had attributed a 'fat and ugly' body image to the patient in childhood and adolescence (an image that seemed to me to be grossly unfounded from seeing photos). Confusingly, the mother had also expected her daughter to have a full social life—even after the emotional disruption of the patient's father's suicide that was violent and public, occurring at the middle of her adolescence.

In insisting that I wanted too much from her, the patient was inviting me into a projective identification. I could readily feel that I was like the unempathic mother who violated her daughter's identity by ignoring her pain and demanding social performance. When I initially responded with an interpretation that sketched out this dynamic, the patient rejected it, saying this was about *me*, not about *her*.

I could feel that the patient's pain and suffering around these issues were communicated mainly through her projection of me as the insensitive mother, but in some ways I did fear that I had missed or left out aspects of the patient's vulnerabilities because she was attractive and intelligent. Instead of being pulled into a power struggle about whether or not I wanted too much, I backed up and looked at the multiple realities that had formed between us. As one middle-aged woman to another, the patient wanted me to acknowledge how difficult it is to meet a friend—whether male or female—outside one's normal social group. She was saying 'Hey, this is difficult and don't act like it's not.' On still another level, she was implying and sometimes saying that she did not believe that I had a clear picture of her—especially her personal style; she feared that I didn't appreciate her introversion and wondered if I was really the therapist for her. When I stepped back from my own feelings, I could notice these multiple realities and not simply push an interpretation of the projective transference.

When a therapist is seen by the patient as unhelpful, inferior, inadequate, or uninformed and she or he protects professional authority too quickly with an implied 'god's eye view' of the mess, then it's very likely that the therapist will get caught in her or his own ego complex—feeling shame, pride, self-doubt, or self-pity. And even more fundamental, a good therapist intuitively fears the destruction of the idealizing transference because then therapy suddenly becomes life. And then the patient and therapist are simply two people victimized by projective identification—both hurt and in a power struggle over what is going on. I have found it helpful to speak for the 'big picture' of what's going on. In this case, I said 'As your therapist I'm looking at what you've said with interest, and concern, and I'd like to look with you at a number of ways that we could understand it.' Together, she and I talked about all three realities—projection of mother, being a woman of about my age without a partner, feeling unhopeful about me as her therapist—examining how each had meaning for the patient. Eventually the patient and I discovered how she had repeatedly wanted me to advise her—and to tell her what I did in my life—even though she also wanted me to respect her own decision-making and style. When I did not tell her about my life, she was dissatisfied, feeling that I did not care enough. When I did give my point of view, she felt intruded upon. And besides, she believed that we were about the same age (we were) and she knew that I was married—happily she thought—and so she wondered if I could really empathize with her. We talked about all of this and other things without reducing anything to a 'just so' story. This was a turning point in her treatment; after it, the idealizing transference was restored and her therapy proceeded successfully.

When patients believe that their views of me are *factually* based, not impressions based on any subjective factors, I must become alert not simply to defend myself through stock interpretations or my own counter-transference—for example, the demand on myself that I should *always* be helpful. Keeping a modest tone of 'this is how I'm seeing it,' rather than 'this is how it is,' acknowledges the complexity of competing realities and the possibility of discovering something that I have not thought of.

CONCLUDING REMARKS

Through the messy work of entering into and understanding projective transference, projective identification, and the multiple realities of psycho-therapy, patient and therapist learn to experience the freedom to choose among different meanings and discover that we are not condemned to repeat the emotional conditions into which we were born. We also learn that everything—from pain to excrement, from delusion to grandiosity, from pride to material wealth—can teach us spiritually because everything emanates compassion when it is perceived in the light of our inter-dependence, a light that shines through the idealizing transference and the transcendent function of effective psychotherapy.

REFERENCES

Byrom, T. (trans.) (1993) *Dhammapada: The Sayings of the Buddha*, Boston, MA: Shambala.

Horne, M. (1998) 'How does the transcendent function?' *The San Francisco Jung Institute Library Journal*, 17/2: 21–41.

Jung, C. G. (1916/1969) 'The transcendent function,' in *The Collected Works of C. G. Jung*, vol. 8, trans. R. F. C. Hull, Princeton, NJ: Princeton University Press.

Modell, A. (1991) *Other Times, Other Realities*, Cambridge, MA: Harvard University Press.

Young-Eisendrath, P. (1997a) 'The self in analysis,' *Journal of Analytical Psychology*, 42: 157–66.

Young-Eisendrath, P. (1997b) 'Jungian constructivism and the value of uncertainty,' *Journal of Analytical Psychology*, 42: 637–52.

Chapter 11

Emissaries from the underworld

Psychotherapy's challenge to Christian fundamentalism

Roger Brooke

It is customary for psychologists not to interfere with a person's religious beliefs (or lack of them); it generally feels unethical to do otherwise. But this 'hands off' approach has meant that psychotherapists are often loath to cross these boundaries and comment at all on religious and spiritual issues. There is also some truth to the popular conception of psychologists and psychotherapists as anti-religious. Freud himself was an atheist, whose essay on religion was iconoclastic (Freud 1928). As Jones says,

> [P]sycho-analytic investigation of the unconscious mental life reveals that [Christian beliefs] correspond closely with the phantasies of infantile life, mainly unconscious ones, concerning the sexual life of one's parents and the conflicts this gives rise to. The Christian story, an elaborate attempt to deal on a cosmic plane with these universal conflicts, can be fully accounted for on human grounds alone.
>
> (Jones 1930/51: 211)

Bronheim reports that 96 per cent of the American population has a theistic orientation but only about 40 per cent of psychiatrists do. The atheists are found most frequently among therapists who have had a psychoanalytic training (Bronheim 1998: 20). The behaviorist images of being human are not very different. Behaviorism originated by jettisoning any conceptual differentiation between person and animal, and it thus regards the spiritual life as merely a certain set of behaviors conditioned by the system of 'reinforcements' operative upon them. Even humanistic psychology, which is more tolerant of religious experience, is limited in this regard. It is rooted in the soil of the French Enlightenment, and it places the ultimate authority for one's life in the self (ego) and the capacity for reason. In its existential versions, a sense of indebtedness to a sacred authority might be regarded as a form of 'bad faith,' an attempt to duck full responsibility for one's life. In the context of such 'psychologism,' Jung's analytical psychology and Boss's Daseinsanalysis (a phenomenological analysis of the world of human existence on its own terms) are perhaps the only two approaches to religious experience that grant it its own authenticity.

However, I and many of the therapists I know have a very real sense of the sacred foundations of our work. This sensibility is a capacity to transcend the boundaries of our own egos, and our impulses to intervene reactively, a capacity that helps us endure with our patients[1] in times of appalling suffering without undue alarm or depression ourselves. Actually, I think that countertransference anxiety and reactivity in the face of psychological distress are often at base a kind of spiritual failure, one that actually prevents our patients from being truly healed. While many of us do have spiritual beliefs, some that are relevant to psychotherapy, we do not talk much about them. For my part, years of listening to people talk blithely about experiences of transcendence while their visible and invisible lives are a mess has also left me with what Paul Ricoeur called the 'hermeneutics of suspicion' towards such things.

On the other hand, silence in this regard means that an essential dimension of psychotherapeutic process remains unarticulated, subliminal, or even frankly unconscious. Further, refusal to comment on spirituality and, more specifically, religious beliefs, leaves us without the means to confront the violence perpetuated by some branches of fundamentalist Christianity on those who are struggling psychologically to make sense of their lives. Psychologists need to rethink the ethics of 'neutrality' with regard to religious beliefs that are psychologically violent; certain Christians might perhaps rethink the meaning of psychotherapy, allowing themselves to face their own defensiveness, where it exists, and perhaps even come to appreciate the way in which psychotherapy participates in, and is made possible by, that sacred moment Christians have called 'grace.'

FUNDAMENTALISM

I shall be addressing only a certain aspect of evangelical Christianity. Although fundamentalism is a style of thinking that is evident in all religions—and even in secular contexts (e.g. theoretical dogmatism)—my concern here is primarily with fundamentalism as a Protestant theology and movement. It is a dominant Christian movement in America, and it defines a part of our cultural and political life. The movement has historical antecedents, especially in American Puritanism, but the term 'fundamentalism' was coined by the Baptist editor of a religious journal in the 1920s. In the 1950s the term evangelism tended to replace it because the earlier term had come to have negative connotations.

Fundamentalism was founded as a conservative moral stance against so-called 'modernism.' Modernist Christianity had accepted that biblical stories were open to various interpretations. It therefore encouraged hermeneutic biblical exegesis and the admission of a certain degree of unknowing and contextual relativity that this implies (see Eliade 1987: 190;

Meagher et al. 1979: 1429). Fundamentalism opposes modernism (and certainly postmodernism!) with the following explicit assertions: (1) the authority of the Scriptures is absolute, and its words are to be understood as literally, empirically true; (2) the human being is born in a state of sin; and (3) there is no salvation without a personal acceptance of Jesus Christ as one's Savior. Thus fundamentalism offers a vision of divine judgment rather than love. It is a conservative moral stance that tends to hypostatize ethical sensibility into moral law, and radically to split the world in two: Christian and non-Christian, God and devil, and so on. To emphasize that I am trying not to perpetuate that dualism here, it deserves repeating that fundamentalism (in general) is a state of mind that touches all of us, no matter our beliefs, when we fear difference and become dogmatic. Thus, while this paper is written with some anger towards fundamentalist Christianity, its deeper purpose is more self-reflective: a meditation on some of those anxieties and defenses that form and deform human spirituality more generally.

ANXIETY

As an analytically oriented psychotherapist, my central concern in a session is usually to try to attend to the patient's anxiety. This is always in some sense threatening work, because it seeks to identify the anxiety-laden fantasies within the patient's defenses (which is why issues such as the therapeutic alliance and timing are crucial). Tracking anxiety is a strange adventure. Grotstein recalls Bion saying, 'We can work forever, for years, to trace the origin of your anxiety, we'll never find it, but we must never stop tracing it. . . . [w]e'll never find out what it is, because it is not to be found' (Culbert-Koehn 1997: 26). The focus on anxiety carries within it the therapist's capacity to remain aware of a sacred movement, or *telos*, on the other side of the anxiety. This awareness is usually unavailable to the patient in the midst of his or her suffering.

Such transcendence on the part of the therapist is not a New Age version of Candide's assumption that we live in the best of all possible worlds (Voltaire 1758/1947): a spiritual indifference borne on the wings of bland equanimity. If the therapist is to maintain a rapport deep enough to meet and contain the patient's suffering, then transcendence is also inaccessible to the therapist insofar as he or she is empathically bound with the patient. In other words, for the therapist, transcendence is not a refuge against the patient's suffering, but a capacity to submit to that suffering in a common humanity.

For the fundamentalist Christian, transcendence has a very different meaning. In this case, transcendence is not a capacity to pass *through* anxiety but, rather, an other-worldly refuge from it. It is a belief in one's personal salvation through Jesus and a belief that one has a privileged access to truth as revealed in prayer and in the Bible. In this form, transcendence is a spiritual clarity which divides the human world into those who are saved and those who remain in darkness, those whose ethical compass is set by biblical law and personal communication with Jesus, and those who are seen to drift in moral relativism, unwittingly subject to Satan's influences. Fundamentalist Christianity involves an identification with the transcendent order and a continual effort to overcome the downward pull of the body's sexuality, aggression, sickness, and death. Such an identification, however, forecloses our capacity for intimate empathy, as well as the aesthetic and embodied foundations of a compassionate ethics (Levin 1985). Further still, as Jung and Hillman argue, it also serves as a defense against the fecund play of the human imagination (Hillman 1979a and b).

My remarks hopefully will become clearer after a few stories.

Rebecca and Karen

'Rebecca,' a young Jewish college student, was depressed, anxious, and rather confused. Her family background was troubled, and her mother had died a few years earlier. The only really good relationship she had had in her life was with her grandfather, who was a supportive old rabbi, but he too had recently died.

Some of Rebecca's friends were members of the Student Christian Association, and they gave her the sort of support they thought she needed. They tried to persuade her that her distress would disappear if she gave herself to Christ, arguing that if she had done so in her early teens her mother would not have died. They said that her grandfather, like her mother, had gone to hell. Rebecca considered consulting a psychologist but was dissuaded from doing so because a psychotherapist would lead her away from the truth and would 'fill [her] head with ideas.' One of Rebecca's friends was 'Karen,' an undergraduate student of mine and a 'spiritual counselor.' She asked my advice. Karen admitted that she 'felt bad about saying these things,' but felt she had to because they might be true. She also admitted that she had some doubt about what she and her Christian friends were doing to Rebecca, but believed that her doubt was literally devil-inspired and had to be suppressed. Karen felt caught between a genuine care and liking for Rebecca and a belief that she was doomed to eternal damnation along with her Jewish family. Karen was torn by a guilt that pulled in both directions: she had enough insight and empathy to feel dreadful about the effect this 'counseling' was having on Rebecca, but she felt equally guilty that she might be betraying God and losing Rebecca's soul, and her own, if she did not manage to save Rebecca from Judaism.

Tom

'Tom' was a seventeen-year-old boy referred to me by his boarding school for hoarding things he bought and never opened, and for being 'unusually tidy.' His school was concerned about him and thought he might benefit from psychotherapy. My assessment, which included the use of projective tests, revealed a deeply schizoid young man. His social skills masked an interior emptiness and brittle fragility that had an ominous feel to it. He reminded me of those vividly portrayed characters in Laing's book, *The Divided Self* (1960). Tom had almost no feelings or even sensations at all, not even sexual ones. I wrote in my notes that I was concerned about schizophrenia in the long term if no intervention was made. The fact that he was also depressed seemed to be a hopeful sign, as it indicated the remnants of feeling and facilitated a therapeutic alliance.

Tom's parents, prominent members of a popular charismatic church, were ambivalent about psychotherapy from the start. They explicitly supported Tom's seeing me, yet they repeatedly told him that no psychologist could help, and that he should 'just' surrender himself to Jesus. Tom's mother explained to me that the devil had populated the world with demons, and these had infiltrated her son. She could see it soon after he was born; she had a mother's intuition; she knew. Several consultations with the parents included interpreting and containing their anxiety, and directly confronting them with the fact that therapy had no chance of success if they continued to undermine the process. In this way the fragile alliance with the parents was sustained for about five months (twenty sessions).

By this time, Tom's bodily and affective life were starting to become more differentiated. He described with real pleasure becoming aware of the smells in his school, such as sweat in the locker room and food in the kitchen. Sometimes he felt lonely, sometimes hurt or angry, and sometimes he became aware of awakening sexual feelings and desires (e.g. daydreaming of inviting a girl on a date). To me, Tom seemed gentler and more vulnerable. There was a tender atmosphere in the room when he was there. Once or twice his eyes softened with tears. He wrote and showed me a poem about the smells and colors of a desert sunrise, and it reminded him of the verses he used to write in secret as a child.

At the same time he was, of course, telling me of a history of experiences that had terrified him out of his mind—and his body. In one of these many memories, for instance, he was having his hair washed in paraffin. He was choking, and there was a foul, poisonous taste in his mouth. Believing that his mother was trying to drown or poison him, he screamed and began to struggle for his life, while his mother's hands continued to hold his head in the basin. Of course, memories such as this have several dimensions. Washing hair with paraffin was a folk treatment for lice, and it was probably not the willful torture he experienced at the time (although Tom's mother came across as a cold, angry, and bitter woman, and I would not rule this possibility out: see Peck 1983). But the fact that he experienced this incident in this way suggests that his relationship with his mother was already filled with anxiety, and in a crucial developmental sense had broken down. Tom and I reflected together how the memory was also in some sense an image of what their relationship *felt* like a lot of the time, even in the present. Following Melanie Klein, I would also say that his terror was partly (but only partly) of his own making: that the hate which terrified him was not only his mother's but also his own. Retrospectively, I also tend to think that what was being shared between mother and son in uncontained projective identifications was psychosis itself. In any event, and not surprisingly, as Tom recounted these images and memories, he was coming to experience significant anger towards his parents. He wondered aloud why his mother hated him.

During the school break Tom's mother took him on a two-week retreat with other members of her church. He was given pamphlets and 'counseling:' a barrage of arguments that psychotherapy was the work of the devil because it pretended to make psychological what were really symptoms of devil possession. These 'symptoms' included depression, irritability, and anger towards one's parents. Before the retreat ended Tom was 'born again,' and, in a painfully angry telephone call, he accused me of being 'Satan's advocate.' I persuaded Tom to come to see me to talk about it, but the session was lost before it started. He looked terrified and refused to sit down. Although he did concede that our relationship was a human one, with human values and human limitations, our therapeutic alliance had been irrevocably broken. There were tears in his eyes when he left, and he did not consult me again.

Five years later Tom's family was reassured by a psychiatrist that his paranoid schizophrenia was purely a neurochemical condition. It included delusions of demons inside him, of being poisoned, and of thought control by unseen forces. The psychiatrist agreed with the family that psychotherapy had been contraindicated. I happened to see Tom in the hospital, standing in a corridor. Behind his smile of recognition and awkward greeting was a look of such unbearable longing and anguish that I am still haunted by it, more than a dozen years later.

THE CHALLENGE OF PSYCHOTHERAPY

These awful stories are not unusual. I recently heard a 'televangelist' telling a group of teenagers that if they married a 'non-believer' Satan would be their father-in-law. Reverend Jerry Fallwell is a regular guest on CNN, where he discusses the 'Christian' view of homosexuality: as a Christian he 'loves' homosexuals, but warns them (us?) of God's damnation if they (we?)

don't change. It is not surprising that psychotherapy should represent such a threat, even though there are numerous Christian writings that are equally appalled at this violence and could pose an equal challenge to it.[2]

The challenge from psychotherapy can be discussed in several ways.

First, psychotherapy has something to offer people in existential distress. People usually get better, often in ways that permanently transform the quality of their lives. This challenges the assertion that there can be no authentic relief except through personal surrender to Jesus Christ as Savior. It also challenges the assumption that psychotherapists who have not been 'born again' have nothing significant to offer, or perhaps are placed there by the devil in order to lead people astray. Psychotherapy, especially psychodynamic therapy, offers people a language and a framework for understanding personal failures and psychic suffering, and it offers a method for promoting genuine personal growth.

Realizing this has helped me understand why it is that, when psychotherapists work with fundamentalists themselves or with their children, therapy is terminated just at the moment of therapeutic change. My hunch is that, because fundamentalist beliefs are used defensively to support ego functioning, particularly its distortions through splitting and projection, the incipient changes brought about through psychotherapy are especially threatening to the whole organization of fundamentalist experience.

Second, psychotherapists have gained considerable experience with people's anxieties and defenses when they are in psychic trouble; the way fundamentalist experience is organized is familiar to us as a way of coping with extreme anxiety and unmanageable psychic pain. (While the defenses are familiar to us for this reason, this is not to say that all fundamentalist Christians are in extreme anxiety and pain—although many are.) Analytically oriented psychotherapists see the twin defenses of splitting and projection (or, as in the cases above, of projective identification, when the Other is actually attacked as the receptacle of unwanted parts of the self). These two defenses are particularly resistant to interpretation and reality testing because they sustain the patient's precarious sense of self and reality.

The Church and the community of the saved form a kind of Noah's ark set against the dark flood waters of the sinful world. One's sense of self and one's hope for a heavenly future are maintained by vigorously fighting this darkness: in preaching to others, praying for strength, giving thanks, and in supportive religious rituals. Since the shadow side of life is an inescapable part of the human condition, it persistently calls for our attention and integration. For the fundamentalist, however, it is split off, disowned, and projected into the world and the devil. Then it is *others* who are sinful, guilty, and in need of salvation. It is also *others* who fail to see the sacred and who supposedly live in profane darkness. There is a terrible irony here, which is of both psychological and spiritual significance. Instead of taking responsibility for the darker aspects of themselves, they shroud the world in darkness through projection. In seeing the world as the devil's domain, they then perpetuate the very darkness they seek to conquer.

Anger is a particular shadow problem for people who are trying their best to live ethical lives and to atone for personal guilt. Fundamentalist Christians, however, seem to believe that they should be free from the vagaries of anger, aggression, and envy. After being 'saved,' normal aggression is denied. It then becomes hostility and, sometimes, rage, which in turn feeds the unresolved guilt and the haunting possibility of despair. It is interesting that Jung believed that St John, the writer of The Book of Revelations, suffered these dynamics in his accounts of Christ's vengeance upon the world. According to Jung, because the figure of Christ was idealized as one-sidedly good, the early Christians, including St John, were increasingly desperate while waiting for Christ's return and their own salvation. 'In [Revelations],' says Jung,

> I see less a metaphysical mystery than the outburst of long pent-up negative feelings such as can frequently be observed in people who strive for perfection. . . . John made every effort to practice what he preached to his fellow Christians. For this purpose he had to shut out all negative feelings, and, thanks to a helpful lack of self-reflection, he was able to forget them. But though they disappeared from the conscious level they continued to rankle beneath the surface, and in the course of time spun an elaborate web of resentments and vengeful thoughts which then burst upon consciousness in the form of a revelation. From this there grew up a terrifying picture that blatantly contradicts all ideas of Christian humility, tolerance, love of your neighbour and your enemies, and makes nonsense of a loving father in heaven and rescuer of mankind. A veritable orgy of hatred, wrath, vindictiveness, and blind destructive fury that revels in fantastic images of terror breaks out and with blood and fire overwhelms a world which Christ had just endeavoured to restore to the original state of innocence and loving communion with God.
>
> (1952: 438; see also Lambert 1977)

When the image of transcendence is split off from the world and our human fallibility, and when projection fails as a defense, one tends to implode into self-loathing. Christian self-loathing is a time-honored tradition. In what was one of the most influential directives and commentaries in Christianity, written in the fifteenth century, Thomas à Kempis wrote:

> Lord, I am not worthy to receive your comfort, or any spiritual visitation—you treat me as I deserve when you leave me helpless and alone. If I could weep an ocean of tears I would still be unworthy of

your comfort. I deserve nothing but torture and punishment, because I have so deeply and so often offended you, and sinned so grievously on so many occasions. If a true account is rendered, I am found unworthy of the slightest comfort.

(1963: 194)

It should not be difficult to see in these lines, too, that the secret side of self-loathing is an inflated grandiosity. When there is no self-forgiveness, there is appalling self-contempt, for which 'torture and punishment' are easily justified.

The Achilles heel of the fundamentalist stance is a lack of faith. Fundamentalists lack faith in the grace and forgiveness that make life possible, whereas depth psychotherapy, at its best, embodies and carries with it those very qualities that should be central to a Christian sensibility. Psychotherapeutic change comes about through humbly grappling with, and accepting, the shadow side of life. Rather than look for the triumph of light over the darkness, the therapist helps the patient enter the darkness with the faith that the acceptance of human fallibility leads to transformation. As Jung once put it: 'One does not become enlightened by imagining figures of light, but by making the darkness conscious,' adding dryly, 'The latter procedure, however, is disagreeable and therefore not popular' (1945/54: 265–66).

Thus the third challenge of psychotherapy is an understanding that the natural tendency to recoil from the source of suffering is ultimately self-defeating. The only way to genuine transformation and greater freedom is to yield to the pull of the snare, to move in the direction of one's own entrapment, and to offer reverend hospitality to what initially appears as malevolent or lethal. Navaho mythology reminds us that the evil trickster, Coyote, is also the bringer of light (Brooke 1993: 62). In terms of psychopathology, Jung said that 'The gods have become diseases' (1929: 113), indicating that the pathway to the sacred is *through* our symptoms, not away from them. Psychotherapists understand the profound sense in which, as once again Jung said, 'A neurosis is truly removed only when it has removed the false attitude of the ego. We do not cure it—it cures us' (1934: 170). If we walk through the world like St George, dressed in armor and carrying a sword, we are inclined to see heathens and dragons. But if we take off our armor and put down our swords, we discover that the world is not so full of dragons and the spirit of Christ is to be found among the 'heathens' too.

Andrew

'Andrew' had wanted to be a doctor. He saw it as a noble calling, one that would lift him out of the violence and degradations of his family of origin.

He saw doctors as holy people doing good in the world, so he worked hard to be accepted into medical school. A year after his residency began he became so depressed that he was tearful much of the day and could barely get out of bed in the morning. He was disillusioned with his medical colleagues, who seemed more interested in making money and chasing women than in their vocation. A trusted colleague of Andrew's prescribed an antidepressant, which he did not take. He came to therapy instead and reported a dream. In his dream he was trying to reach a beautiful golden temple on the other side of a deep canyon which was still in darkness as the early morning sun had not yet reached there. His problem was that he could not find a way down. He watched an eagle soar overhead to the other side, wished he could fly like that, then tried again to find a way down. He was stuck. Then he awoke.

The canyon seemed like 'the valley of the shadow of death.' I interpreted the dream as telling us where his therapy needed to go: he had to make his descent into this dark territory; even in the dream he knew he couldn't fly over it. When Andrew said that he didn't know how to make the descent, I suggested that he might find it useful to talk to me about his background (see Fordham 1965/73). He nodded with understanding—and slowly began his ordeal. Although his clinical depression lifted quite quickly after entering therapy, it was a couple of years before Andrew felt really alive and at home in his work. We returned to the dream image from time to time. He realized with surprise and humor one day that the 'valley' was actually the place of human community in which he did his work and found himself. No longer was his work an heroic attempt to salvage something holy in a spiritual wasteland. In some respects the hospital where he worked was itself, despite its ordinary realities, a sacred place. In that sense he was *already* in a temple of sorts. As the landscape of his previously bifurcated psychic life changed, he discovered that the journey and the goal were not that clearly distinguishable, and that transcendence was a possibility that could be close at hand.

EMISSARIES FROM THE UNDERWORLD

Ironically, fundamentalists who think of psychotherapists as emissaries of the devil have a point. We stand in the shadows of the charismatic world, and are apologists for much of what is regarded as 'Satan's work.' Rather than exorcise the demon, we would ask what the demon might like to say. More prosaically, rather than fight the patient's distress with moral injunctions, however benignly offered, we prefer to illuminate that distress in the faith that it will yield its life-affirming fruit. Our faith in what we do, and in the psyche and its transformative capacities, is not naive; it is more like a humble prayer (Tener 1997). Psychotherapists' abilities differ greatly, and even the best therapists sometimes fail. Our prayer is carried in the attitude of compassionate hospitality for the Beast that Beauty fears; it is in the knowledge that only when Beauty loves the Beast *as a Beast* are his princely qualities revealed. The Beast does not empirically disappear or mutate. The transformation is in the eye of the beholder, and in her relationship to him. It is Beauty that is changed, not the princely Beast.

Helen

'Helen' was the 28-year-old wife of an Episcopalian minister. She came to therapy (for which I was the supervisor, not the therapist) saying she felt depressed and unsatisfied with her life. It emerged that she was particularly distressed about her sex life. She felt guilty about sexual feelings, and hoped that psychotherapy might help her 'integrate' them. She was not sure what this meant, but said that if she did not 'do something' she would be unable to stop herself from sleeping with a parishioner with whom she had begun flirting. Prayer and the loving support of her husband, whom she had told (and who later suggested psychotherapy), made her feel inexplicably worse. She did say that her sexual life with her husband was 'fine,' but it emerged that she felt sexually inhibited and usually unsatisfied.

This short-term therapy of twenty sessions addressed several interrelated themes: the death of her father when she was a teenager, her fear of abandonment, and her sexual anxiety and guilt. As her fear of sexual feeling was persistently questioned, she found herself becoming conscious of considerable sexual pressure. She was preoccupied with sexual fantasies whenever she talked to a man, and wondered as she walked down the street which of the men she passed would make a good lover. Her therapist (the man I was supervising) pushed her further by saying she seemed to be afraid of the sexual feelings she had for him as well. She exclaimed that therapy was turning her into a 'nymphomaniac,' and in agitated excitement said that if she 'let go' she would become a 'female rapist'!

Concurrently with these developments was the therapeutic process of revisiting her terrible feelings regarding her father. His death had left her not only having to deal with his untimely loss, but also without a father to awaken and mirror her sexuality as a potential future belonging to her (Samuels 1985: 31–2). The fact that Helen also had to face the loss of her therapist through impending termination intensified both her mourning process and the meaning of the transference. Termination was only a few sessions away when Helen dreamed that she was being led by her therapist down a pathway into an underground hall. Inside, there was a wild party comprising characters who seemed to belong in a New Orleans Mardi Gras. In the next moment her therapist changed into a sort of totem pole made of flashing lights, with devil's horns on his head. She awoke in some consternation.

Helen felt that she had been led into a strange underworld and abandoned there by a therapist who was an evil trickster. She was angry, and said so in no uncertain terms! But after this session, to her surprise, her sexual love life with her husband improved dramatically, and her fantasies about other men largely evaporated, or at least became easily manageable. She said that over the following days she realized that her sexuality, and that underworld, were really her own, and that her therapist had led her to her self. (I would add that it was Helen's archetypal need that used her therapist as an 'incarnation' of her desire. The transference, for Jung, was most importantly the concrete mediation of *internal* relations (Jung 1916/ 57: 74).)

In her penultimate session Helen reported a dream in which she was enjoying holy communion with her husband. Her therapist was at the back of the church, and they briefly smiled in greeting when their eyes met. Then she turned back to the front and lovingly took her husband's hand. The interior of the church was bathed in sunlight. That mood was still with Helen when she and her therapist said goodbye the following week.

SURRENDER

Every successful long-term psychotherapy in which I have participated, including my own, has freed the patient from the moralistic stance that had been foundational in his or her life. To be engaged, loving, compassionate, and ethical without moralism is the goal! Then one no longer needs to live one's life as a kind of personal concoction, or to be the master in one's psychic house. This is the experience of surrender, which, as Hidas (1981) argued, is common to both depth psychotherapy and the spiritual quest. It is a capacity to experience and yield to that mysterious occurrence called being. A patient once said that she had come to therapy to try to get more control over herself, but discovered that there was a deeper sense in which she never had been in control and that it didn't matter. On the far side of her omnipotent control was grief, and beyond that was, for a while at least, a sense of grace worthy of the word 'transcendent.' More than 'self-forgiveness,' it was for both of us an experience of the Forgiveness without which nothing exists. I am reminded too of a woman who said that, until she had had psychotherapy, she had never truly known the meaning of Christ's saying, 'I am come that they might have life, and that they might have it more abundantly' (*Holy Bible*, John 10:10).

Irene

Irene[3] was unmarried, seventy-five years old, and dying of numerous medical problems. An only child, she had had a grim and punitive childhood, but had dutifully looked after her parents until they died when she was in her mid-fifties. She had always been a God-fearing woman, living a devoutly Christian life. She was fiercely independent. At the age of fifty-eight, she had for the first time in her life allowed herself to fall in love and to experience being loved. She and her lover were devoted to each other for the next ten years, until he died. Now she was terrified and clinically depressed, and was referred to me for psychotherapy. Irene could no longer do even the simplest things for herself: she was doubly incontinent, could not move without assistance, and could not even feed herself. Three years earlier, when her symptoms began, she dreamed of being visited by two angels, but she did not know what to make of this at the time. When I first saw her she wanted to die, but was terrified of the damnation that awaited her. She prayed for forgiveness but felt hopelessly unforgiven. She also felt that her current state was punishment for her sin.

In psychotherapy Irene spoke about her life, and incrementally came to see a different religious story in it. She had to admit that the only love she had felt in her life was with her lover. She wept with relief when it was suggested to her that his entering her life might have been not a Satanic temptation but a sacred gift, which at the time she had *felt* it was. She also came to see that the angels in her dream were present as angels always are: bringing a message from God, announcing the approach of a sacred time. That sacred time was now. Her growing helplessness and dependence were, perhaps, neither a personal failure nor a divine punishment, but an experience of divine forgiveness and love. Why? Because she had never known God's love: that she could be lovingly cared for during her decline, even when she had nothing left to give. In submitting to her dependency, she was putting herself in the hands of God; she had no choice but utter surrender. As she learned to relax when the aides lifted her from bed to wheelchair, or back again, she began to feel, little by little, that their steady arms and kind words were somehow God made flesh. Despite being quite aware that the aides were 'just doing their job,' Irene felt loved again. Perhaps we can suggest that, for the first time in her devoutly religious life, she was knowing the meaning of being a Christian.

In the end, therefore, psychotherapy both assumes and sometimes touches the dimension of the sacred, but it does so in a way that embraces the possibility of radical doubt, failure, and 'sin.' I do not mean to idealize psychotherapy, or to imply that psychotherapists are free from their own fundamentalisms. We are not. But perhaps, at least in the analytic tradition, we are somewhat better at owning our anxieties as our own. Splitting, idealization, and contempt reveal the absence of that transcendent faith which psychotherapy both assumes and attempts to recover. Whether that faith takes a specifically religious form or not is another matter.

NOTES

1. The term 'patient' is controversial because of its medical associations and also the power differential between therapist and patient/client that this implies. Having balked at the term myself, I have come to like it. Stripped of its medical literalisms, the word 'patient' speaks more adequately than 'client' to the sickness of soul in which I find myself when needing psychological help, to my sense of being taken over by something beyond my control, my loss of freedom, and my distress. As a therapist, it also seems important to keep the ethical burden of my power, with its shadows, clearly in mind, which I am less likely to do if I smooth over those issues by pretending those who see me are merely 'clients.'
2. For example, Brinsmead (1985) and O'Donahue (1987). Mention should be made of Peck's (1978) classic and popular book, *The Road Less Travelled*. There has also recently appeared a marvelous new book by Bronheim (1998), which integrates object relations theory and practice with the sacred ground of Christianity.
3. Irene's dying wish to me was that I use her real name. She had no family. She wanted people to know. I do so with deep respect.

REFERENCES

à Kempis, T. (1963) *The Imitation of Christ*, trans. Betty Knott, London: Fontana.

Brinsmead, R. (1985) 'The spirit of fundamentalism,' *Verdict*, essay 19: 2–7.

Bronheim, H. (1998) *Body and Soul: The Role of Object Relations in Faith, Shame, and Healing*, Northvale, NJ: Jason Aronson.

Brooke, R. (1993) 'A coyote barks at Prometheus,' *The Humanistic Psychologist*, 21 (Spring): 58–64.

Culbert-Koehn, J. (1997) 'Between Bion and Jung: a talk with James Grotstein,' *The San Fransisco Jung Institute Library Journal*, 15/4: 15–32.

Eliade, M. (ed.) (1987) *The Encyclopedia of Religion*, vol. 5, New York: Macmillan Publishing Company.

Fordham, M. (1965/73) 'The importance of analysing childhood for assimilation of the shadow', in M. Fordham, R. Gordon, J. Hubback, K. Lambert, and M. Williams (eds), *Analytical Psychology: A Modern Science*, London: Academic Press.

Freud, S. (1928) 'The future of an illusion,' in *Standard Edition of the Complete Psychological Works of Sigmund Freud*, vol. 21, ed. and trans. J. Strachey, in collaboration with Anna Freud, Alix Strachey, and Alan Tyson, London: Hogarth Press, 1953–74.

Hidas, A. (1981) 'Psychotherapy and surrender: a psychospiritual perspective,' *The Journal of Transpersonal Psychology*, 13/1: 27–32.

Hillman, J. (1979a) *The Dream and the Underworld*, New York: Harper and Row.

Hillman, J. (1979b) 'Peaks and vales,' in *Loose Ends*, Dallas: Spring Publications.

Holy Bible (1611) King James Version, Oxford: Oxford University Press.

Jones, E. (1930/51) 'Psycho-analysis and the Christian religion,' in *Essays in Applied Psycho-Analysis*, The International Psycho-Analytical Library 41, London: Hogarth Press and the Institute of Psycho-Analysis.

Jung, C. G (1916/57) 'The transcendent function,' in *The Collected Works of C. G. Jung*, vol. 8, trans. R. F. C. Hull, ed. Sir Herbert Read, M. Fordham, G. Adler, executive editor W. McGuire (Bollingen Series 20), London: Routledge; Princeton, NJ: Princeton University Press.

Jung, C. G. (1929) 'Commentary on "The Secret of the Golden Flower",' in *Collected Works*, vol. 13.

Jung, C. G. (1934) 'The state of psychotherapy today,' in *Collected Works*, vol. 10.

Jung, C. G. (1945/54) 'The philosophical tree,' in *Collected Works*, vol. 13.

Jung, C. G. (1952) 'Answer to Job,' in *Collected Works*, vol. 11.

Laing, R. (1960) *The Divided Self*, London: Tavistock.

Lambert, K. (1977) 'Analytical psychology and historical development in western consciousness,' *Journal of Analytical Psychology*, 22/2: 158–74.

Levin, D. (1985) *The Body's Recollection of Being: Phenomenological Psychology and the Deconstruction of Nihilism*, London and New York: Routledge.

Meagher, P., O'Brien, T., and Aherne, C. (eds) (1979) *Encyclopedia Dictionary of Religion*, Washington, DC: Corpus Publishing.

O'Donahue, J. (1987) 'Fundamentalism: a psychological problem,' *African Ecclesial Review*, 29/6: 344–50.

Peck, S. (1978) *The Road Less Travelled*, London: Arrow.

Peck, S. (1983) *The People of the Lie*, New York: Simon and Schuster.

Samuels, A. (1985) 'Introduction,' in *The Father*, New York: New York University Press.

Tener, E. (1997) 'Is it therapy or is it prayer?' *Self* (December): 165–76.

Voltaire (1758/1947) *Candide*, trans. John Butt, Harmondsworth: Penguin.

Chapter 12

The prism self

Multiplicity on the path to transcendence

Judith Stevens-Long

The Deal
Always there is this tension between
what I think I am
what I want to be and what I am to you.
Shall I tell you
I want to be somebody else just at the point
where I have become predictable to you?

I am a continual source of disappointment.
I am a continual source of joy
      OR
maybe it is you who is the source
of all disappointment, of all joy.
We never know who is the image-maker,
who is the image. It may be you, or my
projection about you, in which case it is
only me, or what I deny I am which changes
constantly with how you are, which may be
only me again. Perhaps the construct
called controller is irrelevant and one
of us should just shut up and deal.

                     J. S. L

'. . . the mature human self is not essentially a center of monological consciousness, often conceived of as an inner space or mind that contains representations of things outside of this container. . . . Rather, it is a scene of dialogue . . . a conversation or struggle among multiple voices, speaking from different positions and invested with different kinds and degrees of authority.'

          (Richardson, Rogers, and McCarroll, 1998: 509)

This chapter reviews some of the growing body of literature in philosophy, personality research, and theory on the development of identity, as well as current thinking about the historical and cultural relevance of that construct as we use it in developmental psychology. I hope this review will raise some questions about the role of ego-integrity in transcendence as well as the notion that a fully developed, separate sense of self is prerequisite to self-actualization. Over the years, I have done a great deal of thinking and writing about theories of human development (see Stevens-Long 1979; 1984; 1988; 1991), and I believe that it is too soon for us to adopt one particular point of view about the nature or direction of optimal development. We still need to challenge all our treasured notions and values, and certainly the idea of integrity qualifies as a treasured value if not a sacred cow. It has also been my personal experience that profound experiences of disintegration can play an important role in a maturing adult personality.

It is not my purpose here to argue about the existence or experience of transcendent states, but rather to note the significant absence of consensual validation of ego-integrity as a prerequisite to the experience of transcendence. In fact, there is little if any work on the lived experience of ego-integrity. Cook-Greuter's (1994) work on post-conventional ego development makes some inferences about such lived experience based on the Washington University Sentence Completion Test. She offers the following thoughts about the experiences of mature (stage 5) adults:

> They have a well-developed *psycho-logic* which enables them to analyze both their own and other's thought, behaviors and feelings. . . . They tend to deal with many variables which interact in a non-linear, organismic mode. They are aware of their multiple roles in society and with often conflicting demands and of contradictory aspects, needs, and perceptions within themselves. . . . A strong, well-developed ego with clearly established boundaries is at the core of the autonomous individual's striving for self-actualization and an objective self-identity.
>
> (p. 122)

In addressing the issue of self-actualization, much less ego-transcendence, many developmental psychologists assume with Cook-Greuter that 'An autonomous, well-integrated ego is the prerequisite for . . . higher forms of self-cognition' (p. 139). Most commonly, it is assumed there is a progression through autonomy and integrity to transcendence.

Some may assume that 'transcendence refers to a felt connection with all things' or the Absolute, but my focus here is on the question of what it is that we transcend, if transcendence is indeed possible. If, as Engler (1986) puts it, 'You have to be somebody before you can be nobody,' what is the sense of somebody that we leave behind? Even the notion that there is a 'somebody' tends to imply ego-integrity. That is, Engler does not consider the possibility that one might leave behind a set of somebodies—a multiplicity of voices or states.

THE SELF

Richardson et al. (1998) distinguish broad ways of thinking about the experience of the self. The first they call a *traditional* understanding of the self: the individual playing a small but meaningful role in both a human community and a wider cosmic drama. The second or *modern* construction is described as the *sovereign self* or an invulnerable front of separateness and mastery. This modern self is also seen as atomistic, free, and rational. Identifying with a modern self, we may treat the social and natural world, even features of our own character, instrumentally as a means to an end. The modern self is not constrained by cultural meanings and practices, but takes culture to be a medium of self-realization or self-actualization.

The third version of the self, originating with the postmodern and post-structuralist thinkers, has been called the *decentered* self and emphasizes the role of cultural context or social processes in the formation of identity. Rather than offering a new definition of self, this view is a strong critique of the notion of a disengaged, masterful self. For example, Foucault (1980) rejects the idea of identity outright.

The fourth version is called a *dialogical* understanding of the self as a locus of self-talk. This self is an internalized, ongoing conversation or dialogue concerning the 'quality of our motivation, the worth of the ends we seek, or the good or right life for us in our time and place' (Richardson et al. 1998: 510). The dialogical self is a stance or attitude toward our values, principles, and goals. It is both permeated by others and yet having a 'significant degree of individual agency and personal responsibility' (p. 511). The dialogical self is best understood as a sort of 'wave and particle theory' of the individual subject. Whether or not the self appears integrated will depend upon where the observer focuses his or her attention. As a stance or attitude, the self appears integrated, and yet it is also an array of discrepant voices each of which makes serious claims on our loyalty and beliefs.

Anderson (1997) also outlines various theories of the self. 'Traditional' views are composed of roles—for example, self as mother, worker, friend, aunt, citizen, or member of the tribe, and so forth. He also describes a 'romantic' view, in which the true inner self can be discovered and nurtured through meditation. Finally, he outlines the 'scientific' view, wherein the self can be measured, characterized, and studied. This scientific approach is congruent with the modern self, defined above. Of the modern self, Anderson has the following to say: 'The modern self was—is—one of the noblest achievements of the human mind, and one of the most inspiring achievements of evolution on the planet. It was a construction of thought that freed people from the tyranny of kings, expanded the horizons of life, opened the mind to the best possibilities of science' (1997: 31).

This modern self began to break down in the 1960s, according to Anderson, although it still dominates our assumptions about personal identity. For example, psychologists and psychiatrists still believe in the value of developing a stable sense of self. The mature modern self is characterized by integrity in the sense of integration or unity. While this kind of self has served us well in developing ideals of individual responsibility, there are a variety of reasons to now take issue with the idea of integrity as a goal. Philosophical, historical, and anthropological perspectives suggest that integrity as an ideal is inconsistent with current research on identity formation.

INTEGRITY

In modern psychological theories, it is usually claimed that the mature self is experienced as autonomous with respect to society, expectations, and conventions. Cook-Greuter (1994) mentions autonomy, objectivity, and stability. Erikson (1982) refers to understanding the single narrative line of one's life and the maintenance of coherence. Anthony Giddens offers a simple but powerful definition of integrity as 'the capacity *for keeping a particular narrative going*' (1991: 54). In other words, identity coheres through the integration of the events of the external world into an ongoing story about the self.

In this view, personal integrity comes from integrating life experiences into a single narrative of self-development. If we are able to tell a sensible, authentic story of the self, we have achieved integration, knowing who we are, how we got to be who we are, and where we are going. Here, identity is understood as knowing one's autobiography as a convincing, rational story.

This notion of narrative implies a knowledge of self that is carried from one domain to another, creating a rational if not predictable trajectory of self-characteristics across situations. One is an honest person or not, loving, kind, compassionate (or not). One does not enter situation B as an entirely different sort of character than in situation A. Erikson (1982) talks about the wisdom, competence, love, and care of the person who achieves integrity in later life. So, not only does integrity usually imply a kind of cross-situational self-knowledge and coherence, it has traditionally implied the existence of many positive attributes in developmental theory.

EPISTEMOLOGICAL ISSUES OF INTEGRITY AND TRANSCENDENCE

Our current understanding of ego development is modern, emphasizing objectivity and the measure of individual differences (Maddi 1993). Survey and interview instruments are developed with an eye to scalability, reliability, and validity. Do these approaches capture self as lived experience? The hegemony of ego psychology has led us to believe that ego development means increasing maturity in terms of greater objectivity and complexity within an integrated ego. Multiplicity or pluralism of the ego is interpreted as a symptom of crisis or pathology.

Research and theory that rely upon the empirical-analytic tradition are likely to lead to conclusions that emphasize ego-logical development—linear and hierarchical progressions. The end-point of this progression is seen as integrity or, ultimately, as self-actualized transcendence. Evidence for this transcendence is based on consensual validation achieved by cross-checking the characteristics of the state amongst those who claim to have had similar experiences (Heron 1997; Wilber 1995). Transpersonal psychology, even the most speculative theories, like those of Wilber (1995) and Grof (1988), make claims for the 'objectivity' of the 'subjective,' even of the transcendent experience.

Jorge Ferrer (1998) has argued that the epistemology of empirical validation among transpersonal psychologists has created the need to objectify the subjective and nearly mandated the adoption of the 'perennial philosophy.' Perennial philosophy is the belief in a unity at the core of all spiritual traditions. 'If there is not a perennial philosophy . . . if there is not a unity in mysticism and a consensus about the world view that spiritual experiences convey, then spiritual knowledge claims would run the risk of being charged again with subjectivism and solipsism or even seen as sheer pathology' (Ferrer 1998: 24). Funk (1993), for example, concludes that transcendent experiences culminate in the conscious apperception of an underlying unity of life, the existence of an Absolute.

The postmodern challenge to this description is captured by White and Hellerich (1998), who suggest that contemporary culture engenders a multiform self best understood as a collection of convenient masks, as the Latin 'personae,' a variety of characters one might play. Or, as Nietzsche wrote in the *Will to Power* (1968) 'The assumption of one single subject is perhaps unnecessary' (p. 490). Because transcendence seems to be the recognition that all structures, including the self, are fabrications, I wonder if transcendence might develop from a 'polymorphous self,' rather than an integrated self. Is it possible that there is more than one developmental path to transcendence?

HISTORICAL AND CROSS-CULTURAL ISSUES

Challenges to the one-path version of transcendence arise from historical and cross-cultural sources. Generally, it is agreed that the modern notion of the self arose in the West at the time of the Enlightenment (Richardson et al. 1998; Anderson 1997). Augustine made one of the first sharp distinctions between inner and outer self, positioning the self as an entity inside looking out. The 'cogito' of Descartes then epitomized the belief that one's self-awareness is beyond all doubt the evidence for existence. Eventually, the self became a masterful self-defining entity, distinct from God and external reality (Tarnas 1991). As I said above, the modern self is an outgrowth of this progression, propounding a coherent biography as an autonomous rational being.

This biography is supposedly transcended, then, through the experience of the transpersonal. And yet, there are many historical figures who reported transpersonal experiences *prior* to the emergence of this modern, separate self. From this fact, I wonder about the following.

- Are the experiences of such mystical and philosophical figures as Plotinus and Teresa of Avila different from the experience of the Absolute which the modern self encounters?
- Are the furthest developments of the personalities of 'wise ancients'—premodern selves—similar to or different from the later stages of modern theories?
- Are there multiple paths to self-transcendence which may or may not include ego-integrity as described in modernity?

Wilber (1995) claims that a few ancient mystics may have traveled the paths of development that we expect of the modern self. This seems unlikely, though, because the self is embedded in historical contexts and individuals cannot leap ahead.

I find more confusion about the one-path theory of transcendence in reviewing the results of contemporary cross-cultural studies of self-identity. Braun (1993) claims, for example, that in India the ego is answerable to many competing and contradictory forces, leading to a self that is experienced as less integrated than our Western ideas suggest. 'The Indian normally has a number of ego nuclei based on conformity to various social rules with a not easily found ideal to judge or coordinate these rules' (Braun 1993: 143).

Furthermore, Indian tribal groups often exhibit close identification of the self with nature, so that changes in the environment lead to changes in identity. As Vasudev (1994) has put it, the Indian woman asks 'What has happened that you have started feeling discontinuous?' Apparently, the Indian self is less autonomous and less separate than the ideal of the modern Westerner.

However, we do not have to go as far afield as India to challenge the notion of the autonomous, integrated self. Feminist psychologists have long argued that the self is more context-dependent and relational than the modern version. Oyama (1993) has gone so far as to imply there is no such thing as individual personality or identity at all. She posits that a person is a moving complex of elements that exist in shifting interpersonal environments, always in dialogic relation to the other. She argues that the conception of the self as a set of traits contained inside persons describes only one dimension of an interactive phenomenon. Looking through a wider lens, individual traits reappear as outcomes of interpersonal events. Different situations evoke different ways of being, acting, thinking, etc. Of course these ideas are not new. Sullivan (1953) and Mischel (1969) were much earlier proponents of a contextualized view, not to mention more radical behavior theories.

All of these interpersonal theories stress the idea that identity is embedded in relational processes. The self is not a static unity that comes to an independent existence in adolescence and is consolidated in young adulthood. Rather, it is a flow of relational dialogues that continue through life. This conception blurs the boundary between self and other. Persons are conceived not as independent, autonomous actors, but as interdependent partners in relationships with family members, romantic partner, friends, co-workers, acquaintances, and strangers. Identity is a dynamic whole comprised of different aspects that dominate, participate, recede, or submerge in accord with established relational patterns. Young-Eisendrath (1997) notes that many interpersonal and feminist theorists have 'cautioned us not to universalize the story of a masterful, bounded self as a necessity for everyone' (p. 162). She refers to the work of Harré (1989) to remind us that a person may have a collective self like the Copper Eskimos, who function almost as a group identity, or a very independent self like the Maori, who see individuality as something like a physical force.

When the self is conceived as interdependent, embedded, and relational, integrity and autonomy may not be necessary for transcendence. Philosophical, historical, and cross-cultural work all suggest the existence of an alternative path for the development of a mature spirituality. In this light, the notion arises that the mature self may be experienced as a multiplicity rather than an integrated entity and may achieve transcendence without a bounded, masterful self.

MULTIPLE SELVES IN PERSONALITY THEORY

Much of personality theory has conceived of multiple centers of subjective identity. James (1890/1963) referred to the *I* and the *me*, being respectively the sense of personal agency, and internalized values and identifications. Psychoanalytic theory offered the structural model of *id*, *ego*, and *superego*, while Jung named a collection of subjectivites in *self*, *persona*, *shadow*, *animus*, *anima*, and *ego*. The mainstream human development literature has ignored almost all of this thinking in favor of Piagetian and Eriksonian ideals of unitary, stage-oriented development.

Contemporary personality theories abound with versions of plurality, including Berne's (1964) *parent, adult, child*; Sullivan's (1953) *good me, bad me*, and *not me*. Gergen (1991) speaks of the *pastiche self*, a multiverse of culturally derived internal images. Harter and Monsour (1992) claim that *human natures* are multidimensional and shift across relations and roles. Markus and Wurf (1987) describe *subsystems* of the self-concept. Breunlin et al. (1992) extend family systems concepts into the realm of the individual psyche by conceptualizing the *interior family*. Watkins and Johnson (1982) refer to *shifting ego states* and Watkins (1986) theorizes about interior voices that she calls *invisible guests* and *imaginal dialogues*. Similarly, Rowan (1990) conceives of the self as an internal community of interactors who 'come out' in various relational cultures, or to use Gergen's (1991) term, *relational nuclei*.

In the cognitive domain, Markus and Cross (1990) refer to plural self-representations, and to a repertoire of *possible selves*: *desirable selves, worst selves*, and *feared selves*. All people have some conceptions of multiple states of identity such as 'not me at all' or self-aspects that are disavowed but nonetheless exist in a person's range of ordinary attributes and behaviors. In one particularly interesting empirical study of this phenomenon, Montgomery (1996) presents a case study in which a variety of aspects of the self are explored using autobiographical and relational diagramming. The researcher describes the existence of a number of sub-systems, such as *me as mother, me as therapist, me as lover*. These various versions of the self show interconnections with each other as well as interconnections with descriptions of significant others, but each version has its own unique characteristics and is distinct as a constellation.

If we admit the possibility of multiplicity, Anderson (1997) contends that we need to pay attention to important differences in approaches to such postmodern selves. He identifies four types of postmodern theories. The first he calls *multiphrenia*—characterizing Gergen (1991) especially. In this version, constant communication, contact, and conflicting messages produce a self that is not consistent and integrated. The self becomes fragmented, shifting, outward-oriented, and accommodating. This construction casts inner multiplicity, such as the idea of the interior family or Markus and Wurf's (1987) subsystems, as a form of derangement, an uncomfortable and distressing adaptation at best, pathology at worst.

The second view, the *protean self*, Anderson traces to the work of Robert Lifton (1993). Unafraid of change and willing to undergo metamorphosis, the protean self is seen in a 'multiplicity of varied, even antithetical images and ideas held at one time by the self, each of which it may be more or less ready to act upon' (p. 8). The protean self seeks to be both fluid and grounded.

In the third view, the idea of separate identity disappears altogether (Derrida 1982; Foucault 1980; 1982). This self is decentered, described as an effect of the rules of discourse and power relations that create and constitute a particular form of life. This impersonal system operates almost entirely outside the control of speakers or actors. In this version, the self is at best a ceaselessly created and recreated 'work of art' (Foucault 1982) and, at worst, an impotent delusion.

The final view, termed 'feminist relationalism,' describes a self which is context-dependent, discontinuous, and contingent (Bateson 1989). This self is similar to Lifton's protean self: accommodating at best, and crazy or dishonest at worst. If we are to regard multiplicity as a mature form of self, it seems necessary to go beyond the vision of the self as socially accommodating and to delineate a human identity that is grounded—as Lifton implies—in some kind of symbolic or ethical connections.

In my view, Richardson et al. (1998) offer something of this sort in their version of the dialogic self, symbolized as wave–particle theory or 'prism' that reflects different views from different perspectives. The dialogic view draws on the work of Bakhtin (1981) to describe the self as a 'double-voiced discourse.' The term *dialogic* emphasizes the struggle among multiple voices internalized from the outside world and suggests an embeddedness and interdependence unrecognized in the modern construction. At the same time, it offers a sense of groundedness conceptualized as perspective, or stance. This self consists not only in a continuous dialogue between voices, images, and ideas that make claims on our attention (particle theory), but also in the existence of a stance or attitude toward those voices (wave theory).

I believe that the perspective that constitutes the groundedness of self is essentially ethical and evaluative. Listening to our own internalized dialogue, we reject some voices, harmonize others, and adopt one or another of many competing perspectives based on our judgments of what produces more penetrating insights, greater coherence, or more focus. We look for what is good and sensible, for what has meaning—the place of integrity in the protean self. The self, then, is not so much what people are as what they seek. It is not so much an experience of self as a quest, a stance toward the constantly shifting discourse of our consciousness.

Using the metaphor of a prism self, I would argue that this stance is what connects us to the transcendent, the Absolute, as we develop an evaluative capacity in relation to our own inner voices. Culture, language, experience, circumstance, and relationships form the prism that splays light along the spectrum of perceived colors. We could then say that the self is both integrated as the white light of the source and dis-integrated in the varied colors of its displays.

No one voice comes to dominate the others within the prism self. Rather, self *is* the interplay of positions through which the individual develops a stance with regard to the quality or worth of his or her motivations and goals. This self is no longer the integrator or synthesizer of experience, but rather the interpreter. It is the source that judges the rightness of an action, the meaningfulness of personae, and the potential in a circumstance. The self-system may be a family of selves that represents both the variety and the unity of voices and stances that allow for fluidity and groundedness, depending on the occasion or situation.

THE SELF AND TRANSCENDENCE

If modernity has opened up our version of the self, then how do we conceptualize that openness? Fragmentation of experience, so common in post-modern society, is often encountered and described as a source of anxiety. The psychiatric literature reported huge increases in Multiple Personality Disorder over time. Between 1791 and 1972, ten cases of MPD were documented worldwide, but in 1986 alone, 6,000 cases were reported. This may be psychopathology or narrative drama, but it expresses the tendency to dissociate or fall apart in today's world. Hundreds of thousands of people experiment every day with altered consciousness—through the use of drugs or prayer or meditation. You can change your identity in a few hours in our modern cities, and no one will be the wiser. On the internet, people take on whole new identities, change their gender and sexual preference, age and personality. Is this creativity or is it pathology?

I am suggesting here that this multiplicity, this prism self, needs to be understood along a continuum that includes many shades of meaning. It is possible that a truly generative, creative self is reflected in some forms of multiplicity. One comes to understand the degree to which identity is constructed, the power of image-making and self-formation. One may begin to see the self as an object that is made and remade through the continuous interplay and evaluation of competing voices and images. Looking at it in this way, it is easier to see how multiplicity offers the possibility of transcendence. This is especially so if, by transcendent awareness, we are speaking of understanding the personal ego as an object of awareness, transcending the notion that 'I am a particular collection of traits, habits, beliefs, attitudes.' In this sense, the self becomes something that I 'have' rather than something that I am.

There are basically two ways in which this transition or path to transcendence might be understood. The first is an appreciation of the plasticity of the self—an understanding of its ephemeralness. That is, if I begin to understand myself as a changing collection of personae, an interior that has developed in various significant relationships, I may begin to experience my inner self as more than, greater than, or emergent from this collection.

Wilber (1995) understands the sense of self in terms of a development position that bridges the personal and transpersonal realms. Here, the self is conceived as a collection of personae by a transcendent Self who is doing the conceiving, much like Jung's supra-personal archetypal Self. In this state, there is freedom of identity—for instance, I become freed or liberated from a fixed concept of who I am. But there is potentially a lack of individual responsibility or accountability if integration has not accompanied the development of a multiplicity of subjectivities.

It is possible that the recognition of multiplicity and plasticity in the self produces a sense of mastery (rather than distress) among people who cope well with the complex, competing, often paradoxical demands of contemporary society. At the outside edge of this development, there is a sense of expediency, bordering on sociopathy, or the possibility of being overwhelmed by and immobilized by the loss of unity. On the inside edge is the potential to produce the experience of Pure Witness, as Wilber (1995: 227) describes the most encompassing, objective transcendent function. Sustained experiences of pure witnessing inevitably lead to the knowledge of the fluid and impermanent nature of the individual subject. Among those who are capable of conscious accountability on the road to a transcendent stage of ego development, we may find those who are both self-aware and dis-integrated.

Young-Eisendrath (1997) argues that analysis can assist: successful, long-term psychotherapy or psychoanalysis involves a developmental movement from the breakdown of ego defenses to the acknowledgment of a 'number of subpersonalities or states of non-ego or not-I that have been disturbing and/or blocking coherence, continuity, agency, and affective patterns in a way that has been destructive or overwhelming' (p. 164). She points out that many adults in our society, perhaps most, resist taking responsibility for these subpersonalities. She defines wholeness as the capacity to reflect metaphorically on the whole personality within a dialogical space. She conceives of the archetype of Self as the predisposition towards unity within the context of multiplicity or diversity in inner and outer life. Again, we have the construction of the self both as white light (stance, predisposition) and as spectrum (diversity, multiplicity).

A second way in which this recognition of multiplicity may serve as a path is in the examination of the self in relationship. The feminist theologians like Ruether and Heywood, and peace activists like Macy along with some Jungian theorists (Welwood 1992) have argued that relationship, particularly intimate relationship, can serve as a crucible for transcendence. This path requires the observation and acknowledgment of the Self in the Other. Kegan (1994) also speaks about the exploration of the self in the service of diversity. If I can experience within me both the oppressor and the oppressed, the angry and the hurt, the rational and the irrational, and so on, I begin to see all the Others in Myself. This perception may move me beyond the illusions of separation and duality to an experience of the Absolute, of connection to others, even eventually to all living beings (Young-Eisendrath 1997).

The feeling of connection is sometimes referred to as transpersonal experience: while remaining oneself, one feels 'inside' the other, lives in and inhabits the other through empathy or a wiser vision of life (Levin 1993). Welwood (1992) compares the practice of mindful relationship to the practice of meditation. 'Just as meditation practice helps us wake up from the war between good and bad, pleasure and pain, self and other *inside* ourselves, relationships can help us see how we enact these same struggles outside ourselves' (p. 307).

Exploration of our internal multiplicity is likely to assist us in being more tolerant and accepting in relationships. If we explore the fluid, changing nature of the self, we will also come to understand how 'our self-identity is, from the very beginning, intertwined with the identity of others' (Levin 1993: 34). Or, as Young-Eisendrath (1997) notes, 'Developing the capacity for complex self-reflection in a clear dialogical space will open the door to empathy and compassion for others and oneself, and finally to the experience of interdependence' (p. 164).

Hermeneutics (the theory of how we interpret and understand) involves a movement back and forth between attending to the object of inquiry—the text, the other, the event—and analyzing its meaning. The hermeneutic inquirer is the subject of change. 'We "dialogue" with the phenomenon to be understood, asking what it means to those who create it, and attempt to integrate that with its meaning to us. . . . Hermeneutics is an exploration that assumes a deep connection to the whole of our culture and tradition' (Bentz and Shapiro, 1998: 111).

One of the clear assumptions of the dialogic/hermeneutic view is that human beings are constantly attempting to make sense of what they are doing and becoming; they care about leading a decent or authentic life. Human life takes place within a space of questions about what is worthwhile, and these questions are answered in the interplay between 'present and past, interpreters and events, readers and texts, one person and another' (Richardson et al. 1998: 507). As our attention flows from present to past, from event to interpreter, from self to other, dialogical understanding grows through openness and application.

Hermeneutic interpretation requires engagement with the world. Contemplation is not sufficient. One must engage, reflect upon, and interpret actions or events in terms of their meanings for one's own development and the development of others. Transpersonal knowing is hermeneutic and, according to Ferrer (1998), transpersonal knowledge is enactive, participatory, and transformative. It is not an experience; it is a participatory event. It is not a movie; it is a party. And so, to revisit the opening poem I used at the outset of this paper with an increased understanding of the role of reflection and action, after so much thinking about the matter, it may be time to 'just shut up and deal.'

ACKNOWLEDGMENT

I wish to acknowledge the work of Bruce La Rue and Lael Montgomery, both graduates of the Fielding Institute, for their help in writing the first draft of this chapter.

REFERENCES

Anderson, W. A. (1997) *The Future of the Self: Inventing the Postmodern Person*, New York: Jeremy P. Tarcher/Putnam.

Bakhtin, M. M. (1981) *The Dialogic Imagination: Four Essays*, ed. M. Holquist, trans. Caryl Emerson and Michael Holquist, Austin, TX: University of Texas Press.

Bateson, G. (1987) *Steps to an Ecology of Mind*, Northvale, NJ: Aronson.

Bateson, M. C. (1989) *Composing a Life*, New York: Atlantic Monthly Press.

Bentz, V. M., and Shapiro, J. J. (1998) *Mindful Inquiry in Social Research*, Thousand Oaks, CA: Sage.

Berne, E. (1964) *Transactional Analysis in Psychotherapy*, New York: Grove Press.

Braun, J. (1993) 'Some cultural sources of ego development,' in J. Braun (ed.), *Psychological Aspects of Modernity*, Westport, CT: Praeger, 143–47.

Breunlin, D., Schwartz, R. C., and Mackune-Karrer, B. (1992) *Metaframeworks*, San Francisco: Jossey-Bass.

Cook-Greuter, S. (1994) 'Rare forms of self-understanding in mature adults,' in M. Miller and S. R. Cook-Greuter (eds), *Transcendence and Mature Thought in Adulthood: The Further Reaches of Adult Development*, Lanham, MD: Rowan & Littlefield, 119–46.

Derrida, J. (1982) *Margins of Philosophy*, trans. Alan Bass, Chicago: University of Chicago Press.

Engler, J. (1986) 'Therapeutic aims in psychotherapy and meditation: developmental stages in the representation of self,' in K. Wilber, J. Engler and D. Brown (eds), *Transformations of Consciousness*, Boston: Shambala, 17–51.

Erikson, E. H. (1982) *The Life Cycle Completed: Review*, New York: Norton.

Ferrer, J. (1998) 'Revisioning the relationship between transpersonal psychology and the perennial philosophy,' Panel on multiculturalism and transpersonal psychology. Palo Alto, CA.: Institute of Transpersonal Psychology.

Foucault, M. (1980) *Power/Knowledge: Selected Interviews and Other Writings 1972–1977*, ed. C. Gordon, New York: Pantheon.

Foucault, M. (1982) 'On the genealogy of ethics: an overview of work in progress,' in H. Dreyfus and P. Rabinow (eds), *Michel Foucault: Beyond Structuralism and Hermeneutics*, Chicago: University of Chicago Press, 229–52.

Freud, S. (1920) *Beyond the Pleasure Principle*, standard edn, vol. 18, London: Hogarth Press, 1–65.

Freud, S. (1923) *The Ego and the Id*, standard edn, vol. 19, London: Hogarth Press, 1–60.

Funk, J. (1993) 'Unanimity and disagreement among transpersonal psychologists,' in M. E. Miller and S. R. Cook-Greuter (eds), *Transcendence and mature Thought in Adulthood: The Further Reaches of Adult Development*, Lanham, MD: Rowman & Littlefield, 3–36.

Gergen, K. (1991) *The Saturatued Self: Dilemmas of Identity in Contemporary Life*, New York: Basic Books.

Gergen, K. (1994) *Realities and Relationships: Soundings in Social Construction*, Cambridge, MA: Harvard University Press.

Giddens, A. (1991) *Modernity and Self-Identity*, Stanford, CA: Stanford University Press.

Grof, S. (1988) *The Adventure of Self-Discovery: Dimensions of Consciousness and New Perspectives in Psychotherapy and Inner Exploration*, Albany, NY: State University of New York Press.

Harré, R. (1989) 'The self as a theoretical concept,' in M. Krausz (ed.), *Relativism: Interpretation and Confrontation*, Notre Dame, IN: University of Notre Dame Press.

Harter, S., and Monsour, A. (1992) 'Developmental analysis of conflict caused by opposing attributes of the adolescent self-portrait,' *Developmental Psychology*, 28: 251–60.

Heron, J. (1997) 'A way out for Wilberians,' http://zeus.sirt,pisa.it/icci/WilbErrs.htm.

James, W. (1890/1963) *Principles of psychology*, New York: Fawcett.

Jung, C. G. (1968) *The Archetypes and the Collective Unconscious*, in *Collected Works*, vol. 9, pt. 1 (Bollingen Series vol. 20), Princeton, NJ: Princeton University Press.

Kegan, R. (1982) *The Evolving Self*, Cambridge, MA: Harvard University Press.

Kegan, R. (1994) *In Over Our Heads*, Cambridge, MA: Harvard University Press.

Levin, D. M. (1993) 'Transpersonal phenomenology,' in J. Braun (ed.), *Psychological Aspects of Modernity*, Westport, CT: Praeger, 17–44.

Lifton, R. J. (1993) *The Protean Self: Human Resilience in an Age of Fragmentation*, New York: Basic Books.

Lucariello, J. (1995) 'Mind, culture, person: elements in a cultural psychology,' *Human Development*, 38: 2–18.

Maddi, S. (1993) 'The continuing relevance of personality theory,' in K. H. Craik, R. Hogans, and R. N. Wolfe (eds), *Fifty Years of Personality Psychology*, New York: Plenum, 85–100.

Markus, H., and Cross, S. (1990) 'The interpersonal self,' in L. A. Pervin (ed.), *Handbook of Personality Theory and Research*, New York: Guilford Press, 576–602.

Markus, H., and Nurius, P. (1986) 'Possible selves', *American Psychologist*, 41: 954–69.

Markus, H., and Wurf, E. (1987) 'The dynamic self-concept: a social psychological perspective,' in M. Rosenzweig and L. N. Porter (eds), *Annual Review of Psychology*, 38: 229–337.

Mischel, W. (1969) 'Continuity and change in personality,' *American Psychologist*, 24: 1012–18.

Montgomery, L. (1996) *Tracking the Inner Tribe: Selves Evoked in Relational Worlds Across Time*, doctoral dissertation, Santa Barbara, CA: Fielding Institute.

Nietzsche, F. (1967) *On the Genealogy of Moral and Ecce Homo*, trans. Walter Kaufmann, New York: Vintage Press.

Nietzsche, F. (1968) *Will to Power*, trans. Walter Kaufmann, New York: Vintage Press.

Oyama, S. (1993) 'How shall I name thee? The construction of natural selves,' Special Issue: 'The Future of Developmental Theory,' *Theory and Psychology*, 3: 471–96.

Richardson, F. C., Rogers, A., and McCarroll, J. (1998) 'Toward a Dialogical Self,' *American Behavioral Scientist*, 41: 496–515.

Rowan, J. (1990) *Subpersonalities*, New York: Routledge.

Rutherford, J. (1990) 'Identity and the cultural politics of difference,' in Jonathan Rutherford (ed.), *Identity: Community, Culture, Difference*, London: Lawrence and Wishart.

Stevens-Long, J. (1979) *Adult Life: Developmental Processes*, Palo Alto, CA: Mayfield.

Stevens-Long, J. (1984) *Adult Life: Developmental Processes* (2nd edn), Palo Alto, CA: Mayfield.

Stevens-Long, J. (1988) *Adult Life: Developmental Processes* (3rd edn), Palo Alto, CA: Mayfield.

Stevens-Long, J. (1991) 'Theories of adult development', in R. Nemiroff and C. Colorusso (eds), *New Dimensions in Adult Development*, New York: Basic Books.

Sullivan, H. S. (1953) *The Interpersonal Theory of Psychiatry*, New York: Norton.

Tarnas, R. (1991) *The Passion of the Western Mind*, New York: Harmony Books.

Vasudev, J. (1994) 'Justice, and the unity of life: postconventional morality from an Indian perspective,' in M. E. Miller and S. R. Cook-Greuter (eds), *Transcendence and Mature Thought in Adulthood: The Further Reaches of Adult Development*, Lanham, MD: Rowman & Littlefield.

Walsh, R., and Vaughan, F. (1993) *Paths Beyond Ego: The Transpersonal Vision*, Los Angeles: Tarcher.

Watkins, M. (1986) *Invisible Guests: The Development of Imaginal Dialogues*, Hillsdale, NJ: Analytic Press.

Watkins, M., and Johnson, R. J. (1982) *We, the Divided Self*, New York: Irvington.

Welwood, J. (1992) 'Intimate relationship as a practice and a path,' in J. Welwood (ed.), *Ordinary Magic: Everyday Life as a Spiritual Path*, Boston: Shambala, 289–308.

White, D. R., and Hellerich, G. (1998) *Labyrinths of the Mind: The Self in the Postmodern Age*, Albany, NY: State University of New York Press.

Wilber, K. (1995) *Sex, Ecology and Spirituality*, Boston: Shambala.

Young-Eisendrath, P. (1997) 'The self in analysis,' *Journal of Analytical Psychology*, 42: 157–66.

Chapter 13

Wholeness and transcendence in the practice of pastoral psychotherapy from a Judeo-Christian perspective

Terrill L. Gibson

> The practice of depth psychology with a religious sensibility belongs within the contemplative tradition, because it represents an active attempt to experience and understand the ways of the divine as they operate within the human psyche.
>
> (Corbett 1996: 220)

This chapter takes a radical stance. It declares that pastoral psychology is neither one of the helping professions, nor a health behavioral science. Pastoral psychotherapy is what its name implies—a pastoral engagement with the psyche (see Clebsch and Jaekle 1964; McNeill 1951). It is a psycho-spiritual praxis on ancient themes, a mystical art, a contemplative craft. It seeks a voicing of the transcendent in an immanental context, a context that can be felt in our physical bodies and be experienced in our phenomenal world. By extension, I would also advocate that all psychotherapy, regardless of originating theory, is a contemplative, sacramental craft. Contemplative defines here both the attitude and the method by which the sacred–transcendent is constellated within the secular–immanent. Con-templation is fundamental to psychotherapy, a required attitude of mind for both patient and therapist.

> I am sitting on a church bench at a familiar suburban bus stop. It is midday on a sunny day. A funeral procession from church, kind of like Mardi Gras, comes by. It is for a dearly beloved older parishioner. The crowd is celebrative of this man's life. The priest sees me and comes over. He gives me a nativity set in a wrinkled paper bag and tells me that the dead man had been its guardian and now that is my job.
> (Patient dream)

Psychotherapy moves us into the sun. It takes us (sometimes it drives us) from the dark closets of avoidance, agony, and abuse. Psychotherapy takes us from painful spirit-death to soulful nativity. Like the best of the Mardi

Gras spirit, psychotherapy gives death a melody of dignity and passion, bringing loss into the streets where it can cook up a community gumbo of rebirth and transformation.

In the achingly beautiful culmination scene of the Kurasowa film *Dreams*, an old woman dies and the whole village turns out and dances, plays tubas, and revels in her honor. The old man teacher tells a quizzical young man visitor that hers

> is a nice, happy funeral. It's good to work hard, and live long, and then be thanked. We have no temple or priest here. So all the villagers carry the dead to the cemetery on the hill. We don't like it when a young adult or children dies. It's hard to celebrate such a loss. But, fortunately, the people at this village lead a natural way of life. So they pass on at a ripe old age. Some say life is hard. That's just talk. In fact, it's good to be alive. It's exciting.

This dream-man speaks of the individuated, sacramental whole implied in the woman's dream above. It is this individuated, sacramental whole that pastoral psychotherapy seeks for all its patients.

Pastoral therapy invokes the guardians. We function like the Japanese peasants who wrenched up the mighty cedar guardian-gates at the 1998 Nagano Winter Olympics, all the while chanting ancient melodies of spirit protection and invocation. We build and maintain sacred enclosures for those in our care. Many shamanic traditions talk of practitioner soul journeys and retrievals, taken on behalf of frightened wounded clients. The shamans actually enter other worlds to beseech or do battle with numinous forces on behalf of the healing needs of those for whom they care. Sometimes shamans even go beyond beseeching to bribe, barter, or battle for the curing condiments required (Eliade 1972; Sandner and Wong 1997: 63–9).

Psychotherapists are soul journeyers. We traffic across frontier tollgates between physical and spiritual worlds, between inner world and outer worlds, between earth medicine and sky medicine. Though I resent the cheapened 'New Age' sloppiness which too often defiles the sacred in our consumerist culture, I deeply respect these genuine realities of transcendent meaning embedded in everyday life.

The secular varnishings of recent decades have created an amnesia for the sacred contexts of the profession. I hope to awaken a provocative debate about the transcendent contexts of therapy, in which the transcendent is defined as the perceived wholly Other whose incorporated encounter in our lives brings a sense of grounded meaning and destiny to our existence. These assertions emerge out of my 25-year practice as a pastoral psychotherapist, marriage and family therapist, supervisor, and Jungian analyst working in community-based, non-profit, pastoral counseling centers. In this chapter, I will outline and ground the above assertions through four frameworks. Each assumes and evokes a transcendence-and-wholeness model of psycho-spirituality applicable to all arenas of psychotherapeutic practice: (1) that pastoral psychotherapy is a confessional sacrament; (2) that pastoral psychotherapy seeks, at its core, a transformative immanental encounter with the animate, non-dualist, transcendent Other; (3) that depth pastoral psychotherapy is a contemplative, feminist depth-therapy; and (4) that pastoral psychotherapy is a mystical, playful, heretical craft.

DEPTH PASTORAL PSYCHOTHERAPY AS A CONFESSIONAL SACRAMENT

You cannot preach to a man who does not understand the language. To shout and repeat makes no sense. But you feel as I do that the theologian ought to learn a new language. . . . It is a gigantic task indeed to create a new approach to an old truth. . . . The old way of interpreting has itself to be interpreted.

(Jung, letter to Dominican Victor White, in Lammers 1994: 28)

The revelation of secret . . . was the seed from which early psycho-analytic theory grew.

(Hymer 1988: 2)

We live in a bizarre time. How strange that the conversation with one's attorney is more sacrosanct, more protected, than the conversation with one's psychotherapist, lover, or religious elder. Therapy session records are the prime prize of legal auction houses, attempting to subpoena and exploit precious secrets for unholy gains. Managed care has become synonymous with abusive care because profit-engorged insurance companies insist on exposing the private annotations of therapy sessions for their self-serving financial benefit. The bottom line is the only line in such a world order.

Such crass respect for vulnerable therapeutic secrets violates core professional vows in our healing craft. Pastoral psychotherapy is inherently a confessional craft. It is the most recent expression of the ancient and always living *cura animarum*. All modern psychotherapies were spawned by this merciful guardian tradition at its original shrines in Altamira, Thebes, Delphi, Jerusalem, Chartres, or Stonehenge (see Meier 1968; 1986). All psychotherapies are confessional craft and, therefore, have common cause in defying the growing forces of economically and politically motivated violations of its necessary privacies.

Confessional containers create the elemental protection necessary for the fragile sacrament of new psychic meaning to appear and to work its healing wonders. The great *cura animarum* lies at the heart of the confessional craft. Confession is a dialogic conversation of disclosure and discovery between an empathic, merciful receiver and a candid, courageous enunciator. Darkness is disclosed—all the primal pain, grief, rage, and terror that goes with that abyss inside ourselves.

The most perennial forms of confessional practice in the West were never fundamentally about forgiveness of sin, but were about seeking psycho-spiritual insight and connection to the transpersonal. The therapist is a medium of protected space, a non-anxious witnessing deployed to facilitate insightful encounter with the broader dimensions of the self. Less about 'relief' or 'catharsis' than discovery, confession allows us to fashion a map of our own enduring personal meaning within the vastness of things (see Hymer 1988: 3–4). Confession is about containment, catharsis, and most importantly, renewed creativity—defined here as psychic rejuvenation in the unceasing quest for meaningful existence.

For example, a talented, depressed woman in her fifties came into therapy. She had a persona of outer animation and friendliness that had masked her core despair from all but the most discerning of friends and family. She had been abandoned by her father, stepfathers, and mentoring males (except for a maternal grandfather) in her childhood. Her chronically narcissistic mother often left her emotionally neglected, so unmonitored that my patient, as an early adolescent, addictively provided sexual favors to a wide variety of older males in a public park as a way to achieve some human warmth and contact.

This information came out very cautiously over a protracted period of time—the containment part of the confessional process. This woman's inner psyche knew the grave danger of trusting another with her core being. She had experienced too much savage abandonment to believe otherwise. As she gradually, over several years, began to remember and announce this accumulation of early life traumas, the connective bond of therapy deep-ened significantly. There were numerous dream images of her flying over rivers or journeying through mountains with animal beings, witches, spirits, or me as guide. The dreams often led from the ordinary world of despair to extraordinary worlds of peaceful presence and transformation.

And, most significantly, deep affects began often to accompany the images and recovered memories—this was the catharsis stage of the con-fessional process engaged in the essential operation of connecting narrative to heart, mind to body, spirit to intellect. During this phase, often she would grieve, rage, confront, exhort, or huddle exhaustedly into the therapy couch.

And, finally, she had clearly transpersonal dream images which seemed to release her from her recovered core agony and family-of-origin inheritance of pain. One example will illustrate. In one of her dream journeys between worlds with me as her guide, we arrived at a high and far-off magical place.

We stared at each other in mutual wonder and awe. We kissed. Not a profane, exploitative, sexual kiss, but an otherworldly kiss during which the elemental wind of the cosmos passed between our lips and was exchanged back and forth between our bodies. We were simultaneously connected to every other living being in all creation through that kiss. It was the breath of god. She awoke aglow and vibrating with an embodied spiritual energy and creativity unlike anything she had experienced before. This was the capstone phase of the creative aspect in the confessional cycle.

Genuine confession is not an isolationist activity. It is not a community-hostile dialogue. In fact, true confession should function as part of the core of conscious collective community, not as its periphery. The confessional encounter might be in a monk's cell, in a wilderness retreat, or in a therapist's office, but it happens only under the wary community eye of a tradition-respecting, liturgically enveloped, sacramentally sanctioned process. Community, the community of both the respectful living and the wise dead, is the collective witness of every tear and every dream. A confession outside community is a heartbeat out of the body. Confession heals not only through understanding and greater wisdom, but also through the community sanction of the healing ritual.

If all psychotherapy is confessional craft, then certain problems arise. The overseeing guild organizations, state licensing bodies, and codes of ethics are too thin and frail to provide the kind of consumer and practitioner protection required by deep confessional practice. Does psychotherapy know who its community of accountability really is and where its deep tradition can be located? Certainly, it is not the state or managed-care companies that provide the ethical foundation for such a sacred craft. Beyond the guilds and the conscience of individuals, I believe that we need new kinds of psycho-spiritual accountability and proficiency similar to those ancient academies of Athens, Alexandria, Harran, Cordoba, or Florence. These were not just learning centers, but centers of psycho-spiritual formation where professional character was tempered by continuous dialogue and accountability with fellow journey-persons, the community at large, and the gods themselves. Craft knowledge was seen as ultimately grounded and authored in the transpersonal realms (see Baigent and Leigh 1998).

Confession is at the heart of all modern psychotherapies. Remember, again, psychotherapy, in the West, has roots in the paleolithic cave, ancient synagogue, Greek temple, and Christian basilica. All therapies are increasingly concerned with the ethical issues that emerge about confidentiality and privacy. Bollas and Sundelson's recent volume, *The New Informants* (1996), broadly and elegantly broadcasts this concern. The psychotherapeutic profession is waking up to what we have allowed to happen in the last several decades; where legal adventurism and entrepeneurialism have compromised our profession with their market-place concerns of financial gain and secular power.

Therapy is not designed for a courtroom. This may be hard to explain to an eager client whose own attorney tries to convince her or him of the benefits of opening confessional records to a judicial process. There, a barrister can instantly turn the most benign information into hurtful weapons that wound in unexpected and permanent ways.

In the pastoral psychology center where I work, we refuse to comply with such legal requests, except in relation to any charges that might be made against our own professional conduct. We assert that any records of the therapeutic process are confessional annotations, not healthcare records. They are religious private documents by definition. We believe this is a First Amendment protected act of clinical ministry. If secular psychotherapy were to recover a sense of its basic religious function, it too could claim such protections.

Our psycho-spiritual forebears honed the complex alchemy of the confessional out of a careful, deep listening to what ignites spontaneously between two or more persons when they begin to tell the raw, genuine, jagged truth in a protected space. It is that reverent vessel which permits what the alchemists called the *tertiam non dator*—the third not given—to appear. That other is the psyche, the Self, the *imago Dei*—the transpersonal Other. This Other-Presence cannot emerge, cannot survive, without confessional protection from harsh secular intrusions.

DEPTH PASTORAL PSYCHOTHERAPEUTIC ENCOUNTER WITH THE ANIMATE TRANSPERSONAL

> Jung sees the primary human drives as reflecting the existence of an a priori transcendent reality. Freud, on the contrary, finds any so-called transcendent reality an illusion generated unconsciously from unmet infantile desires. Jung also reverses Freud's evaluations of culture and symbol: Freud sees language, art and religion as 'disguise' for the repressed incestuous instinct, whereas Jung sees these symbolic expressions as generated by a spiritual drive. The spirit is a primary 'instinctive' reality of human existence, Jung says, equal in power to sexuality.
>
> (Lammers 1994: 75–6)

The divine that appears in the flesh of therapeutic relationship is the true voice that emerges from a genuinely constellated depth-of-transference. The therapist stands in for the healing image of the restorative divine until the patient can recognize the true, living divine that has been resident under her or his wounds all the time.

Regardless of our training and origins, we engage in a prayer-full methodology, where prayer is understood as the attentive concern of a compassionate observer. It is a prayer introduced, guided, and deepened by the client's lead. We do not need to guide or problem-solve or lead. We do not need to inject our own symbols or language, but simply to receive and follow the language that the client's experience constellates.

Therapy serves and honors the sufferers, their symptoms, their sexualities, and their spiritualities. A confessional therapeutic *cura* is a perspectival *cura* knowing the symptom as a voice thrown towards the transpersonal, not a reductive defect to be searched out and destroyed or fixed. From a Jungian viewpoint, symptom seeks meaning, the future, the whole. In this way, the sexual is also profoundly spiritual. The spiritual is the eros-bridge to the divine. Our patients unknowingly seek the mature spirituality of connection to something transcendent, though they may seek it only through their symptoms and suffering. It is the transformative encounter that drives people into therapy and that drives the therapeutic process itself.

Depth therapy cannot promise a cure, happiness, peace, or normalcy. It can only reasonably hold out the possibility of an enhanced sense of meaning about one's life narrative. And this narrative, when it is respectfully received, protected, and honored by a therapist, can suggest something of the transcendent contours of a patient's existence, because the language and symbols of the process begin to cut into deeper dimensions of one's psycho-spiritual core. As a patient begins to relax and feel safer, their very language and syntax change. The deeper layers of her or his life begin to be expressed in aesthetic, compacted, and archaic images in dreams and other metaphors. In a carefully attended therapy process, there are recognizable laments, psalms, parables, and chants, as old categories of good and evil, right and wrong, sin and guilt take on relevance (see Menninger 1973). So much liturgical aliveness seems to me to address the animate Other to whom it is ultimately spoken and from whom reply is expected.

DEPTH PASTORAL PSYCHOTHERAPY AS A CONTEMPLATIVE THERAPY

Shekinah is the catalyst of our passion,
Our inner spiritfire, our knowledge of self-worth,
Our call to authenticity.
She warms our hearts, ignites our vision.
She is the great turning round,
Breathing and pulsating, pushing life toward Illumination.
Womb and Grave, End and Beginning.
All these are her names.

(Gottlieb 1995: 28)

For millennia the *cura animarum* tradition has been characterized by a contemplative quest for the transcendent (see Bergsten 1950; Fiorenza 1988; Jung 1970a; Jung 1970b; McNeill 1951; Schaer 1950; and Woods 1981). Pastoral psychotherapy is a contemporary clinical version of that quest. A familiar core image in this tradition is what Judeo-Christian contemplative practice has called the Shekinah (a figure primarily from Jewish mysticism) or Sophia (a figure from Christian and hermetic mysticisms).

In Luc Bresson's hilariously unsettling film *The Fifth Element*, a blue diva arrives at a twenty-first-century spa, Planet Fhloston, to be the opera-house headliner, the evening's entertainment for holidayers who have been beamed up from the paradise planet's cyber-beaches. The diva is both exquisitely beautiful and grotesque. Her delicate, aqua-blue hands ripple sensuously to a soprano voice borrowed from the gods. Her face is full of compassion and mercy like the celestial music she sings. An earth-blue planet floats in crystalline serenity in the enormous windows behind her. Bulbous-blue tubes flow out of the elongated back of her head. Her lips are vampire-red. The diva's music touches her audience. She is the life, eros, spirit that survives all the tortuous paradoxes and maddening contra-dictions that living on this planet evokes. This figure both promises redemption and becomes that redemption. In the middle of America's Friday night movie, she expresses our urgent desire for something that transcends our cultural psyche. The personal self and the transpersonal Other are what the blue diva sings about in cinematic opera house.

The old masculine icons and realities of the divine no longer work. They have run out of steam. Once mighty forces of a vigorous new age of consciousness and productivity, they have dissipated into an often abusive caricature of their former selves. The old god of the primal mountain has become a bitter, abusive old man in a postmodern secular world.

In image after image from the contemporary arts, the transcendent–divine adopts a feminine visage. Shekinah–Sophia is our new voice of wisdom (see Gottlieb 1995). Apparently, her ministrations can fuse the broken shards of this late-patriarchal culture into some new wholeness. For example, in the spirit-gouging confrontations of the bleak Scottish film *Breaking the Waves*, Sophia is an innocent young woman of simple devotion, abused by her family, her village, and her oil-rigger husband. Her husband suffers a severely disabling accident on his North Sea drilling tower, and she agrees to go out into the streets as a whore to provide him vicarious sexual experience.

Watching the film, we are confused as to whether this young woman is mentally retarded, terribly naive, or profoundly loving. How best can we understand her horrible sacrifices and John-induced beatings, her shunning family, and her cynically uninterested community? How best can we comprehend the meaning of this Sophia figure beaten to death in the hold of a dirty freighter, abandoned by all, and seemingly left bereft of any transcendent meaning for her sacrifices.

The mystically literate viewer recognizes this character as that divine aspect of being which has fallen into the abusive hands of our cynical commercial culture. In that dirty freighter she is willing to endure death if she can gather the shards of divine light into some whole fabric of love and compassion for human needs and loss. This contemporary feminine character of Sophia–Shekinah gathers the fragile fragments of the transcendent and guides them into a slow ascent back to their still possible reunion with the divine. Even in the gloom of a hostile millennial world, she will not surrender her compassionate grip upon our hearts. Skillfully but humbly, pastoral psychotherapy replicates or mirrors that process of salvific descent and ascent in search of a transcendent perspective that allows us to endure our commercialized earthly existence. Sophia loves unconditionally despite, not because of, the degradation of patriarchy gone awry.

DEPTH PASTORAL PSYCHOTHERAPY AS A GNOSTIC BODY-MYSTICISM

And for the hermeticist, as opposed to the dualist, 'gnosis' entailed direct apprehension of, and integration with, the all-inclusive harmony.
(Baigent and Leigh 1998: 27)

There is a Yu'pik (Alaskan First People) creation tale. The primal wo/man wakes up startled. The celestial heavens are falling down upon her. They fall and fall until they are hovering just above where she lies. In her fright, she starts to sit up and pierces these heavens and finds herself in another world, where the vaults of the heavens are high as they should be. But soon they, too, begin to fall and sit just barely above her head.

Startled even more, she sits up further and finds herself in a third world, where the heavens are held in their rightful place. Then they, too, begin to collapse upon her. She pierces them into yet another world, where she espies the first ceremonial lodge. She enters it and finds ceremonial gear laid out for her. She takes these sacred animal rattles, masks, and dancing regalia as an inner voice tells her their use. She lies back down, and descends to the first world, where she creates a replica lodge and enacts the first ceremonies in the bottom world. The skies have stayed in place to this day. (My very free paraphrase of Seattle Art Museum Yu'pik installation, 1998.)

People come for pastoral psychotherapy in a panicked state; their skies are falling. They need help in sitting up, in piercing the claustrophobic thoughts and images that besiege them. They need encouragement to reach the fourth heaven and to seize the ritual tools and chants of healing that almost inevitably await them there.

The Yu'piks were indigenous gnostics. Their lore is full of parallel stories of falling and rising worlds, descending and ascending spirits. The universal pattern of these tales intimates that we are all mystical accompanists on esoteric journeys which may begin in the exoteric world but soon cross over into the divine.

The ancient and unfairly maligned mystical/gnostic systems of the West are some of our best technological predecessors for pastoral care. The gnosticism referred to here is the non-dualist hermetic traditions that reach back to ancient Egypt, run through Islamic culture, to medieval centers such as Languedoc in Provence and to the High-Renaissance Florence Academy, and lastly emerge in aspects of contemporary Jungian thought. The essence of these traditions is to live by the knowledge of one's deepest experiences—the flowering of the *cura animarum* craft (see Baigent and Leigh 1998).

Gnosticism is more a way of life than an institution, which is both its curse and its blessing. It is a curse because, without organizational support and defense, followers of gnosticism have frequently been misunderstood and persecuted for their beliefs. It is a blessing because, freed from a particular social structure, or cultural identity, gnosticism has repeatedly escaped the clutches of society's political and material erosion of Big Ideas.

My brief interpretation of the movie *Breaking the Waves*, above, sketched a contemporary gnostic story. Boil away gnosticism's complexity and you get a relatively simple narrative: The Creator has lost contact with our corner of creation, a fallen parcel of the cosmos full of a dark materiality that threatens to squeeze out the light and parch our souls forever. There then appears a feminine companion of the divine who wanders to the edge of her perfect heaven to look down on imperfect creation until she is moved to compassionate tears by the misery and pain she sees. She falls toward us, seeing that there is still light in our world, especially the spark in our beings. Her cosmic compassion has her tumble head over heels into our agonizing abyss. The faster and deeper she falls, the more she is moved by our plight and committed to do whatever it takes to find us, and lead us back to our real, divine selves. She falls, in many tales, into our worst environments— often into brothels, where she is a prostitute—and serves to transform our pains and miseries from this hidden place.

She attempts to redeem all that is devastated on this plane and to make real the ancient hermetic truths: as above, so below she wants to show us the *Unus Mundus* (see Jung 1970a)—one world of transcendent divinity where personal and transpersonal, sacred and profane, are irrelevant distinctions (for another similar account see Hoeller 1989).

After every great historical whirlwind, this gnostic seed survives and blossoms anew. My patients' lives are filled with such gnostic realizations.

A middle-aged stockbroker comes into therapy 'because I am so depressed over the conflicts with my colleagues at work and my wife at home, and I keep hearing this voice. She talks to me going up the same hill on the interstate every night on my way home. She says "look inside and to the east—I will listen, I will be there." Do you think I am crazy?' I know Sophia when I hear her, and so did this patient. He and I set to work tuning in to her frequency as deeply as we both could manage. Listening and attuning to dreams, bodily signs and symptoms, and passing moods allowed us to invite this voice into the conscious sphere of my patient's awareness.

The alchemists (mystical practitioners of a chemical gnosticism) talk of a process called 'decoction,' in which raw, often foul, elements are 'boiled' in order to leech out the special flavor or unique 'active element' of the material soul (Fabricius 1994: 104). I find this to be an apt image of the process of pastoral psychotherapy. The therapist provides a space and stokes up a heat to sweat out the psyche's unique gnostic flavor and destiny. The often acrid and subtle horrors of spiritual suffering can produce an ultimately sweet and abiding flavor of soul. Pastoral psychotherapy, at its best, is a full encounter of the immanental moment with transcendent beings.

REFERENCES

Baigent, M., and Leigh, R. (1998) *The Elixir and the Stone*, New York: Penguin.
Bergsten, G. (1950) *Pastoral Psychology: A Study in the Care of Souls*, London: George Allen and Unwin.
Bollas, C., and Sundelson, D. (1996) *The New Informants*, New York: Jason Aronson.
Clebsch, W., and Jaekle, C. (1964) *Pastoral Care in Historical Perspective*, Louisville: John Knox.
Corbett, L. (1996) *The Religious Functions of the Psyche*, London: Routledge.
Eliade, M. (1972) *Shamanism*, Princeton, NJ: Princeton University Press.
Fabricius, J. (1994) *Alchemy*, London: Diamond.
Fiorenza, E. (1988) *In Memory of Her*, New York: Crossroads.
Fox, M. (1994) *The Reinvention of Work*, San Francisco: Harper San Francisco.
Gottlieb, L. (1995) *She Who Dwells Within*, San Francisco: Harper San Francisco.
Hoeller, S. (1982) *The Gnostic Jung and the Seven Sermons to the Dead*, London: Quest Books.
Hoeller, S. (1989) *Jung and the Lost Gospels*, London: Quest Books.
Hymer, S. (1988) *Confessions in Psychotherapy*, New York: Gardner Press.
Jung, C. G. (1970a) 'Psychoanalysis and the Cure of Souls,' in *Psychology and Religion West and East*, New York: Pantheon Press.
Jung, C. G. (1970b) 'Psychotherapists or the Clergy,' in *Psychology and Religion West and East*, New York: Pantheon Press.

Lammers, A. C. (1994) *In God's Shadow*, New York: Paulist Press.

McNeill, J. T. (1951) *A History of the Cure of Souls*, New York: Harper Torchbooks.

Menninger, K. (1973) *Whatever Became of Sin*, New York: Hawthorn.

Meier, C. A. (1968) *Ancient Incubation and Modern Psychotherapy*, Evanston, IL: Northwestern University Press.

Meier, C. A. (1986) 'The dream in ancient Greece and its use in temple cures (incubation),' in *Soul and Body*, Santa Monica: Lapis Press, 190–209.

Miller, A. (1996) *The Drama of the Gifted Child*, New York: Basic Books.

Noll, R. (1997) *The Aryan Christ*, New York: Random House.

Otto, W. (1965) *Dionysos: Myth and Cult*, Bloomington: Indiana University Press.

Sandner, D. F., and Wong, S. H. (eds) (1997) *The Sacred Heritage*, London: Routledge.

Schaer, H. (1950) *Religion and the Cure of Souls in Jung's Psychology*, New York: Pantheon Books.

Segal, R. A., Singer, J., and Stein, M. (1995) *The Allure of Gnosticism*, Wilamette, IL: Open Court Press.

Seattle Art Museum (Spring 1998) *Installation: Agayuliyararput: The Living Tradition of Yup'ik Masks*.

Woods, R. (1981) *Mysterion*, Chicago: Thomas Moore Press.

Chapter 14

Green spirituality

Horizontal transcendence

Michael C. Kalton

> To have an environmental education is to live alone in a world of wounds.
>
> (Aldo Leopold)

> The homing instinct of the heart is the path within every path.
>
> (David Steindl-Rast)

Eyes accustomed to seeing the systemic interdependence of all forms of life observe the manicured green lawns of suburbia, or the endless acres of uniform crops on industrial farms, with a feeling of disquiet. Where others see enrichment, they see impoverishment. When Leopold (1949) wrote the words above, such eyes were rare: he was indeed alone. Now, nearly five decades later, their way of seeing is at the core of a growing national and international movement. Outwardly its missionaries fight on varied fronts, for the salvation not of souls, but of rainforests, of whales, of endangered creatures of every type. The media pick up readily on these outward causes, the more so because they often involve very real and dramatic conflict with the established order.

Less attention, however, has been directed to the inner revolution that for many has accompanied this new way of looking at the world. For the way we see the world is in the end inseparable from the way we see ourselves. Environmental consciousness, a sense of connectedness with and obligation to the life of the earth, has penetrated and found a place within all of the great historical religious traditions. My academic background is in philosophy and comparative religion, with a specialization in the traditions of East Asia. But the broad interdisciplinary program in which I teach has given me ample scope to explore the complex intersection of contemporary social developments with the increasingly borderless domain of world religious traditions. In my courses I frequently encounter students for whom a new sense of the environment inspires a new religious identification as well: it seems that Zen, various forms of neo-paganism, and Native American traditions have a particular appeal to those who sense an insufficient earthiness in the more familiar Christian traditions. But there are also students who embrace emerging forms of green Christianity as well, students who are quick to introduce 'stewardship' and argue that anthropocentric dominion is no fundamental nor genuine part of the Christian heritage.

But environmentalism also provides a central life orientation for many even without the benefit of traditional religious frameworks. When I teach environmental ethics, an entirely new contingent shows up in addition to the regulars, students who would not think of taking a religion course. For the 'hard core' of these green students, the environment itself provides a framework within which they organize their values and map their life paths. They may even welcome the inconveniences of a greener lifestyle, the feeling for self-sacrifice in the name of ultimate values. Courses in environmental science and related subjects show up on the transcripts of these students with the frequency of religion on others—or one might say, in place of religion.

Yet this bio-centric movement is separated by a widening gap from traditional cultural and religious moorings. The common refrain of the movement is the vigorous assertion that 'humans are parts of the system, and no part is better than any other.' This expresses a fundamental awareness that comes with even a rudimentary understanding of ecosystemic interdependence. Its clear intent is to flatly contradict the perceived wrongness of anthropocentrism: we make a fundamental mistake, it says, if we regard ourselves as separate from the natural system of life, or prefer ourselves as uniquely valuable over other 'parts' of the system. Anthropocentrism, long a fundamental assumption of our philosophic and religious heritage, thus now moves to center stage as an issue of urgent practical import.

Questioning and even undermining the assumption that humanity is the pinnacle of some hierarchy demands a profound theoretical shift for Western cultures. But while the reframing of theory adequate to the task lags, for many a fundamental reorientation of values has already taken place. The shift is evident if one considers the contemporary scene in comparison with the attitudes historically (and still, for many) associated with Darwin's theory of evolution. The idea that we might be intrinsically related to 'lower animals' was initially both threatening and demeaning; even to its adherents, evolution seemed more a matter of living by hard scientific truth than a matter for celebration. In contemporary writing, the attack on human distinctness, far from the earlier overtones of a reluctant relinquishing of a prized but unavailable status, often seems to celebrate our status as members of the biosystem as a sort of homecoming. The tradition of human supremacy finds continued expression in certain forms of evolutionary theory that see the emergence of human abilities as some kind of culminating achievement or systemic warrant of a dominant and controlling role. But the unreformed anthropocentric implications of such theories now are highlighted and attacked by a growing constituency that finds itself far more comfortable with Leopold's land ethic that 'changes the role of *Homo sapiens* from conqueror of the land-community to plain member and citizen of it' (Leopold 1949: 201).

Traditional religion undercut mundane greed and acquisitiveness with the observation, 'We have no lasting home here.' Now a trenchant critique of capitalist values is mounted from the seemingly opposite direction: 'The earth is our home, and we must make it last.' In both cases the appeal to 'our true home' has the power to challenge our conduct through the presence of a dimension that might be called 'transcendence.' But if the new sense of home has some sort of functional transcendence, it is nonetheless virtually the antithesis of the supernatural transcendence common to Western religious tradition. Indeed, one of the best windows on the implications of this new sense of home is furnished by an inquiry into its contrast with its opposite in the philosophic and religious traditions of transcendence.

TRANSCENDENCE AND CONTINGENCY: THE PROBLEM

The classical discourse regarding transcendence is inseparable from the problem of time, change, and meaning. Just as Greek culture idealized youth and beauty as the natural accompaniments of nobility and goodness, it also wrestled with the question of impermanence and change. The problem of finding meaning in the world of flux overshadowed the celebration of youth and beauty in Greek art and literature and found a brilliant crystallization in the philosophy of Plato, Aristotle, Neo-Platonism, and the Christian world that succeeded them, leaving their mark indelibly on Western thought.

In the Platonic Dialogues the quest for knowledge moved to the center of human life. The problem of change moved beyond the transience of youth and beauty to encompass the realm of true knowledge, which Plato contrasted with the changing world of opinion and common sense. In his dialogues Socrates (Plato's voice) shows how obvious answers may fit one situation but turn problematic or contradictory when applied to others, and hence are inadequate. The quest for universality versus particularity, or necessity versus contingency, is inherent in this method: the questions cannot end until the world of contingent, flowing time is grounded in a transcendent, unchanging realm of Beauty, Truth, and Goodness.

Aristotle brought the Platonic forms back to earth with his doctrines of substantial forms and teleology. But his identification of real knowledge with the apprehension of necessary causes simply moved the flight from contingency to a new arena. Aristotle's change itself is necessarily a matter of limit and imperfection. The entire universe of contingent motion must be grounded securely in the ultimate Unmoved Mover. Christian thinkers picked up both versions of the Greek problematique by identifying their God with Truth, Beauty, and Goodness, the Eternal and Unchanging Creator of all contingent being.

From this easy synergy of Greek and Christian thought emerged the paired dichotomies fundamental to the history of Western philosophy and theology: finite and infinite, temporal and eternal, contingent and necessary poles of existence for both thought and spirituality. Within this conceptual scheme 'transcendence' described both a metaphysical structure grounding the contingent in the Absolute, and a practical spiritual quest of rising above changing worldly affairs to ultimate union with the Eternal. Within this perspective, the finite, temporal, and contingent cannot stand alone without meaninglessness and absurdity, for the basic Platonic questions would then have no answer, and our existence no direction or purpose.

Naturally, this approach to transcendence and contingency is clearly historical and the product of a particular sort of culture and worldview. But minds nurtured in this tradition find it an almost irresistible way of understanding how meaning becomes Meaning as the deeds of daily life are subsumed under some sort of transcendence. Eliade brilliantly adapted this structure to elucidate the religious meaning of myth and ritual in *The Sacred and the Profane*. In planting his yams or repairing his canoe in the manner the gods originally performed these tasks, the tribesman is able to live in a space of Ultimate Meaning as he goes through motions that otherwise would fall into the realm of mere contingency and only evanescent meaningfulness (Eliade 1957: 87). In a similar vein the diminished role of myth in our secular society has been persuasively explicated by commentators such as Joseph Campbell, as a source of social ills.

For the heirs of this tradition of transcendence, losing one's grip on the Absolute and falling into unredeemed time is the recipe for absurdity, an option explored at some length in both the literature and the philosophy of the twentieth century. In spite of heroic attempts to turn absurdity itself into a spirituality, absurdity has remained trivial and unredeemed. The emerging biocentered life orientation has little patience for self-engrossed musings on absurdity, but it also locates its center of value, meaning, and purpose squarely within the realm of the contingent. Indeed, contingency itself is a central element of its salvific message. The problem is rather the people who cannot recognize and live by the implications of contingency, which environmental advocates perceive as bearing the most important meaning of all.

REEVALUATING CONTINGENCY

Science now offers us an unprecedented perspective on the earth and its history that is taken seriously by many. Human beings, it appears, are rather latecomers in the earth's 3.8 billion year bio-history: over 99.9 per cent of the history of life on this planet has not included us. In the evolution of life, 100 million years is a respectable span for a species; dinosaurs survived about 165 million. Humans and proto-humans have been around, by best estimates, about 3.5 million years, and the entire history of our civilized way of life—urban living supported by agriculture—is no more than ten thousand years old. And so the human species belongs to only the last one-tenth of one per cent of the history of life, and 99.7 per cent of human history has preceded the rise of civilization.

In evolutionary time human civilization has more the status of a brief experiment than an established fact. Studies of the overall evolutionary record of species do little to reassure us that the experiment will be successful. Estimates vary considerably, but there is a wide consensus that of the many millions of species that have arisen, fewer than one per cent still exist. And long-term survivors seem to be simple life forms such as blue-green algae, rather than complex organisms such as dinosaurs or humans. The message is clear: we have not always been here, need not be here, and almost certainly will not be here to witness the final solar conflagration.

What we make of such information depends on how we think of evolution, the theoretical framework to which the information belongs. Below I examine interpretations of evolution that remain anthropocentric, leaving traditional transcendence theories essentially intact. In the popular mind evolution is often considered a progressive process crowned with the emergence of humans, but science is more wary of importing purposeful direction into the picture. Contemporary genetics and theoretical understanding of self-organizing complex systems yield a much richer picture of the way a selective system becomes increasingly complex. A development in such a system remains radically historical and contingent on circumstances grounded on earlier circumstances. The only guarantee is change, with systemic collapse and redirection an ever possible feature. On the tree of life, we as a species are more a probing twig than an established branch, and civilization, let alone industrialization, is a radical experiment that depends on conditions civilization itself may systemically undermine.

Radical environmentalists favor this non-teleological scientific interpretation for very practical reasons. The feasibility of the experiment remains an open question. This can be salvific knowledge: if we can see that we are embarked on a mighty experiment, then we might scrutinize with a more observant and questioning mind just how the experiment seems to be working and what we might do about it.

This view takes as salvific knowledge the very kind of irredeemable contingency identified with meaninglessness and absurdity within conventional transcendent frameworks: until we grasp our radical contingency, we have small chance of really understanding the nature of what is at stake. Here we are at a profound parting of the ways. Classical transcendental frameworks seek reality and meaning by a transcendental grounding of the historical and contingent, and write humans into the very fabric of existence. The radical environmental perspective, on the other hand, claims that the conventional approaches make it impossible to confront the true nature of our situation and that they imprison us in destructive anthropocentrism as the price of a meaningful existence. The historical contingency of random self-organizing evolutionary systems brings us home into our biosystem, but that homecoming seems in the traditional perspective to undercut the very meaning of our existence. How are we to understand this alternative framework within which undirected historical process and profound meaning are compatible?

As a first step of this exploration, it will be useful to examine more closely the anthropocentric turn involved in the common transcendental grounding of meaning. Understanding this linkage clarifies how to frame an alternative spirituality that avoids an over-confident centrality of our species and our projects.

The grounds of the anthropocentric twist in conventional theories of transcendence are evident in the way Darwinian evolution has been made safe for meaning. Liberal Christianity, freed from the constraints of literalistic biblical interpretation, can explain the whole evolutionary process through the creative will and intention of God. Human life is then founded on the self-validating purpose and intention of the creator. But there is also latitude beyond maintaining the creator/creation framework. Teilhard de Chardin moved to a more radical centering on the evolutionary process as such, describing it as a trajectory of increasing complexity leading to the emergence of consciousness and beyond to Christ. This has resonated strongly with New Age orientations, where it easily combines with Hindu sources and becomes the story of the cosmic evolution of consciousness. The infinite, eternal, personal creator by whose will we may live, and cosmic consciousness—the process and ultimate directional reality of one's own mind—are different metaphysical expressions of the familiar transcendence. They succeed equally in furnishing meaning by supplying a non-contingent purpose within all existence, described as the product of divine will or as the inner nature of Being identified as consciousness.

Both succeed in securing for humans a central place in the fabric of existence. Positing mind or consciousness as the ultimate origin entails this anthropocentric consequence. Once this is done, human consciousness, however described, becomes a central feature in a cosmos founded on consciousness. Rationality, ethics, or an enlightened human understanding thus emerges as the highest value. Within this framework, one cannot but imagine that the emergence of our kind of consciousness represents the highest achievement in our world.

A spin-off of this vision has played a critical role in our secular confidence in the ability and suitability of our minds to comprehend and perhaps control the world through science and technology. If mind is somehow at the basis of all things, then it is plausible that human minds are proportioned to grasp and perhaps control the nature of things. It is an ironic historical unfolding that allowed us to become so fascinated with our own rational powers that we could displace the cosmogonic Mind in determining a purposeful ordering of the world.

Here is where Darwinian evolution poses its most radical challenge. That Darwin would relate us to other primates was a shock to the sensibilities of his time, but systemically the blow was relatively superficial. The real problem was that he posed a vision of the evolution of life in which mind or consciousness was neither an original nor a purposeful end achievement. Mind within the framework of natural selection has no inherent claim to superiority, nor can it escape the pragmatic question, 'what is it good for?' Consciousness comes with no cosmic warranty. Nothing in this system supports New Age expectations or the technocratic dreams envisioned by the likes of Buckminster Fuller: there is no reason to think that Spaceship Earth has finally evolved its own pilot. And yet reflective consciousness does pilot myriad earth-transforming projects. Instead of celebrating this as a self-evident peak of evolution, evolutionary theory asks the same question that confronts every emergence of life: does this work in the context of this set of systemic conditions?

Humans remain either explicitly (religion) or tacitly (expectations of science/technology) at the center of any worldview premised on mind or consciousness. A radically non-anthropocentric spirituality does not incline towards such a premise. In the search for bio-centric alternatives there is a revival of Native American and other primal traditions that integrate humans into the community of life. The same may be said of the fertility-based Mother traditions of Gaia, Wicca, various forms of neo-paganism, and East Asian Tao-based traditions. Green spiritualities are in the process of being called into existence, and what might evolve is unclear. Directions for the future merit careful consideration.

GREEN SPIRITUALITIES

An environmentally aware spiritual movement seeks relational wholeness in terms of an inclusive life community that encompasses and extends beyond human society. The devastation caused by humanity in this larger community is a primary motivating force in the development of this movement. The meaning that can guide self-cultivation in this context must both encompass the traditional issue of situating humans within a relational whole, and include the new intuition that recognizes the entire biosystem as vulnerable and hence contingent. What, then, might be the meaning-full story of our relatedness and our contingency?

Our participation in the biosystem of life on earth is a cogent contemporary insight richly figured in primal traditions. Stories that help us find our place in the community of life take on new meaning for urban dwellers at the turn of the millennium. Ritual traditions that allow us to relate to mountains, rivers, and wind, or to the mysterious power of life itself, have a new-found power. My brother the bear, my sister the singing waters, my mother the earth, these are modalities that allow us to express the awe, reverence, joy, and love for the process of life in which we have our own being and from which, along with all other forms, we have emerged. Once this was sufficient as the whole story. Its contemporary retelling includes the poignant awareness that the bear, the singing waters, the fertility of the earth are products of a history that is at risk. Awe, reverence, and love for the shape of that history motivate a fierce desire to preserve, foster, and continue it, giving a new point to the ancient stories. And for some, that may encompass a total life path and direction, much as the values of secular humanism were sufficient to make sense of the lives of the unchurched of an earlier generation.

But for many in contemporary society the terms in which the primal traditions find expression are too inextricably bound with a way of life that has little to do with the daily reality of an urban setting. Ancient civilizations were already at pains to move beyond the immediate natural world and ground the structures of their complex societies in some kind of broad cosmic framework. And for the modern urban world the vocabulary of science has become the shared vehicle of serious knowledge. The web of life depicted in terms of familial relationships in primal traditions is described by contemporary environmentalists in the scientific language of information and systems theory.

We would expect, then, that in addition to drawing on various sorts of primal traditions, a green spirituality might move towards grounding itself in a cosmic framework elaborated in the respected vocabulary of science. Harbingers are already with us. Swimme and Berry's *Universe Story* (1994) consciously strives to weave a spiritually cogent cosmogony in scientific terms. Less deliberately but with similar effect, scientific work on self-organizing systems such as Kaufman's *At Home in the Universe* (1995) depict a cosmic process bound to eventuate in life. Goodenough's *The Sacred Depths of Nature* (1998) explores a religious sense of mystery and awe emerging from scientific theory and insight. Clearly the resacralization of nature is emerging as a trajectory beyond the traditional divide between the worlds of religion and secularity.

The mechanistic reductionism of Newtonian and Cartesian models is being challenged now by a more holistic approach that emphasizes systemic emergence. Given a supernova producing heavy elements plus about ten billion years, we find that carbon reaches a state of complexity where it can give lectures and miss publication deadlines, or perform an intricate dance to signal hive mates where to locate new flowers in bloom, or mutate and change essential metabolic processes quickly enough to survive the latest insecticide onslaught.

In many applications, contemporary systems theory sounds as rationalistic as traditional mechanistic reductionism. But when its holistic character finds full form, it can easily lead to expressions of reverence and even mystery: What kind of amazing, awesome stuff is emerging here? The move from an inanimate mechanistic cosmos to a living cosmos requires no new evidence, only a new way of seeing the evidence already here. The life system that evolved into us can be permitted a full historical contingency, and yet be moored in a wider life process, a religiously enshrined becoming.

The meaning framed above finds its anchor in life rather than mind, thus displacing human consciousness from its privileged place. The movement from earth to cosmos, from biosystem to life, is a form of transcendence that is characteristic of degrees of abstraction, rather than a movement towards some kind of Absolute metaphysical dimension. There is no cosmos posited apart from the historically ongoing one within which we find ourselves, nor is there life apart from ongoing living, at whatever level it is considered. Instead of the typical vertical transcendence of the Greek-inspired tradition, the movement of this kind of spirituality is horizontal, perfecting our relationship with the world of life about us.

In this kind of horizontally framed spirituality the question of belonging acquires a new meaning. Recovering a more sacral sense of the earth and universe is only the beginning. Many of our habitual, ordinary ways of thinking and acting carry the imprint of the assumed discontinuity between us and the rest of the natural world. Belonging is an achievement as well as a statement of fact, and the path to that end involves a reexamination of our basic assumptions.

How are we to conduct ourselves in a manner appropriate to our place and role in the order of things? Our mind-centered habits naturally lead us to imagine that if we belong, then the first order of business is to identify our place, our ideal fit in the life system; then we will know how to act. But this is akin to trying to find how a given part fits into a complex mechanism, and we have scant warrant for expecting that such an understanding of the earth is within our grasp. An approach more in keeping with our concrete and situated reality is to rephrase such questions into a consideration of relationships. We exist always and only enmeshed in the relational reality of surroundings and situation. The question of fitting is really not a matter of how we fit in some ideal scheme but a question of the appropriateness of our response to the situation in which we find ourselves.

We ask how we are to act, as if we were autonomous initiators of deeds. In a situated, relational existence, there is no action which is not in fact a response. This has major consequences. Action sets goals and succeeds or fails; response is ongoing, dealing appropriately with what is at hand and looking to the feedback from an always evolving situation. Our favorite modern language of goal-setting, problem-solving, competence, and control has only limited meaning in the borderless process of a continuously transforming life situation.

Questions regarding human nature are important because they set the immediate stage for spiritual cultivation: what are we dealing with, what is it that we attempt to remedy or complete as we cultivate our humanity? Traditional Western answers have variously emphasized our godlikeness and our sinfulness; 'self-interest' is the most common contemporary evaluation, perhaps reflecting the depth to which economic thought has saturated our sense of self. Certainly the environmental movement is afflicted with an overwhelming feeling of an almost futile battle against the forces of self-interest and greed.

If we are indeed co-evolving situated existences, then inquiries regarding our particular nature inappropriately look for some kind of distinctive, self-contained characteristic. A co-evolutionary understanding of a particular nature would look to the relational process within which the creature emerged. On the genetic level the feedback loop of selective environments and gene pools means that an atmosphere rich in oxygen is patterned into our lungs and the presence of the flora and fauna of the earth is anticipated by the form of our digestive tracts and metabolic systems. Organs of sensation arise in terms of the available vibratory patterns of light, sound, and heat, or the chemical effects we register as taste and smell. And cultural, mental, and social processes continually condition one another and co-evolve. On all levels we are immersed in selective processes which shape and are shaped by what we become, so that our nature may be best described as a node of relations with the world.

The world-life process is ultimately one of dynamic flux and change: the history of extinctions is simply the history of disappointed expectations. Considered in this light, the ability to learn from experience and flexibly adapt to changed circumstances seems a great advantage. Humans are at the forefront of this line of evolutionary development. In particular our communication abilities enable us to amplify learning by sharing and accumulating it at an exponentially accelerating pace. Through this process our ability to anticipate and manipulate have grown to the point where the prime mandate of adaptive fit is less evident than our spectacular ability to adapt the environment to fit our purposes.

This is the cluster of characteristics often cited as distinctive of human beings. But the inclination to congratulate ourselves on our evidently superior status neglects the relational matrix within which every evolved character has its meaning. As we transform earth, air, water, and biotic environs, less rapid adaptive strategies are overwhelmed by unexpected conditions and we are surrounded by cascading extinctions. Concern for the well-being and relative continuity of the life community with which we co-evolved requires no altruism; we understand now that we ultimately interdepend in the web of biotic life so that concern for other creatures operates in synergy with self-concern. This is the spiritual dynamic of systemically grounded horizontal transcendence, where the part and the whole are never two.

We thus return to the troubling phenomena that have given rise to contemporary environmental consciousness and a critical turn from anthropocentrism. Speed, the rate at which we can drive change, is our problem, though not our fault. The growth of civilization on a trajectory of accelerating accumulation of learning may be seen as a dynamic of self-organizing complexity characteristic of the entire biotic process. Far from being stable, evolving life seems to continually probe, push, and eventually overshoot systemic limits (Kaufman 1995: 235–43). One such limit may be a speed limit, and we are the probe testing it.

This gives a larger perspective on the question and allows us to locate the human problem more precisely. In dimensions of geologic time and the changing, ever-probing process of evolving life, this is one more critical moment in a systemic process in which crisis, collapse, and reorganization may well be the deep pattern of patterns. In a sense everything is operating perfectly, and there is nothing wrong with our being as we are, even if that means an ecosystemic crisis. Replacing anthropocentrism with a misanthropic dislike of civilization is surely shortsighted. But from the position of historically and systemically situated humans, there is indeed a problem. We are responsive and responsible, not to geologic time but to our own moment, with success and failure measured in terms of passing on a flourishing life to our kind and to the web of all kinds with which we are interwoven.

Knowing that nothing guarantees, or even favors, the success of our efforts to save a slipping ecosystem easily fuels a burst of desperate activity all too often followed by frustration, bleakness and despair. The history of profound environmental concern, like all idealisms, includes a large measure of despair. Traditional vertical transcendence could offer another dimension as a buffer against the way our ideals and efforts refuse to take lasting shape in the contingent processes of our lives. And as illustrated in the consideration of evolutionary life in geologic time, a similar transcendent buffering is possible in a horizontal mode.

The buffering offered by these two kinds of transcendence—against frustration and despair amidst the vicissitudes of a world of open, contingent process—appear structurally similar. Both move beyond the context of this human life and incorporate it in another dimension which supports the meaning of our efforts, even while absolving them from the onus of worldly success. But there is a great difference in the spiritual process each entails. God, heaven, and afterlife can represent a dimension in which my intentions and activities in this world receive their ultimate and appropriate consequences. Or, in an enlightenment-oriented tradition, a similar effect is achieved by positioning the suffering worldly as less than ultimately real, the product of ignorance from which we may finally awaken. Horizontal transcendence to the vast scope of temporal process, prior and consequent to human or even earth existence, is a different challenge. It does not relate to our goals and projects with either an ultimate affirmation or negation. Rather it connects with the effort itself, as our mode of manifesting and experiencing a dynamic that is coextensive with the process of life.

The inner dynamic of horizontal transcendence is to associate the life process with which we identify with the universe itself. Earth-oriented biocentric works such as James Lovelock's *The Ages of Gaia* (1988) or Gribbin's *The Breathing Planet* (1986) can inspire an intense spirituality of belonging. A parallel might be the experience of God's love and caring providence, or the all-encompassing compassion of the Buddha-nature. The transcendent must be present to daily life. It must also reach beyond, so the living-earth library is complemented by a growing shelf of books with titles such as *Universe Story*, *At Home in the Universe*, *Belonging to the Universe*, and *The Conscious Universe*. Such works adhere to the traditional scientific language of random process rather than the mind-centered language of purpose.

The rough outlines of a spirituality of horizontal transcendence are thus already in place. The story of the emergence of life has been the natural pivot of this revisioning of ourselves, the earth, and the universe. But correlative points beg for further elaboration. One of the most urgent is thinking through the transformation the traditional concept of matter must undergo in this new context. The assumption that matter is lifeless, and yet that from it emerges all the rich and varied phenomena of life and consciousness, has long been a stumbling-block for those who approach the question of evolution framed in a mechanistic universe. The consequence of this implausible combination has been a reductionist science that has insistently explained the vitality of our bodies and minds in terms of chemicals and complex electric functions that presumably themselves have no vitality.

The thrust of a holistic approach moves in the opposite direction. Instead of reducing the higher to the lower, we recognize that we do not really know what an element such as carbon is if we do not take into account its performance at highly complex systemic levels such as plants and animals, as well as its functioning at simple levels such as lamp black. If we can recognize matter as alive when it is at the complex level of metabolic and self-reproductive processes, what are we to think of it at less complex levels? This is the line of thinking that leads towards a living universe, in which all life is understood as a phenomenon just waiting for the right level of complexity to appear.

How then are we to see life in the elemental forces and forms of the universe? The direct attribution of life and consciousness as we experience them in less complex levels of physical reality seems inadequate to the newness of emergent phenomena, while the total denial of some kind of presence that could eventually manifest as life, ignores the demands of continuity. We have already advanced in understanding our connectedness with all life, but much remains to be understood as we expand the sphere of life to include what has been regarded as non-living.

We can expect multiple perspectives as this question is pursued. It already is a magnet for scientific investigation from both the reductionistic and the holistic perspectives. Philosophers might devote more attention to phenomena at the undecidable border between what is now regarded as life and non-living. And spiritual experience will offer another kind of window, for spiritualities premised on unity or continuity invite, beyond intellectual apprehension, direct experience of the reality they frame.

This reexamination of how we regard the 'non-living' aims to open the possibility of a mode of self-identification which transcends the boundary of biotic life. What the poet Robinson Jeffers has referred to as 'the massive mysticism of stone' (1987: 167) surrounds us, inviting us to discover the patterning that lives in geologic time or even cosmic time, substrate to patterns manifest in the rapid complexity of life time. What is it from which we have emerged, and to which we return at death? It cannot be less than us, for we are formed of it, belong to it, manifest it.

CONCLUSION

Contingency plays an urgent role in the environmental consciousness that is a primary force moving many towards a biocentric life orientation. I have argued that traditional Western forms of transcendence negate contingency not only by creating an absolute dimension, but also by writing humans into the very fabric of existence in framing mind or consciousness as the origin of the cosmos.

An alternative, green spirituality, I have suggested, needs to move from the vertical transcendence of the Absolute to the horizontal transcendence of belonging to the universe. Premised on life rather than mind, such transcendence does not deny our contingency, but it provides a deeply grounded belonging that extends beyond human life or even the earth itself. In discovering a dimension of life running as a fundamental thread in the forces and processes of the universe, we find grounds for an affirmation that reaches beyond the life of our kind. This horizontally transcendent affirmation does not delude us with a questionable sense of permanence, but no less than other forms of transcendence, it sustains us with a sense of awe and reverence for the mystery that encompasses us.

REFERENCES

Capra, F., Steindl-Rast, D., and Matus, T. (1992) *Belonging to the Universe: Explorations on the Frontiers of Science and Spirituality*, San Francisco: Harper.

Eliade, M. (1957) *The Sacred and the Profane*, New York: Harcourt, Brace, and World.

Goodenough, U. (1998) *The Sacred Depths of Nature*, New York: Oxford University Press.

Gribbin, J. (1986) *The Breathing Planet*, Malden: Blackwell.

Jeffers, R. (1987) *Rock and Hawk: A Selection of Shorter Poems*, ed. R. A. Hass, New York: Random House.

Kafatos, M. (1996) *The Conscious Universe: Part and Whole in Modern Physical Theory*, New York: Springer Verlag.

Kaufman, S. (1995) *At Home in the Universe*, New York and Oxford: Oxford University Press.

Leopold, A. (1949) *A Sand County Almanac*, Oxford: Oxford University Press.

Lovelock, J. (1988) *The Ages of Gaia: a Biography of Our Living Earth*, New York: Bantam Books.

Swimme, B., and Berry, T. (1994) *The Universe Story: From the Primordial Flaring Forth to the Ecozoic Era: A Celebration of the Unfolding of the Cosmos*, San Francisco: Harper.

Author index

Adams, C. 109, 112
Alonso, A. 36
Anderson, W. A. 162, 164, 167–8
Apter, T. 92
Aristotle 106, 189
Atwood, G. E. 93
Avery, Nancy 58

Bacal, II. A. 36, 40
Baigent, M. 179, 183, 184
Bakhtin, M. M. 168
Baltes, P. B. 111
Bateson, M. C. 99, 168
Baynes, C. 14
Beebe, John 12, 13
Bellah, R. N. 64
Benjamin, J. 94, 96
Bennett, W. 14
Bentz, V. M. 171
Bergsten, G. 182
Berne, E. 167
Berry, T. 194
Bion, W. R. 37, 38, 39, 41, 147
Birren, J. E. 89, 111
Blanchard-Fields, F. 112
Bollas, C. 179
Boss 145
Bradley, C. L. 88, 90
Braun, J. 165
Brazier, D. 113, 114
Breunlin, D. 167
Brinsmead, R. 158n2
Bronheim, H. 145, 158n2
Brooke, R. 153
Bruner, J. 89
Buber, Martin 43, 93
Buddhaghosa 25
Byrom, T. 135

Calhoun, C. 12
Campbell, Joseph 190
Canin, E. 14
Cassirer, E. 105
Chandler, M. J. 88
Charet, F. X. 77
Chinen, A. B. 109
Chödrön, P. 114, 115
Clayton, V. P. 111
Clebsch, W. 175
Clinchy, B. M. 89
Commons, M. L. 111
Confucius 12
Cook-Greuter, S. 161, 163
Corbett, L. 175
Crittenden, P. 12
Cross, S. 167
Culbert-Koehn, J. 147
Cushman, P. 64

Darwin, Charles 188, 192, 193
de St Aubin, E. 88
Derrida, J. 168
Descartes, René 62, 165
Donald, M. 105
Dreyfus, Hubert 62

Edelman, G. 78
Eliade, M. 146, 176, 190
Engler, J. 161
Erikson, Eric 35, 87–8, 90, 94, 97, 98,
    100nn1,2, 110, 163, 167; integration
    and wisdom 120-9
Erikson, Joan 87, 88

Fabricius, J. 185
Ferrer, Jorge 164, 171
Fiorenza, E. 182
Fisher, L. M. 89

Subject index